COASTAL
DISTURBANCES

COASTAL
DISTURBANCES

Four Plays by
TINA HOWE

Theatre Communications Group
NEW YORK
1989

Published by Theatre Communications Group, Inc., the national organization for the nonprofit professional theatre, 355 Lexington Ave., New York, NY 10017.

Owing to limitations of space, all acknowledgments of permission to use quotations will be found following the text.

Coastal Disturbances originally produced by The Second Stage, New York City; presented on Broadway by The Circle in the Square. *Painting Churches* originally produced by The Second Stage; Lamb's Theatre production presented by Elizabeth I. McCann, Nelle Nugent, Ray Larsen, Lee Guber and Shelly Gross. *The Art of Dining* originally coproduced by The Kennedy Center and the New York Shakespeare Festival, Joseph Papp, producer. *Museum* presented by the New York Shakespeare Festival, Joseph Papp, producer.

Front cover photo: "Ballston Beach, Truro, 1976"
by Joel Meyerowitz
Design by G&H/SOHO Ltd.

Library of Congress Cataloging-in-Publication Data

Howe, Tina.
  Coastal disturbances: four plays by Tina Howe.
  p.   cm.
  Contents: Museum—Art of dining—Painting churches—Coastal disturbances.
  I. Title
PS3558.0894C6 1989   88-37053
812'.54—dc19   CIP
ISBN 0-930452-85-2
ISBN 0-930452-86-0 (pbk.)

For Norman, Eben and Dara

 PREFACE

Since plays are all about creating illusion, there's something inherently self-defeating about revealing one's moves. It's sort of like a magician pausing mid-trick to say, "Wait a minute, wait a minute, let me show you how I'm doing it. See the bottom of this top hat? Tap, tap, tap. It's really fake!" The sad truth is, we show-biz types are so desperate for attention, we'll clamber up on a soapbox faster than you can say spit. Be warned though, it's not where we belong, and we're liable to just fling more dust in your eyes.

The obvious common denominator of the plays in this book is the extravagance of their settings—a museum, a restaurant, a surreal Beacon Hill townhouse, a beach complete with heaving ocean and twenty tons of sand. I seem to go out of my way to make putting them on as hard as possible. It's probably a reaction to my schizophrenic New England upbringing. During the week, all was thrift and simplicity—buying our school uniforms at the secondhand stores and reading the classics aloud at bedtime—but once Saturday morning hit, the family motto of plain living and high thinking was turned on its head. It was off to Marx Brothers movies and howling delirium. My father would laugh himself into a weeping coma, and my mother would disgrace herself in more personal ways. My brother and I were in heaven because everyone around us was going berserk. And it was *allowed*. The Marx Brothers didn't just celebrate lunacy, they turned it into a high art form. Just when you thought Groucho's stateroom couldn't hold one more living soul, a whole phalanx of waiters with teetering trays would show up. The whole point was to keep piling excess on top of excess—more props, more pratfalls, more dizzy language. Why shouldn't it be the same in the theatre? *The Art of Dining* has always been my favorite of my plays because of the chaos it whips up. Once the food starts to fly, everything leaps into an ecstatic gear. It's like when the clothesline is destroyed in *Museum*, or when Holly Dancer is buried up to her chin in *Coastal Disturbances*. I sometimes think the whole reason I write plays is so I can ignite these lunatic climaxes when all hell breaks loose.

There's that, and my fascination with food and artists . . . and of course my love of slinging language around. For a while there it looked as if my plays were getting smaller in scope, moving from a crowded museum to an intimate Boston interior . . . but then *Coastal Disturbances* came along. I was tired of examining artists at work and wanted to write about falling in love. And blam! I had this enormous beach on my hands. My new play is even bigger. It suddenly occurred to me, I've never had the guts to move *out* of my fancy settings. The time has come for a road play. It's the ultimate indulgence: to hop around from an interstate highway to a mountain stream to an aviary. Why didn't I think of it before? Well, that's the appalling thing about the form. Because plays are essentially internal landscapes, the poor writer can never make out the forest for the trees. It's not so much "See the bottom of this top hat? Tap, tap, tap. It's really fake!" as . . . "*What* hat? There's no hat up here. It's just us rabbits!"

Tina Howe
New York City
September 1988

CONTENTS

MUSEUM

ABOUT THE PLAY

Museum premiered at the Los Angeles Actors' Theatre in 1976; it was codirected by Dana Elcar and Richard Jordan. The play was produced in 1978 by the New York Shakespeare Festival under the direction of Max Stafford-Clark; and by the Folger Theatre Group at Kennedy Center, under the direction of Leonard Peters, in 1980.

Characters

THE GUARD, guardian of the exhibit
MICHAEL WALL, first photographer
JEAN-CLAUDE, French visitor
FRANÇOISE, French visitor
ANNETTE FROEBEL, lost woman
LIZ, college girl
CAROL, college girl
BLAKEY, college girl
ELIZABETH SORROW, bewildered woman
PETER ZIFF, silent man
MR. SALT, man with recorded tour
MRS. SALT, wife, attached to recorded tour
MAGGIE SNOW, lost woman
BOB LAMB, art enthusiast
WILL WILLARD, art enthusiast
FRED IZUMI, second photographer
MIRA ZADAL, inquiring woman
FIRST MAN IN PASSING
SECOND MAN IN PASSING
BARBARA CASTLE, fashion plate
BARBARA ZIMMER, her mirror image
MR. GREGORY, man with loud recorded tour
CHLOE TRAPP, curator
ADA BILDITSKY, Chloe's first guest
GILDA NORRIS, sketcher
TINK SOLHEIM, friend of Agnes Vaag
KATE SIV, friend of Agnes Vaag
BILL PLAID, Chloe's second guest
LILLIAN, laughing lady

HARRIET, laughing lady
MAY, laughing lady
GIORGIO, art buff
ZOE, his wife
JULIE JENKINS, third photographer, a knockout
FIRST GUARD, guard from another area of the museum
SECOND GUARD, guard from another area of the art museum
STEVE WILLIAMS, artist
MR. AND MRS. MOE, an elderly couple

Time

The present.

Place

The second-floor gallery of a major American museum of modern art on the final day of a group show, titled "The Broken Silence." The artists and works on display are:

ZACHERY MOE
Born 1950, Fort Wayne, Indiana

Four gigantic white canvases, all identical.

Landscape I, 1989
Acrylic emulsion and wax on canvas
On loan from the Sidney Rubin Gallery

Landscape II, 1989
Acrylic emulsion and wax on canvas
On loan from the Sidney Rubin Gallery

Seascape VII, 1989
Acrylic emulsion and wax on canvas
On loan from the Sidney Rubin Gallery

Starscape XIX, 1989
On loan from the artist

AGNES VAAG
Born 1965, St. Cloud, Minnesota

Nine small, menacing constructions made of animal teeth, feathers, fur, claws, bone, shell, wings, horn, scales, sponge and antennae.

Sacred Inquisition, Daylight Savings Time, 1989
On loan from the Minneapolis Institute of Fine Arts

When the Archangels Abandon Their Grace, 1989
On loan from the Minneapolis Institute of Fine Arts

Prometheus, Singed, 1989
On loan from the Minneapolis Institute of Fine Arts

Socratic Dialogue, 1989
On loan from the Corcoran Gallery of Art

The Temptation and Corruption of William Blake, 1989
On loan from the Whitney Museum of American Art

Abraxas, 1989
On loan from the Whitney Museum of American Art

Ode to Emily Dickinson, 1989
On loan from the Rhode Island School of Design

Metaphysics Revisited, 1989
On loan from the private collection of Igmar Vaag

The Holy Wars of Babylon Rage through the Night, 1989
On loan from the private collection of Igmar Vaag

STEVE WILLIAMS
Born 1943, Santa Rosa, California

A clothesline runs twenty-five feet across the room. On it hang five life-sized cloth figures. They are spookily realistic and are made so they can come apart and be put back together again.

The first figure is a businessman dressed in a pin-striped suit. One of his shoes is missing.

Second is a bride billowing in satin and veils.

Third is a Mexican boy in a tee shirt.

Fourth is a self-portrait of the artist wearing blue jeans and a plaid lumber jacket.

Fifth is a naked Chinese woman with bound feet.

A basket of round-headed clothespins sits under the clothesline. The piece is titled *Wet Dream Left Out to Dry*, 1989. Construction of rope, cloth, papier-mâché, wire, leather, wood, plaster and fiber glass.
On loan from the Los Angeles County Museum of Art.

Playwright's Notes

The dates of completion of the paintings should correspond to the year the play is being read or performed. As the years pass, the dates of the artists' births should also be moved ahead to keep them suitably young.

The audience should be encouraged to walk through the exhibit before the play begins.

It's morning, several minutes before the museum opens. The gallery is in darkness. Nothing happens; then faraway sounds of footsteps and clanging doors are heard.

The Guard walks briskly into the room and turns on the lights. First the Agnes Vaags are illuminated with pinpricks of light, then the Moes are revealed, and finally the clothesline. As The Guard brings everything to life, a voice sounding something like a combination of God and a newscaster announces:

VOICE: Sandro Botticelli's priceless masterpiece *The Birth of Venus* was attacked and virtually destroyed yesterday afternoon by a hooded man armed with a handgun who opened fire on the painting while screaming, "Cursed is the ground for thy sake." Before he was finally overcome by three guards and numerous bystanders, the heavily built assailant pumped more than eighteen bullets into the nude Venus figure, literally shooting her off the face of the canvas. The Acting Director of the Uffizi Gallery, which houses the masterpiece, said in an interview last night that it was the most violent attack ever made against a Renaissance painting. Restoration will be impossible.

The Guard stores this information along with everything else he knows and begins his daily process of becoming watchful yet as unobtrusive as possible. He rocks on his heels, sucks his breakfast out from between his teeth, picks fuzz off his uniform, hoists up his underwear, and waits.

Michael Wall enters carrying an arsenal of photographic equipment including a camera attached to a tripod. He looks around the room, finds the Zachery Moes, and sets his gear down in front of Landscape I. *He walks up to it, backs away, walks up close again and takes out his light meter for a reading. He adjusts his camera and prepares to shoot, all with enormous concentration, energy and flair. The Guard is mesmerized by him. After several moments, Wall poises his finger on the shutter release.*

THE GUARD: It's against museum regulations to photograph the artworks.

MICHAEL WALL *(Whirling around, furious)*: You're kidding!

THE GUARD: It's against museum regulations to photograph the artworks.

MICHAEL WALL: Thanks a lot for waiting to tell me until I was all set up . . .

THE GUARD: I'm surprised they even let you in with all that stuff . . .

MICHAEL WALL *(Shaking his head)*: Too much!

THE GUARD: The attendant downstairs is supposed to see that all photographic equipment is left in the Checkroom . . .

MICHAEL WALL: I don't believe this . . .

THE GUARD: . . . and that includes binoculars, telescopes, folding—

MICHAEL WALL: You wait until I'm all set up, tripod locked, camera attached, f-stop set—

THE GUARD: I've seen the attendant downstairs refuse visitors admittance who were just carrying . . . film!

MICHAEL WALL: —AND WHEN ALL OF THAT IS DONE, THEN YOU TELL ME IT'S AGAINST MUSEUM REGULATIONS TO PHOTOGRAPH THE ARTWORKS!

THE GUARD: And not just film either, but radios, tape recorders, typewriters and sandwiches . . .

MICHAEL WALL: Who do I see to get permission?

THE GUARD: I've seen the attendant downstairs stop visitors who had bulging pockets.

MICHAEL WALL (*Detaching his camera from the tripod*): The Head of Public Relations? The Administrative Assistant?

THE GUARD: The public has no respect for *place* anymore.

MICHAEL WALL: The Curator? The Chairman of the Board?

THE GUARD: They wear tennis shorts to church. They drink soda at the opera. They bring flash cameras to museums . . .

Michael Wall, his camera in hand, walks up to The Guard and starts snapping his picture.

MICHAEL WALL: Come on, who do I see for permission to photograph the artworks? (*Taking a picture with each guess*) The Cinematic Representative? The Acting President of the Exhibition? The Liaison for Public Information? (*Pause*) You have an interesting profile.

THE GUARD: I've caught men exposing their genitals in this room!

MICHAEL WALL (*Getting involved with The Guard as a model*): Good cheek bones!

THE GUARD: Certain shows . . . inspire that!

MICHAEL WALL: Strong chin . . .

THE GUARD: Nineteenth-century French Academy nudes encourage . . . flashing.

MICHAEL WALL (*Adjusts The Guard's head for a shot*): Hold it . . .

THE GUARD (*Voice lowered*): You'd be surprised, the shortest men have the most swollen genitals . . .

MICHAEL WALL: Nice . . . nice . . .

THE GUARD (*Flattered, shyly poses for him*): And there don't even have to be women in the room in order for these . . . shorter men to expose their swollen genitals . . .

MICHAEL WALL *(Still snapping)*: Come on, give me a hint. Do I see the curatorial staff or the administrative staff?

THE GUARD: Very few women expose themselves.

MICHAEL WALL *(Taking closeups)*: Nice, very nice . . .

THE GUARD: Though I *have* seen a few younger women lift their skirts and drop their panties.

MICHAEL WALL: Please! Who do I see to get permission to photograph the artworks?

The Guard and Michael Wall are still as Jean-Claude and Françoise, a French couple in their thirties, enter. They are very serious museum-goers. They advance to the Moes. Jean-Claude looks at Landscape I, *then consults his bilingual catalogue.*

JEAN-CLAUDE: Voici, Zachery Moe!

FRANÇOISE: Ah oui, Zachery Moe!

JEAN-CLAUDE *(Reading from his catalogue)*: "Le publique qui s'intéresse à l'art est tenté de ne voir que chaos dans la profusion des tendances de la peinture contemporaine . . ."

FRANÇOISE *(Looking at the painting)*: Il a un style . . . un style . . . tout à fait . . .

JEAN-CLAUDE *(Reading)*: "Trop près pour distinguer l'authentique du factice, il est le témoin trop passionné de la frénésie d'être divers qui est le propre des artistes de notre temps—"

FRANÇOISE: . . . tout à fait . . . tout à fait . . . FRAGILE!

JEAN-CLAUDE: "Il est troublé par la surproduction de la matière peinte. C'est une des singularités les plus cocasses de notre siècle . . ."

FRANÇOISE: Mais viens voir, Jean-Claude! Regarde la peinture!

JEAN-CLAUDE: ". . . qui abonde pourtant en duperies de toutes sortes . . ."

FRANÇOISE: C'est une fragilité . . . mystique . . . une fragilité . . . religieuse . . . une fragilité . . .

JEAN-CLAUDE *(Finally looks at the painting)*: PLASTIQUE! Une fragilité plastique, Françoise!

FRANÇOISE *(Disagreeing)*: Une fragilité . . . symboliste!

JEAN-CLAUDE: Une fragilité . . . moderne!

FRANÇOISE: Une fragilité dix-septième siècle!

JEAN-CLAUDE: Une fragilité psychologique!

FRANÇOISE: Une fragilité . . . fragile!

JEAN-CLAUDE: AH OUI, SURTOUT UNE FRAGILITÉ FRAGILE!

FRANÇOISE: C'est le mot juste . . .

JEAN-CLAUDE: Fragile . . .
FRANÇOISE: Un adjectif exact!
JEAN-CLAUDE: Comme . . . futilé *futile*!
FRANÇOISE: Ou . . . frivolité *frivole*!
JEAN-CLAUDE: Fraternité *fraternelle*!
FRANÇOISE: Ou même de la . . . folie *folle*!
JEAN-CLAUDE *(Kissing her in appreciation)*: Françoise, je t'adore!

They gaze up at Landscape I.

THE GUARD *(Softly to Michael Wall)*: The Director!
MICHAEL WALL: What?
THE GUARD: The Director.
MICHAEL WALL: What about the Director?
THE GUARD: It's the Director who gives permission to photograph the artworks!
MICHAEL WALL *(Incredulous)*: THE DIRECTOR?
THE GUARD: The Director!
MICHAEL WALL: It just . . . never occurred to me that . . . the Director . . .
THE GUARD *(In unison, smiling)*: . . . the Director.

Michael Wall, amazed, gathers his equipment.

MICHAEL WALL *(Hurrying out of the room)*: The Director . . . son of a bitch . . .
THE GUARD *(Yelling after him)*: Main floor to the left of the Checkroom.
JEAN-CLAUDE *(Pointing to his catalogue)*: Regarde Françoise, un photo d'artiste . . .
FRANÇOISE *(Looking at it)*: Tiens . . .
THE GUARD *(To himself)*: I still don't understand how he got past the attendant downstairs.
FRANÇOISE: Quelle bouche!
JEAN-CLAUDE *(Looking closely at the picture)*: C'est une bouche . . . extraordinaire!
THE GUARD: I mean, Raoul is tough on photographers!
FRANÇOISE: Une peu . . . chimpanzé, n'est-ce-pas?
JEAN-CLAUDE: Chimpanzé! Mais voyons, Françoise, qu'est-ce que tu veux dire? Que c'est artiste extraordinaire resemble . . . un chimpanzé? Un bête sauvage? *(Looks at the picture, more and more troubled)* C'est une erreur, une faute de photographe . . . *(Looks closer)* C'est . . . *incroyable*!
FRANCOISE: Eh? Eh?

Jean-Claude approaches The Guard with his catalogue opened to the page.

JEAN-CLAUDE *(Speaking in pidgin English)*: Excuse me please. The photograph in my catalogue. Here. This picture of Zachery Moe. There must be some mistake. This is a photo of a chimpanzee!

THE GUARD: Chimpanzee? *(Takes the catalogue and looks)*

JEAN-CLAUDE: You see, that is not a photograph of the artist. It's a photograph of a chimpanzee!

FRANÇOISE *(Leaning over The Guard's shoulder)*: C'est toute à fait fantastique!

THE GUARD *(Looking at the picture very closely)*: It sure looks like a chimpanzee.

Françoise, delighted, breaks into a light giggle, followed by monkey-chattering noise.

JEAN-CLAUDE *(Snatching the catalogue away from The Guard)*: Monsieur, I am shocked. I have never seen such a thing before. Such an insult as this! You should be ashamed!

FRANÇOISE: C'est absolument ridicule!

JEAN-CLAUDE: It's a disgrace.

Françoise chatters in his ear, teasing, laughing. Jean-Claude realizes how foolish it all is, succumbs and joins her in an answering chatter. Never for a moment do they abandon their French precision or dignity. Annette Froebel enters. She can be any woman of any age. She looks around, confused.

ANNETTE FROEBEL: Where did the Colonial Quilts and Weathervanes go?

THE GUARD *(Shaking his head)*: No, that was no chimpanzee. I've seen his picture in the papers, and he doesn't look like no chimp!

ANNETTE FROEBEL *(Remembering them as clear as day)*: Colonial Quilts and Weathervanes used to be in this room . . . right over there!

THE GUARD: Colonial Quilts and Weathervanes are on the third floor, Miss!

ANNETTE FROEBEL: The *third* floor?

THE GUARD: Third floor.

ANNETTE FROEBEL: Are you sure?

THE GUARD: Colonial Quilts and Weathervanes are on the third floor.

ANNETTE FROEBEL: I could have sworn they were on this floor. *(She exits)*

LIZ *(Offstage)*: Did you hear what happened to Botticelli's *Venus* this morning?

CAROL *(Offstage)*: No, what?

LIZ *(Offstage)*: Some maniac shot it with a gun.

Liz, Carol and Blakey enter, enthusiastic college girls who are taking an art course together.

CAROL: Someone *shot* it? People don't shoot paintings. They slash them!

LIZ: I heard it on the radio this morning. A hooded man pumped eighteen bullets into the Venus figure at the Uffizi.

CAROL: I've never heard of anyone . . . shooting a painting.

BLAKEY: You're right! They usually attack them with knives or axes.

CAROL: There's something so . . . alienated . . . about shooting a painting.

BLAKEY: And then there was the guy that wrote slogans all over *Guernica* with a can of spray paint!

LIZ *(Laughing)*: That's right: spray paint!

BLAKEY: Red spray paint . . . and he misspelled everything, remember?

LIZ *(Leading them to the Moes)*: Carol, Blakey, guys, YOU'RE GOING TO LOVE HIM!

They look at his work with reverence.

LIZ *(Softly)*: You know, his parents are deaf mutes . . . *both* of them . . . profoundly deaf . . . *(Blakey and Carol gasp)* Can you imagine what it must have been like growing up with parents who couldn't hear you? I mean, when would you figure out that it was *their* affliction and not yours? How could a baby realize there was anything unusual about his parents? *(Pause)* Since he never heard them utter a word, he must have assumed he couldn't speak either. He could hear his own little baby sounds of course, but he had no idea what they were. . . . *(Blakey and Carol exhale, impressed with the dilemma)* When he cried . . . no one heard him.

Pause.

BLAKEY: Maybe he never did cry!

LIZ: Of course he cried! All babies cry. Even deaf babies.

CAROL *(Lost)*: He assumed he couldn't speak either . . . ?

LIZ: Don't forget, his parents could always *see* him cry. Sooner or later he must have realized that in order to get their attention he didn't really *have to cry,* all he had to do was go through the motions . . . *(She opens her mouth and cries without making a sound)*

BLAKEY *(Musing)*: If a deaf, *mute* baby had hearing parents . . . they couldn't hear *him* cry either . . .

Pause.

CAROL *(Still lost)*: Go through the motions?

LIZ *(To Blakey)*: The deaf aren't necessarily mute, you know, some of them can make some sort of residual sound . . .

CAROL *(She's got it)*: WHEN HE CRIED . . . NO ONE HEARD HIM!

LIZ: . . . but it's not the case with Zachery Moe's parents. They are consigned to absolute and lifelong silence.

Her head spinning from it all, Blakey turns her back on the Moes and notices the clothesline.

BLAKEY: OH MY GOD, WILL YOU LOOK AT THAT?! IT'S IN-CREDIBLE!

LIZ *(Reaching for Carol)*: When Moe finally realized that his meandering attempts at speech fell on deaf ears—

BLAKEY *(Pulling Carol with her)*: THIS IS THE MOST BEAUTIFUL THING I'VE EVER SEEN IN MY LIFE! *(Touches the clothesline gently)*

THE GUARD *(To Blakey)*: Please don't handle the artworks.

BLAKEY: It's . . . fantastic!

THE GUARD: DON'T HANDLE THE ARTWORKS!

BLAKEY: Oh, I'm sorry. *(To Carol)* Imagine thinking of making a clothesline . . . with the bodies left inside the clothes . . .

CAROL *(Torn between her two friends)*: Yeah . . .

BLAKEY: It's a reality grounded in illusion!

Carol, feeling trapped, detaches herself from Blakey.

CAROL: You know, this is the first time I've ever been in this museum!

BLAKEY: Oh no! There's even a little kid wearing a tee shirt!

THE GUARD: DON'T TOUCH.

BLAKEY: I'm not touching, for Christsakes, I'm just looking!

CAROL *(Walking around the room)*: I've lived in this city my whole life, and this is the first time I've ever been to this museum!

BLAKEY: It's our bodies that give our clothes meaning, just as without our clothes we—

CAROL *(Looking out the window)*: You know, you can always tell the quality of a museum by the view out the windows.

BLAKEY *(Kneels by the basket of clothespins)*: Do you see this? He even left out the basket of clothespins?!

THE GUARD *(Walks over to her)*: Please don't handle the basket of clothespins!

BLAKEY *(Rises)*: If you're not supposed to handle the basket of clothespins, how come the artist put them there?

CAROL *(To Blakey)*: The Tate Gallery has just about the shittiest view of any museum in the world!

BLAKEY *(To The Guard)*: He put them there so we *would* touch them!

CAROL: The view from the Del Prado isn't so hot either.

LIZ *(Still enthralled with the Moes)*: He chose painting as his voice! *(Opens her catalogue; stops at a page)* Look at his early sketches! The drawings he did of his toys when he was only three! Do you believe this technique? Look at his handling of perspective . . .

Jean-Claude and Françoise have worked their way to the Agnes Vaag sculptures.

FRANÇOISE: Jean-Claude, elle resemble Tougache, tu sais?

JEAN-CLAUDE: Il est beaucoup imité, tu sais, Tougache!

FRANÇOISE: C'est le même esprit que Tougache!

JEAN-CLAUDE: Tougache est trop admiré!

FRANÇOISE: C'est un style un peu comme Kavitsky aussi . . .

JEAN-CLAUDE: Mon chou, tu sais très bien que je n'aime pas Tougache de tout!

FRANÇOISE: Kavitsky est sombre . . .

JEAN-CLAUDE: ÉCOUTE, FRANÇOISE, TOUGACHE EST BETE!

FRANÇOISE: Elle choisit les objects simples comme Kimoto . . .

Jean-Claude flings down his catalogue in a rage and starts storming around the room, raving in French.

JEAN-CLAUDE: TOUGACHE EST DE LA SALOPERIE! JE DÉTESTE TOUGACHE! TOUGACHE EST DE LA MERDE.

FRANÇOISE *(Upset and embarrassed)*: Jean-Claude . . . chéri . . .

Jean-Claude and Françoise stand at opposite ends of the room, sulking.

BLAKEY: The image of people being . . . laundered . . . washed . . . soaking wet . . . pinned up on the clothesline of life to dry out . . .

CAROL *(Standing next to a window)*: If I designed a museum, there would be no art on display . . . just windows. The public would come *inside* the museum in order to look *outside* the windows. The object of study would be nature itself . . . as seen through many different types of windows. There'd be . . . elevated windows, dropped windows, stained-glass windows, broken windows, bricked-up windows, open windows . . . all looking out at exactly the same view . . .

LIZ *(Still enthralled in front of the Moes)*: I don't know which I like more, his landscapes or seascapes . . .

CAROL: And then there'd be windows that weren't really windows at all, but *paintings* of windows . . .

Blakey starts laughing in delight over the clothesline. Mr. Hollingsford enters. He could be anybody.

MR. HOLLINGSFORD *(Speaking to The Guard)*: Where would I find the . . . uh . . . the uh . . . *(He looks at Blakey and gets more confused)* . . . Colonial Quilts and Weathervanes?

THE GUARD: Third floor.

MR. HOLLINGSFORD: Colonial Quilts and Weathervanes.

THE GUARD: Colonial Quilts and Weathervanes are on the third floor!

MR. HOLLINGSFORD: I was told they were on this floor. *(He consults his catalogue)*

Blakey can't contain her delight over the clothesline and sways her head back and forth laughing and moaning gently.

THE GUARD: "The Broken Silence" is on this floor.

MR. HOLLINGSFORD: What?

THE GUARD: I SAID, "THE BROKEN SILENCE" IS ON THIS FLOOR!

Everyone is startled and instantly quiet.

MR. HOLLINGSFORD: Broken . . . what? *(Looks through his catalogue with rising alarm)* Broken quilts?

THE GUARD: Colonial Quilts and Weathervanes is on the third floor.

Michael Wall reenters with his photographic equipment minus the tripod, drops it to the floor underneath Landscape I *and waves a paper in his hand.*

MICHAEL WALL: I got permission from the Director!

THE GUARD: COLONIAL QUILTS AND WEATHERVANES IS ON THE THIRD FLOOR!

Blakey, still on the floor, sways and croons with renewed feeling.

MICHAEL WALL: I just got permission from the Director himself. You can see, he signed it!

MR. HOLLINGSFORD *(Bewildered)*: The broken silence?

MICHAEL WALL: He was very nice about it. He took my tripod, but he invited me back to the next show.

THE GUARD *(To Mr. Hollingsford)*: This is the last day of the show.

MR. HOLLINGSFORD: Thank you very much, I will. *(He exits)*

MICHAEL WALL: I know it's the last day of the show, that's why I'm here!

Blakey emits a peal of delighted laughter.

LIZ: Just as sound and speech were irrelevant to him, so line and form became irrelevant. *(Pause)* It makes you wonder where he'll go from here . . . *(She dreams in front of the Moes)*

THE GUARD *(Takes the permission slip from Michael Wall)*: It's against museum regulations to photograph the artworks without permission from the Director.

Blakey advances on the clothesline, wedges in between two of the figures as if she's part of the work.

BLAKEY: Do you know what this makes me want to do? It makes me want to grab some of the clothespins and pin myself right up there alongside the others. . . . I want to be laundered . . . hung up to dry . . . all limp and dripping wet with the sun slowly drying me out . . .

THE GUARD *(Going up to Blakey)*: All right Miss, that's enough. I'm going to have to ask you to leave . . .

BLAKEY: They look so at peace, cleansed . . . flapping in the sun . . .

THE GUARD *(Guiding Blakey out of the room)*: That's it. . . . We've had enough . . . quietly, quietly . . . just move it right along . . .

BLAKEY *(From offstage)*: I want to join them! I want to be cleansed! I want to feel the sun on my face . . .

CAROL: And then at some point, the structure of the museum would . . . just end . . . everyone would suddenly be . . . outside . . . *in the view* . . . they'd actually *become the view,* the objects on display. You'll stand in line and pay admission . . . to see . . . *yourself!* And then the guards will be hired to watch the people . . . watching each other . . . GOD! I'VE GOT TO WRITE THIS DOWN! *(She exits)*

LIZ *(Seated before the Moes, falls into a revery)*: They must be so proud of him, his parents . . . so very proud.

A silence descends. It's finally broken by the entrance of Elizabeth Sorrow. She is a highly sensitive woman who has tremendous difficulty orienting herself to the artworks. She doesn't know how long it takes to "see" them. She flits from one to the next like a yo-yo spinning on a string that keeps getting shorter and shorter. When she's through looking at something she doesn't trust her impressions, but rushes back to it for another glance, then on to the next one to compare, then back again.

In the midst of her confusion Peter Ziff enters. He is a silent and nervous man who glitters with a strange menace. His moves are stealthy and ambiguous. He should give the impression of having visited this show many times. Like Elizabeth Sorrow, he rarely notices other people. Time passes in absolute silence as they alternately explore their hidden worlds. This silence is finally broken by the sound of a lively voice intoning on an acoustiguide.

Mr. and Mrs. Salt enter, attached to an acoustiguide and to each other by twin wires they have plugged into their ears. They are not experienced museumgoers and are terrified by the voice babbling into their ears. Furthermore, they've never worn an acoustiguide before, and keep getting hopelessly tangled up in all the wires. The machine hangs around Mr. Salt's neck, Mrs. Salt follows him timidly. Eventually overwhelmed by the difficulty of keeping pace, following the instructions of the guide, and maneuvering with all the wires that keep getting in their way, they collapse on the nearest bench.

THE RECORDED TOUR: On behalf of the trustees of the museum, it give me great pleasure to welcome you to our current exhibition, "The Broken Silence." Before we start on our tour, let me say a few words about the operation of the cassette you are now wearing around your neck. The small red button on the left allows you to turn me on or off at your own discretion. When you hear this beep sound *(Beep sound)*, it is the signal that my commentary about a specific work is finished and that you may turn the button to the "off" position and enjoy the painting or sculpture at your own leisure. When you wish to rejoin me, simply turn the button back to "on" and our tour will continue. If you inadvertently miss any of my remarks and would like to hear them again, switch the red button to "off" and then turn the adjacent white button to the "replay" position. My comments will then be repeated until you are caught up and ready to proceed. At that time, just return the white button to "play" and be sure to remember to flip the red button back to the "on" position. To raise and lower the volume on the earphone element, just turn the large black dial at the center of the cassette clockwise or counterclockwise. If the quality of your recorded tour is defective in any way, simply exchange it for another cassette at the front desk, main floor, to the left of the checkroom.

Jean-Claude and Françoise find themselves in front of the clothesline, and are horrified by it.

FRANÇOISE: Mon Dieu, Jean-Claude, regarde!
JEAN-CLAUDE: Quelle horreur!
FRANÇOISE: C'est affreux!
JEAN-CLAUDE: Un insult!
FRANÇOISE: Dégoutant . . .
JEAN-CLAUDE: Déplorable . . .
FRANÇOISE: Débraillé . . .
JEAN-CLAUDE: Décadent . . .
FRANÇOISE: Déclassé . . .

They get angrier and angrier.

JEAN-CLAUDE: Décomposé . . .
FRANÇOISE: Défectif . . .
JEAN-CLAUDE: Défoncé . . .

And faster and faster.

FRANÇOISE: DÉFORMÉ!
JEAN-CLAUDE: DÉGÉNERÉ!
FRANÇOISE: DÉGRADANT!
JEAN-CLAUDE: DÉMODÉ!
FRANÇOISE *(Weepy)*: Je veux partir, Jean-Claude.
JEAN-CLAUDE: Moi aussi, Françoise.

Jean-Claude takes Françoise's arm and with the utmost grace and disdain, they exit. At this point the following people are in the gallery. The Guard watching over Liz. Liz watching the Zachery Moes and thumbing through her catalogue. Elizabeth Sorrow resting on one of the benches. The Salts at the mercy of their recorded tour, Michael Wall taking pictures, and Peter Ziff, moody and restless. Maggie Snow enters, a woman in a hurry.

MAGGIE SNOW *(To The Guard)*: Excuse me, where is the Puritan Pewter and Hooked Rugs?
THE GUARD: You mean, Colonial Quilts and Weathervanes.
MAGGIE SNOW: No! Puritan Pewter and Hooked Rugs!
THE GUARD: We don't have Puritan Pewter or Hooked Rugs on exhibit here, only Colonial Quilts and Weathervanes!
MAGGIE SNOW *(Exits, running)*: Typical! Typical!

Maggie Snow almost bumps into Bob Lamb and Will Willard, who glide into the room like elegant swans. They are experienced museumgoers, close friends, and arbiters of good taste.

WILL WILLARD: Bruce said the show was shit!

BOB LAMB: Bruce says everything is shit!

WILL WILLARD: Well, Bruce said *this* show was especially shit. *Merde de la merde!*

BOB LAMB *(Looking around the room)*: Pretentious . . . ?

WILL WILLARD: This wasn't my idea . . . !

BOB LAMB *(Looking at the Moes)*: Ad Reinhardt was doing those in black twenty years ago!

WILL WILLARD: I would never in a million years—

BOB LAMB: And Yves Klein did them in blue before you were even born!

WILL WILLARD: I'm sorry, my taste is more—

BOB LAMB: It's pure Rauschenberg, but without the emotion.

WILL WILLARD: Wait a minute, I love Rauschenberg!

BOB LAMB: Willard, I love him too, but . . . *this* . . .

WILL WILLARD: Rauschenberg is a giant!

BOB LAMB: Rauschenberg is *the* giant!

Fred Izumi enters. He is another photographer, a second-generation Oriental who's been completely Americanized save for a residue of old-world politeness. He starts setting up his equipment in front of one of the Moes.

BOB LAMB *(Looking at the clothesline)*: I like Segal better.

WILL WILLARD: You do?

BOB LAMB: Don't you?

WILL WILLARD: I thought you've said Segal was shallow.

BOB LAMB: I've never said Segal was . . . shallow. Just a bit . . . muted for my taste.

WILL WILLARD: Well, what about Duane Hanson?

BOB LAMB: Hanson . . . *(Laughing with pleasure)* is divine!

THE GUARD *(Noticing Fred Izumi)*: Hey mister, it's against museum regulations to photograph the artworks!

WILL WILLARD: Hanson is . . . insane!

FRED IZUMI *(To The Guard)*: Excuse me, but I notice there is another man here taking photographs.

WILL WILLARD: Of course my all-time favorite is . . .

WILL WILLARD: Claes Oldenberg!	BOB LAMB: Claes Oldenberg! I know!

FRED IZUMI *(Going over to The Guard)*: I'm sorry for troubling you again, but unless I'm very mistaken, that fellow over there is taking photographs.

THE GUARD: He has permission.

FRED IZUMI: Oh . . . he has permission.

BOB LAMB *(Reads the title of the clothesline)*: "Wet Dream Left Out to Dry, 1989." *(He starts to laugh)*

Will Willard laughs with him.

BOB LAMB *(Reading in an affected voice)*: "On loan from the Los Angeles County Museum of Art"!

FRED IZUMI *(To The Guard)*: Would there be some way I might get permission as well?

Liz comes out of her revery over the Moes. She looks around the room for her friends, who have disappeared.

LIZ: Carol? Blakey? Guys? Hello? CAROL? GUYS? *(She exits in a panic)*

WILL WILLARD: Isn't it terribly loud in here? I can't see a thing!

BOB LAMB: This has always been a noisy museum.

FRED IZUMI: If there is some procedure to follow to get permission, perhaps you'd tell me what it is.

THE GUARD: If you want permission to photograph the artworks, you'll have to see the Director.

FRED IZUMI: Oh, the Director?! That's curious, usually it's the Administrative Assistant who authorizes permission to photograph the artworks. *(He exits)*

BOB LAMB: Oh no, look at that! He put a basket of real clothespins under an imaginary clothesline. Now, that's what I call . . . *panache*!

WILL WILLARD: You mean, *pastiche*!

BOB LAMB: *Pastiche*?

WILL WILLARD: Real clothespins under an imaginary clothesline!

BOB LAMB: Willard, *pastiche* is collage, I mean, *panache* . . . dash!

WILL WILLARD: Robert, the word is . . . *panacea*!

BOB LAMB: *Panacea* . . . ?

WILL WILLARD: No wait, *paradigm*!

BOB LAMB *(Thinking back, confused)*: *Pastiche* . . . ?

WILL WILLARD *(Also confused)*: *Placebo* . . . ?

BOB LAMB: PARADIGM . . . ?

Fred Izumi reappears.

FRED IZUMI *(To The Guard, slightly out of breath)*: Excuse me again, but
. . . uh . . . where would I . . . uh . . . find the Director?
THE GUARD: Main floor, to the left of the Checkroom.
FRED IZUMI: Yes of course! The main floor! *(He exits again)*

*Bob Lamb absentmindedly picks up one of the clothespins to help him
find the mot juste.*

THE GUARD: Please don't handle the clothespins!
BOB LAMB *(Drops it)*: Oh, sorry. *(To Willard, but also taunting The
Guard)* Did you read that the Metropolitan Museum of Art is only
going to be open four days a week?
WILL WILLARD: The Metropolitan?
BOB LAMB *(To The Guard, pointedly)*: The museum doesn't have enough
money to pay its force of two hundred and twenty-seven security
guards.
WILL WILLARD: The Metropolitan has two hundred twenty-seven
security guards?
BOB LAMB *(Eyeing The Guard)*: The Metropolitan *had* two hundred
twenty-seven security guards. They just let eighty-two go.
WILL WILLARD: I had no idea Metropolitan had two hundred twenty-
seven guards.
BOB LAMB: They just let eighty-two go.
WILL WILLARD: I thought they had fifty or sixty guards . . . but *two
hundred and twenty-seven*?!
BOB LAMB: All the museums are being forced to cut back.
WILL WILLARD: Two hundred and twenty-seven security guards is a lot
of people!
BOB LAMB: They don't have enough money to meet operating costs
anymore.
WILL WILLARD: Robert, two hundred and twenty-seven security guards
is a crowd!
BOB LAMB: They're all closing down a few days during the week.
WILL WILLARD: Jesus!
BOB LAMB: That's right, "Jesus!" Pretty soon there won't be any fucking
culture left!

*Mira Zadal enters. She's very pretty and flirtatious. She sidles up to
The Guard.*

MIRA ZADAL: Hello. Where are the museum engagement calendars
sold?

THE GUARD *(Sweating under her gaze)*: In the museum Gift Shop. Main floor, to the left of the Checkroom.

MIRA ZADAL *(Starts to exit)*: Thank you so much.

FIRST MAN IN PASSING *(Rushing through the room on the way to somewhere else)*: Did you hear what happened to Botticelli's *Venus* this morning?

SECOND MAN IN PASSING: No.

FIRST MAN IN PASSING: Shot and killed with a gun!

SECOND MAN IN PASSING: Shot and . . . *killed?*

FIRST MAN IN PASSING: Shot right off the face of the painting!

SECOND MAN IN PASSING *(As they both exit)*: Son of a bitch!

Mira Zadal reenters, sashays up to The Guard.

MIRA ZADAL: Do you also have reproductions of ancient Egyptian jewelry in the museum Gift Shop?

THE GUARD *(Blushing)*: Books, catalogues, foreign publications, postcards, blown . . . glass . . .

MIRA ZADAL *(With a tremulous sigh)*: Blown . . . glass?

THE GUARD *(With rising ardor)*: Pewter figurines, ceramic reproductions, needlepoint kits, table linens . . . dried flowers . . .

Mira Zadal groans.

THE GUARD: Silver ladles, cloisonné key rings, solid gold cuff links . . . rare spices!

MIRA ZADAL: Oooooooh, you're so . . . helpful! *(She exits)*

THE GUARD: Main floor, just a little bit left of the Checkroom!

Elizabeth Sorrow exits in her fashion, trying to make doubly sure she has taken everything in. Peter Ziff starts stalking the same artworks Elizabeth has just left. He's bothered by them, but for more destructive and obscure reasons. The Guard watches him like a hawk. Peter Ziff, frustrated by this scrutiny, sits down on one of the benches. There is a silence into which step Barbara Zimmer and Barbara Castle, enormously stylish mirror images of each other. They have come to the show to be seen and display themselves with languorous grace.

BARBARA CASTLE: Gloria said the show was wonderful!

BARBARA ZIMMER: Gloria would!

BARBARA CASTLE: She came to the opening with Misha.

BARBARA ZIMMER: I saw Misha last week!

BARBARA CASTLE: Really?

BARBARA ZIMMER: He was wearing his fur cape!

BARBARA CASTLE: Oh, I love that cape! Did he have on his linen vest with it?

BARBARA ZIMMER: The linen vest . . . *and* an incredible raw silk shirt!

BARBARA CASTLE: Ooooooooh, what color? *What color?*

BARBARA ZIMMER: Bright . . . green!

BARBARA CASTLE: Perfect!

BARBARA ZIMMER: And his tweed cap . . .

BARBARA CASTLE: He was wearing his tweed cap?

BARBARA ZIMMER: Yes!

BARBARA CASTLE: But not his tan boots . . .

BARBARA ZIMMER: Not his tan boots . . .

Pause.

BARBARA ZIMMER: His black ones! *(A groan)*	BARBARA CASTLE: His black ones! *(A groan)*

Pause.

BARBARA CASTLE: What I wouldn't give for that linen vest of his!

BARBARA ZIMMER: Well, you'd have to give a great deal, believe me!

BARBARA CASTLE: Can you see that vest with my gabardine slacks?

BARBARA ZIMMER: Barbara, they don't *make* linen like that anymore!

BARBARA CASTLE: Or, with my Halston skirt . . .

BARBARA ZIMMER: There's a worldwide shortage of natural fibers. We have quite simply used them all up.

BARBARA CASTLE: And it's reversible too. On the inside, it's a lightweight cream wool!

BARBARA ZIMMER: Drained them . . .

BARBARA CASTLE: Reversed, I could wear it with practically anything!

BARBARA ZIMMER: Barbara, within the next few years, all our fabric will be synthetic.

BARBARA CASTLE: *Synthetic?* Did you just say *synthetic,* Barbara?

BARBARA ZIMMER: Yes, Barbara, I just said *synthetic,* Barbara! They hardly grow any cotton in the South anymore, it's just too expensive to harvest.

BARBARA CASTLE: Barbara, I can't wear synthetics!

BARBARA ZIMMER: Who can, Barbara? WHO CAN?!

BARBARA CASTLE: Last week I bought a slip I was told was pure silk, only to read the label two days later and discover it was Cresulon. Do you know what Cresulon does to my skin?

BARBARA ZIMMER: Chinese silkworms are as scarce as hen's teeth!

BARBARA CASTLE: It coats it with a thin layer of petroleum!

BARBARA ZIMMER: And as for wool. Because the cost of feeding sheep has skyrocketed, the sheep farmers are going bankrupt. Soon, there will be no more wool, cashmere, or angora!

BARBARA CASTLE: Barbara, I've got a rash. A white rash all over my body!

BARBARA ZIMMER: From now on, it's the manmade substitutes: Orlon, Acrylic, Lycra Spandex, Quiana Nylon, Fortrel Polyester, and Celanese Arnel Triacetate!

BARBARA CASTLE: And it won't go away! I've tried everything. Barbara, I'm desperate!

Pause.

BOB LAMB: As the costs of running museums keep rising, the price of admission is bound to go up. Museum officials are now talking about ten dollars as a fixed single admission fee.

WILL WILLARD: *Ten dollars to get into the Metropolitan?*

BOB LAMB: Ten dollars for admission into the Metropolitan will be a bargain, Willard, it will be twenty-five before the end of the decade. The only way people will be able to afford visiting museums in the future will be in chartered groups!

WILL WILLARD: Chartered groups?! Robert, I go to the Met by myself, or I don't go at all!

BOB LAMB: The fifty-dollar "Budget" chartered tour will include admission into the Metropolitan, the Modern, and the Whitney . . .

WILL WILLARD: I would *pay* fifty dollars to avoid a "Budget" chartered tour . . .

BOB LAMB: The "Imperial" chartered tour will include those three, and for twenty-five more, admission into the Guggenheim, Cooper-Hewitt, and the Hayden Planetarium!

WILL WILLARD: Stop, stop!

BOB LAMB: And don't think the private galleries aren't hurting either . . .

WILL WILLARD: I have to be alone with the things I love!

BOB LAMB: The day will come when you'll have to use MasterCharge to get into Pace and Castelli!

WILL WILLARD: The Morgan Collection of Renaissance jewels, snuff boxes, and enameled jeweled cups!

BOB LAMB: Write checks for admittance into second-story Soho galleries!

WILL WILLARD: Do you *know* the Morgan Collection at the Met? Have you ever *seen* the Rospigliosi Cup?

BOB LAMB: Pay cash to—

WILL WILLARD: Robert, when I'm in front of that cup, I can't stand two people within ten feet of me!

Pause.

BARBARA CASTLE *(To Barbara Zimmer)*: This is the first time I've ever had a . . . *white* rash!

WILL WILLARD *(To Bob Lamb)*: The last time I was there, there was a swarm . . . of screaming children.

BARBARA CASTLE *(Revealing some bare arm)*: Look! *(She blows on it, a fine white powder rises)* Did you see that?

WILL WILLARD: I broke out in a sweat . . .

BARBARA CASTLE: I think I'm on fire . . .

WILL WILLARD: It's called agoraphobia!

BARBARA CASTLE: It keeps getting worse!

WILL WILLARD: I'm told it's incurable . . .

BARBARA CASTLE: . . . and Barbara, it's spreading!

A pause.

BARBARA ZIMMER *(To Barbara Castle)*: The handwriting is on the wall!

BOB LAMB *(To Will Willard)*: Our troubles have just begun!

BARBARA ZIMMER *(Agreeing with Bob Lamb, but for her own reasons)*: We could lose everything!

BOB LAMB *(To Barbara Zimmer)*: Exactly!

BARBARA ZIMMER *(To Bob Lamb)*: We're only beginning to wake up . . .

BOB LAMB: . . . and when we finally do, it will be too late!

BARBARA ZIMMER: Of course, this is not the first time.

BOB LAMB: No, we've been through it before.

BARBARA ZIMMER: This is the first time I've ever had a white rash!

WILL WILLARD: I just hope we can retain what's most precious to us.

BARBARA ZIMMER: We've tried so hard!

BOB LAMB: Sacrificed so much . . .

BARBARA ZIMMER: Given our all . . .

WILL WILLARD: Gone more than halfway . . .

BARBARA ZIMMER: Stinted on nothing . . .

BOB LAMB: Held out for the best.

BARBARA CASTLE: Fought a fair fight . . .

WILL WILLARD: And stuck to our guns!

A pause.

BARBARA ZIMMER: He's right!

BOB LAMB: You said it!

BARBARA CASTLE: Well put!

WILL WILLARD: Culture, as we know it . . .

BOB LAMB: Is on the way out!

BARBARA ZIMMER: On the way out . . .

BARBARA CASTLE: . . . and disappearing round the bend!

A pause. The Guard suddenly launches into a tap dance of private protest. It rises in spirit and magnificence. Everyone waches him in amazement. The Salts start to applaud and then check the gauche impulse. The dance suddenly stops and The Guard returns to his post as if nothing happened.

THE GUARD *(To himself)*: It's the last day of the show.

Everyone resumes their former activities and the room falls into silence. Mr. Gregory enters, a shy man with a recorded tour that's playing much too loud.

THE RECORDED TOUR: ON BEHALF OF THE TRUSTEES AND ADMINISTRATION OF THE MUSEUM, IT GIVES ME GREAT PLEASURE TO WELCOME YOU TO OUR CURRENT EXHIBITION, "THE BROKEN SILENCE." FIRST, LET ME SAY A FEW WORDS ABOUT THE OPERATION OF . . . *(It continues)*

Everyone eyes him with hostility, their hands over their ears.

THE GUARD: WILL YOU PLEASE TURN THAT DOWN?

WILL WILLARD: WHAT'S GOING ON IN HERE?

BOB LAMB: I TOLD YOU THIS WAS A NOISY MUSEUM!

MICHAEL WALL: HEY, MISTER . . .

The Barbaras shake their heads and cluck. Fred Izumi reenters, goes up to The Guard, hands him a slip.

FRED IZUMI: My permission slip from the Director! *(He sets his gear down by the Moes)*

THE GUARD: *WHAT?*

FRED IZUMI: PERMISSION SLIP FROM THE DIRECTOR!

THE GUARD: I SAID, IT'S AGAINST MUSEUM REGULATIONS TO PHOTOGRAPH THE ARTWORKS!

FRED IZUMI: MAIN FLOOR TO THE LEFT OF THE CHECKROOM!

THE GUARD: THE GUARD DOWNSTAIRS . . .

FRED IZUMI: YES, I SAW THE DIRECTOR . . .

The recorded tour mysteriously regulates itself.

THE GUARD: IT'S AGAINST . . .

Mr. Gregory somehow manages to turn the sound completely off.

FRED IZUMI *(Hands The Guard his slip)*: My permission slip from the Director.

THE GUARD *(Taking it)*: Wonderful!

FRED IZUMI: Main floor, to the left of the Checkroom!

THE GUARD: Terrific!

Mr. and Mrs. Salt's recorded tour suddenly goes berserk in sympathy with Mr. Gregory's. It plays insanely loud and then very, very fast. Everyone groans and mutters in angry disbelief.

THE GUARD: LOOK . . . WOULD YOU PLEASE TURN DOWN THE VOLUME . . .

MR. GREGORY *(Cowering in a corner)*: THE SAME THING HAPPENED TO MINE, JUST SHAKE IT . . . *(Etc.)*

Mr. and Mrs. Salt, frantic with embarrassment, bang on the controls.

MRS. SALT: TURN THE RED BUTTON, NOT THE WHITE BUTTON. . . . NO, NO. . . . *THIS* ONE. . . . NOT SO FAR . . .

MR. SALT: SOMETHING'S GONE WRONG SOMEWHERE!! I'M TURNING THE WHITE BUTTON, BUT NOTHING HAPPENS . . . GODDAMNED MACHINE! . . .

THE GUARD: LOOK, I'M GOING TO HAVE TO ASK YOU TO LEAVE!

The Guard strong-arms Mr. Salt out of the room. Mrs. Salt is pulled helplessly after him on her attached wire. Peter Ziff seizes the moment and quickly rushes over to one of the Moes, takes out a small pencil and scribbles on one corner. With sweat pouring down his face, he looks to see if anyone saw him, and then quietly sneaks out of the room.

FRED IZUMI *(To The Guard)*: Both he and his assistant were very courteous. It turns out we have mutual friends in Cincinnati. *(He paces down the length of all the Moes, reading their titles out loud to himself)* "Landscape I, 1989. Acrylic emulsion and wax on canvas. On loan from the Sidney Rubin Gallery."

BOB LAMB *(To Will Willard)*: Not only will it cost ten dollars to get into the Metropolitan, but because of the shortage of guards, certain galleries will be roped off on odd and even days of the month.

FRED IZUMI: *"Landscape II,* 1989. Acrylic emulsion and wax on canvas. On loan from the Sidney Rubin Gallery."

BOB LAMB: Medieval helmets will only be on view even days, from noon till one. Renaissance stringed instruments, odd days, from two to three.

FRED IZUMI: *"Seascape VII,* 1989. Acrylic emulsion and wax on canvas. On loan from the Sidney Rubin Gallery."

BOB LAMB: Sooner or later, the less popular exhibits will close altogether: Etruscan bronzes, Mideastern glazed bricks . . .

FRED IZUMI: *"Starscape XIX,* 1989. Acrylic emulsion and wax on canvas. On loan from the artist."

BOB LAMB: Eventually, entire periods and forms of art will be lost completely as the public is denied access!

FRED IZUMI *(Amazed)*: "On loan from the . . . *artist*"?!

BOB LAMB: One by one, all the treasures of Western civilization will be dismantled, put into storage . . . lowered into fiberglass crates and buried underground . . . to be grouped and catalogued by art historians wearing thick, lint-free asbestos gloves. *(Pause)* We will never again stand face to face with an original painting or sculpture. And if there is no place where that painting or sculpture can be shown, the artist is bound to ask: *Who am I doing it for . . . and why am I doing it?* The impulse to create will be shattered. Willard, this may be our last day in the presence of live art!

WILL WILLARD: Wait a minute! Yesterday I was standing one foot away from probably *the* most live and stunning object of art made by man in the last four hundred years! Robert, have you ever studied the Rospigliosi Cup? It's a fucking dazzler! *(Pause)* It's this . . . incredible scalloped seashell which rests on the back of an enameled dragon . . . which in turn rests on the back of an enameled turtle. It's carved out of solid gold and is no more than ten inches high and eight inches across. Instead of a handle, a winged sphinx perches on the rim of the cup, a gigantic baroque pearl hanging between her golden breasts. I mean, the workmanship, the detail . . . the fantasy! Tiny seed pearl earrings dangle from her ears . . . and instead of having the traditional legs and paws of a lion . . . she has flippers! Indigo blue flippers etched in enamel. You can *count* each iridescent scale!

BOB LAMB: Well, you'd better get ready to kiss it good-bye. . . . It won't be there in two weeks. All the museums are closing.

WILL WILLARD: Robert, what on earth are you talking about?

BOB LAMB: The museums . . . are . . . shutting . . . down!

WILL WILLARD: Robert, no museums are shutting down.

BOB LAMB: Willard, we've got to do something!

As Bob Lamb is tensed for some sort of desperate act, there's a gradual slowing down. The visitors become languid artworks themselves. The Guard paces, Michael Wall keeps taking pictures, Fred Izumi prepares to take his, Mr. Gregory doggedly follows his tour, the Barbaras pluck at each other's beautiful clothes, and Will Willard stares straight ahead.

This moment of serenity is broken as Chloe Trapp enters. She's on the curatorial staff of the museum. Her life and passion center on discovering and explaining the mysteries of modern art. Ada Bilditsky enters with her, a patron of the arts who's being given a special private tour. Liz suddenly careens into the room.

LIZ: Carol? Blakey? Guys? *(She looks around, then exits)*

CHLOE TRAPP: This is the final day of our group show, "The Broken Silence," and here we have the work of an extraordinary young Post-Conceptual painter, Zachery Moe.

Everyone looks up at the sound of her voice. They are held by her seriousness and authority.

CHLOE TRAPP: Most significant painting since Matisse's *Joie de Vivre* has been reductive. Reductivism does not belong to any one style: it is as operative in painting conceived as a gesture . . . as in painting cut down to a line or square. The traditional aim of reduction has been to push painting to its farthest limits by reducing it to its bare essentials. In slicing away residues of imagery that have lost their relevance, the artist seeks to transform the apple . . . into a diamond.

A pause.

ADA BILDITSKY: I'm so grateful!

Everyone except The Guard gathers around Chloe Trapp for more.

BARBARA CASTLE: Oh, we're all grateful!

WILL WILLARD: *I'm* grateful!

BOB LAMB: No one . . . is more grateful than me!

MR. GREGORY: I had no idea anyone was going to . . .

FRED IZUMI: Thank you very much.

CHLOE TRAPP *(Moves to the next Moe)*: There is left the void—not Yves Klein's empty sky, but a void that seeks the cancellation of art as it has been until now and supplanting it with works from which adulterating impulses have been . . . purged. It is evident that Moe saw that a traditional commitment to the theoretical picture plane was no longer relevant.

ADA BILDITSKY: Absolutely evident and no longer relevant.

EVERYONE *(Except The Guard, who's lost in the rhythms of his own job)*: Absolutely evident and no longer relevant.

CHLOE TRAPP: For such American artists, the concern was mainly with the surface of the canvas and the nature of the pigment applied to it. What states more plainly the literal character of the picture support covered by canvas . . . than a piece of canvas . . . covering that picture support . . . *painted white?*! If the first mark on a surface destroys its flatness, then Moe contradicts this by painting a picture whose first and *only* mark . . . is an all-over white one.

ADA BILDITSKY *(Letting it sink in)*: All-over white!

EVERYONE *(Understanding, joyous)*: All-over white!

CHLOE TRAPP: White . . . of course, is the one color carrying in it the potential for all other colors.

A pause. These colors should spill out rapid-fire, creating a verbal rainbow.

ADA BILDITSKY: Red!

MICHAEL WALL: Yellow!

FRED IZUMI: Orange!

BARBARA CASTLE: Violet!

BARBARA ZIMMER: Blue!

BOB LAMB: Green!

WILL WILLARD: Sepia!

MR. GREGORY: Purple!

ADA BILDITSKY *(Breathing deeply, her favorite color)*: Rose!

MICHAEL WALL: Turquoise!

FRED IZUMI: Umber!

BARBARA CASTLE: Mauve!

BARBARA ZIMMER: Lavender!

BOB LAMB: Cobalt!

WILL WILLARD: Magenta!

MR. GREGORY: Saffron!

CHLOE TRAPP: The difference between historic Dada and the current fundamentalist version lies in the treatment of the spectator . . . *(Everyone turns and faces Chloe, suddenly aware that they are the spectators she's talking about)* Instead of goading you into indignation at the desecration of art, the new Dada converts you into an aesthete.

Everyone, flattered, congratulates themselves, murmuring "aesthete."

CHLOE TRAPP: The monotonous shapes and bleak surfaces presented to you as objects wrapped in their own being compel you to embrace a professional sensitivity to contrasts of tone, light, and dimension. The more a work is purged of inessentials, the closer the scrutiny required to see it . . . and the more precious the sensibility required to respond to it!

A reverential silence.

ADA BILDITSKY: Oh, you were just . . . wonderful! Really . . . wonderful!

Everyone breaks into applause.

CHLOE TRAPP *(Suddenly made shy by their outpouring, ducking her head to one side and rushing from the room)*: How kind . . . you're too kind . . .

ADA BILDITSKY: I've never heard anything so . . . lyrical . . . so inspired . . . so informative . . . so apt! *(She runs after Chloe)*

Everyone is stirred by their new vision. They move around the Moes, not daring to speak for fear of breaking the spell. Gilda Norris enters; intense and serious, she carries a folding chair and sketchbook. She settles down in front of one of the Moes and starts copying it with as much fury as if she were reproducing a Rembrandt.

THE GUARD: I'm sorry, Miss, it's against museum regulations to sketch from the artworks!

GILDA NORRIS: I can't sketch without permission from the Director?

THE GUARD: I didn't tell you it was the Director who gave permission to sketch. How did you know the Director gives permission to sketch?

GILDA NORRIS: Because I have sketching permission from the Director.

THE GUARD: You have *sketching* permission from the Director? I've never seen sketching permission from the Director!

GILDA NORRIS: I'm the Director's daughter!

THE GUARD: Oh, you're the Director's *daughter* . . .

GILDA NORRIS: The sketching Director's daughter . . .

THE GUARD *(Laughs)*: Sketching Director's daughter . . .

GILDA NORRIS *(Still sketching)*: The . . . *fetching*, sketching Director's daughter!

The Guard laughs lightheartedly.

GILDA NORRIS: The . . . *letching*, fetching, sketching Director's daughter!

The Guard laughs, with embarrassment.

BOB LAMB: Willard, now's the time to make our move. See that basket of clothespins over there, I'm going to steal one dozen of them!

GILDA NORRIS *(Rises and advances on The Guard)*: The . . . *kvetching*, letching, fetching, sketching Director's daughter!

WILL WILLARD: Robert, you're crazy!

Bob Lamb, checking that The Guard is engrossed with Gilda Norris, starts stuffing clothespins in his pocket.

WILL WILLARD: Robert, please!

THE GUARD *(Rushes over to them)*: HEY, WHAT'S GOING ON OVER HERE? I TOLD YOU, YOU ARE NOT TO TOUCH THE CLOTHESPINS! THEY ARE PART OF THE SCULPTURE!

BOB LAMB: For your information, this is not a *sculpture*, it's a *construction*.

WILL WILLARD: I'm so embarrassed!

THE GUARD: I DON'T CARE WHAT YOU CALL IT, MISTER, IT'S AGAINST MUSEUM REGULATIONS TO TOUCH THE ARTWORKS. NOW, PUT THOSE CLOTHESPINS BACK!

BOB LAMB: Are you accusing me of . . . theft?

THE GUARD: All I said was put the clothespins back!

BOB LAMB *(Tossing them back into the basket)*: I hope you realize this is the first time a museum guard has *ever* raised his voice to me . . .

WILL WILLARD: The poor man is just doing his job!

BOB LAMB: And let me assure you, I've been to every major art museum across the country! The Hirschorn, the Carnegie Institute, The Philadelphia Museum of Art, the Walker Art Center . . .

THE GUARD: ALL BACK. PUT THEM ALL BACK!

BOB LAMB: Furthermore, this is just about the worst show I've ever seen, anywhere! Real stinko!

WILL WILLARD: Rooooooooooooobert . . .

BOB LAMB: I'd be embarrassed to work here!

THE GUARD: COME ON, HURRY IT UP! *(Clamping his hands on Bob Lamb)* Each one of those pins is a valuable piece of art!

BOB LAMB: *You touched me!* That does it! *(He throws back the last remaining ones)* I'm reporting you to the Director of the museum . . .

BOB LAMB: . . . main floor, to the left of the Checkroom!　　THE GUARD: . . . main floor, to the left of the Checkroom!

BOB LAMB: *(Exiting)*: Bruce said this show was shit!

WILL WILLARD *(Following him)*: BRUCE IS AN ASSHOLE!

THE GUARD: This is just the beginning, just the beginning . . .

BARBARA ZIMMER *(Gazing at* Landscape I): Barbara, I want one!

BARBARA CASTLE: They are lovely!

BARBARA ZIMMER: *This* one!

BARBARA CASTLE *(Considering it)*: Mmmmmmmmmmm . . .

BARBARA ZIMMER: It would be perfect in my bedroom!

BARBARA CASTLE *(Indicating* Seascape VII): *That's* the one for your bedroom, Barbara. This one's more for your family room.

BARBARA ZIMMER: Are you crazy, Barbara? It would be terrible in the family room!

BARBARA CASTLE: Well, it would be heaven in *my* family room!

BARBARA ZIMMER: Your family room and my family room are two different places!

BARBARA CASTLE *(Pointing to* Landscape II): *That's* the one for your bedroom, Barbara!

BARBARA ZIMMER: You mean, that's the one for *your* bedroom . . .

BARBARA CASTLE *(Gazing at* Landscape II, *picturing it in her bedroom)*: No. *(Then looking at the others, settling on* Seascape XIX) *That's* the one for my bedroom, and . . . *(After considering, indicating* Landscape I) . . . *this* is the one for your family room!

BARBARA ZIMMER: Well, what about *my* bedroom?

BARBARA CASTLE: Barbara, these aren't easy decisions!

BARBARA ZIMMER *(Pulling her friend's arm)*: Come on, we've got to get out of here. The cafeteria's probably jammed. We'll be in line forever!

BARBARA CASTLE *(Exiting with Barbara Zimmer)*: What are you going to order?

BARBARA ZIMMER: Oh, I don't know, I feel like a quiche . . .

BARBARA CASTLE: I'm more in the mood for a salad.

BARBARA ZIMMER: Their spinach salads are excellent!

BARBARA CASTLE *(As they exit)*: Yes, I know . . .

BARBARA CASTLE: Tarragon and dill dressing . . .　　BARBARA ZIMMER: Tarragon and dill dressing . . .

Mr. Gregory's tour suddenly goes berserk again, louder and faster than before. He pounds on it. Everyone looks at him and groans.

THE GUARD: HEY, WILL YOU TURN THAT DOWN? LISTEN, I'M AFRAID YOU'RE GOING TO HAVE TO TAKE THAT BACK DOWN TO THE DESK AND GET ANOTHER ONE . . . MAIN FLOOR. . . . I SAID, MAIN FLOOR . . . TO THE LEFT OF THE . . .

MR. GREGORY: IT'S STUCK, THE BUTTON'S STUCK. . . . IT'S JAMMED. . . . I CAN'T . . . WHAT? I CAN'T TURN IT OFF. . . . YES, I'M TRYING, I'M TRYING, BUT IT'S JAMMED . . .

The Guard drags Mr. Gregory from the room. Tink Solheim and Kate Siv enter. They're friends of the artist Agnes Vaag. They're dressed in exotic yet flattering clothes, and both exude a high-strung sensitivity. They've come to the show practically every day.

TINK SOLHEIM: The last day of the show!
KATE SIV: I can't believe it! The last day!

The Guard has returned, worn out from Mr. Gregory.

THE GUARD: Last day.
TINK SOLHEIM: The last day!
KATE SIV: Ed called this morning, he said Aggie might come.
TINK SOLHEIM: I know . . .
KATE SIV: He thinks she'll come around noon and bring Hilton with her.
TINK SOLHEIM: That's odd, Hilton told me it would be closer to three.
KATE SIV: Ed said Aggie has some appointment later on.
TINK SOLHEIM: Hilton didn't mention anything about it to me.
KATE SIV: Hilton probably hasn't been in touch with Ed.
TINK SOLHEIM: Aggie's busy at noon.
KATE SIV: Not according to Ed.
TINK SOLHEIM: But Aggie would never call Ed!
KATE SIV: You mean, Hilton would never call Ed!
TINK SOLHEIM: Well of course *Hilton* would never call Ed . . .
KATE SIV: Neither would Aggie.
TINK SOLHEIM: That's true.
KATE SIV *(Getting depressed)*: She'd never call Hilton, either.
TINK SOLHEIM: But Hilton called *her!*

KATE SIV: She'd never call anyone!

TINK SOLHEIM: And then he called *me*!

KATE SIV: She's the problem!

TINK SOLHEIM: Ed's the problem.

KATE SIV: And I don't trust Hilton.

TINK SOLHEIM: She'll come.

KATE SIV: What time is it?

TINK SOLHEIM: She'll be here.

KATE SIV: Maybe she already came and left . . .

TINK SOLHEIM *(In front of one of Agnes Vaag's pieces)*: Every time I see her work, it moves me more than the last time.

Chloe Trapp enters again with Bill Plaid, a man who is bewildered by art, and infuriated by modern art. That he is Chloe's guest at all is the result of some horrible mixup.

CHLOE TRAPP *(Advances to the clothesline)*: This is the final day of our group show, "The Broken Silence." *(Pause)* In his earliest work, Steve Williams experimented with such typically surrealist devices as totemic imagery, often incorporating assemblages of unrelated objects. The idea of indicating a magically demarcated environment . . . *(She indicates the length of the clothesline)* for his sculptures appeared early in his work as did his reliance on cloth and rope for basic materials.

BILL PLAID *(Confused and depressed)*: Yes. Cloth and rope.

CHLOE TRAPP: A surrealist cast persists in his most recent work, particularly in his use of erotic imagery and in his unexpected variations of color and scale.

Tink Solheim, without knowing what she's doing, picks up one of Agnes Vaag's sculptures and presses it against her cheek.

BILL PLAID: Yes, highly erotic.

CHLOE TRAPP: What makes Williams' work of unusual contemporary relevance, however, is his attitude towards the materials he uses and the processes he employs.

BILL PLAID *(Dimly)*: Cloth and rope.

CHLOE TRAPP: Rather than imposing his will upon materials in order to force them into a preordained form, Williams obeys the inherent capabilities of a given material and follows the suggestions offered by its particular qualities.

Bill Plaid, depressed, sits on one of the benches, head in hands. Tink Solheim is now rubbing the Vaag statue up and down her face.

CHLOE TRAPP: Gesture is a crucial factor in Williams' work, a means of indicating the participation of the artist in the—

Kate Siv notices that Tink has seized the statue and screams. Chloe Trapp screams because Kate screamed. Tink Solheim screams because their screams have startled her. Bill Plaid screams because he can't take it anymore.

THE GUARD: WHAT'S GOING ON?
KATE SIV: TINK, WHAT ARE YOU DOING WITH AGGIE'S STATUE?
TINK SOLHEIM *(Lost in her own reverie)*: What?
KATE SIV: WHAT . . . ARE . . . YOU . . . DOING . . . ?
CHLOE TRAPP: *The Temptation and Corruption of William Blake!*
KATE SIV: It's *The Temptation and Corruption of William Blake!*
TINK SOLHEIM *(Clutching it tighter)*: No!
CHLOE TRAPP: On loan from the Whitney Museum of American Art.
THE GUARD: Put that statue down, Miss.
CHLOE TRAPP: Her first attempt to combine porous with nonporous objects.

Bill Plaid groans.

KATE SIV: Tink, put it down!
THE GUARD: Please, Miss . . .

Tink Solheim, feeling cornered, dashes to the clothesline and stands among the bodies.

CHLOE TRAPP: Tink, we'd all like you to put the statue down before something terrible happens . . .

KATE SIV: Oh Tink, you're going to drop it, and it will shatter into a million pieces . . .

FRED IZUMI: It's all right. Everything's going to be all right . . .

GILDA NORRIS *(Ready to pounce)*: SURROUND HER!
THE GUARD: Sssssssssh, calm down. Let's everybody just . . . calm down . . . take it easy . . .
MICHAEL WALL: Hey, could I look at it for a minute?

Michael Wall holds out his hands to Tink Solheim with great gentleness. She eyes him, frightened, but then softens and starts to hand him the statue.

KATE SIV: Oh Tink, what's happened to you?

THE GUARD: Sssshhhhhh . . .

MICHAEL WALL: I'll give it right back. It's so beautiful . . .

GILDA NORRIS: GRAB IT!

TINK SOLHEIM *(Lifts the statue high over her head)*: DON'T TOUCH ME!

KATE SIV: Oh Tink . . .

THE GUARD: Miss, you'd better—

CHLOE TRAPP: It's my favorite one, my very—

BILL PLAID: Go ahead . . . SMASH THE UGLY THING!

A silence.

TINK SOLHEIM: Yesterday . . . I was remembering a day I spent with Agnes Vaag.

KATE SIV: Aggie!

TINK SOLHEIM: Aggie . . .

KATE SIV: We're friends of the artist. *Old* friends . . . she's such a wonderful—

TINK SOLHEIM: Agnes Vaag invited me to spend a day with her in the country. Looking for her things; bones, wings . . . teeth . . .

THE GUARD *(Reaching up for the statue)*: WATCH IT!

CHLOE TRAPP: ALL OF HER MATERIALS ARE FOUND MATERIALS!

MICHAEL WALL: I've never seen anything like this . . .

KATE SIV: She'll be here later, with Hilton.

TINK SOLHEIM: She finds all her objects in Connecticut state parks. *(Fitfully caressing her face with the statue)* At least once a month she gets on a Greyhound bus carrying two blue suitcases filled with soft polyester batting for wrapping her objects in . . . and scours one of Connecticut's state parks. The last time she invited me to go with her. I said I'd bring along an extra suitcase and a picnic lunch. We met at the Port Authority Bus Terminal. It was so . . . odd. Going with Aggie to look for something. I mean, whenever you see her in her studio, her hands are always full: molding something, gluing something. Her studio is bursting with the exotic: bird beaks, fish skeletons, turkey down, fox claws . . .

KATE SIV: I'm Aggie's oldest friend, I've known her for years!

TINK SOLHEIM: So I just assumed she always *had* these things, that they were part of her, not something separate she had to seek out. So it was odd meeting her at Port Authority carrying those two blue suitcases stuffed with polyester batting.

KATE SIV: She's invited me on her expeditions millions of times . . . of course I—

TINK SOLHEIM: I don't remember the name of the park we visited, but Aggie seemed to know her way around and before I realized it, we were walking through deep woods. Deep woods is the best place to find small animal skeletons, she told me. While I looked up at the trees and sky, she bent close to the ground, scooping her hands through the underbrush like some human net. In the first hour she found a bat skeleton, several raccoon skulls, a fresh rabbit carcass, patches of fur . . .

KATE SIV: Aggie's only twenty-four, you know . . . and so beautiful . . . !

TINK SOLHEIM: At one moment she was crouched out of view, the next she was holding fragile white bones up to the sun exclaiming over their perfect—

KATE SIV: She has this amazing blond hair. It's as thick as rope and falls down her back in golden cascades . . .

TINK SOLHEIM: After a while she had filled both her blue suitcases and asked if she could borrow mine. We stopped for lunch and she gave me a long speech about how calcium is formed in the bones of vegetarian animals . . .

KATE SIV: And her eyes are this deep . . . green . . .

TINK SOLHEIM: It wasn't long before my suitcase was filled too and it was starting to get dark. I suggested we walk back along a different route, but she said no, she couldn't stop yet.

KATE SIV: MEN DIE OVER HER!

TINK SOLHEIM: It was then I noticed something . . . strange. Well, I didn't notice it, I heard it because it was getting too dark to see. As she was combing the underbrush, I heard this soft kind of . . . licking noise . . . a slight kind of . . . slurping . . . like eating, but not really chewing and swallowing . . . just licking and tasting. "Is that you, Aggie?" I asked her. But she never answered, and it was such a light muffled sound, she could have been sucking on a mint. *(Deep breath)* I told her I really thought we should leave before it got any darker and we got lost, and this time with real anger in her voice, she said . . . NO! And then the nibbling, or kissing . . . or whatever it was . . . got louder. We reached a clearing, the trees dropped away, the moon shone down on Aggie's bent form as clear as day, and then I saw . . . she was holding one of the little skeletons up to her mouth and . . . was licking it, nibbling on it . . . running her tongue over it. I screamed. She dropped the little thing and turned white. The next thing I knew, she was hitting me with her fists, socking me hard all over my body, screaming and crying, "I hate you! I hate you! I HATE YOU!"

KATE SIV *(Near tears)*: I'm not listening to this.

BILL PLAID: Oh boy, oh boy, oh boy, all artists are *crazy!*

CHLOE TRAPP: Her perceptual gifts are extraordinary!

BILL PLAID: NUTS! ALL OF THEM!

KATE SIV: You made it up. You made it all up! That didn't happen! NONE OF IT . . . HAPPENED!

BILL PLAID: YOU HAVE TO BE NUTS TO MAKE THE STUFF!

TINK SOLHEIM *(Puts the sculpture back on its pedestal)*: Agnes Vaag's breath reeks!

THE GUARD: Thank you very much.

TINK SOLHEIM: Her breath is . . . foul!

KATE SIV: You made it up! You've never been invited on one of her expeditions, and you know it. It's your jealousy, Tink . . . your relentless jealousy . . . and it's hateful . . . hateful . . . hateful . . . *(She runs from the room, sobbing)*

TINK SOLHEIM *(Giddy)*: I always noticed a certain animal quality about her breath, a certain . . . rancidness . . . something sour. You know how certain people have breath that doesn't smell quite . . . human?

CHLOE TRAPP *(Shattered)*: It was at my insistence that Agnes Vaag was invited to exhibit in the show. *(She exits)*

THE GUARD: For a minute there, you had me worried.

Lillian, Harriet and May enter. Their arms are linked and they're on the verge of a belly laugh. Harriet and May have covered their eyes with their hands as Lillian leads them to the Moes.

LILLIAN: Will you look at that?

Harriet and May uncover their eyes and let out a piercing shriek of laughter.

LILLIAN *(Also laughing)*: Modern art!

HARRIET AND MAY *(Clutching one another)*: I don't believe it . . . stop . . . oh stop . . . please . . .

LILLIAN *(Advances to the first Moe and reads the title)*: "Landscape I, 1989. Acrylic emulsion and wax on canvas. On loan from the Sidney Rubin Gallery."

All three roar.

BILL PLAID: AND YOU HAVE TO BE NUTS TO LOOK AT IT! *(Rises to exit)* Sucking on statues . . . I mean, normal people don't go around sucking statues, do they? *(Going up to The Guard)* I've

never seen a *normal* person sucking on a statue, have you? First of
all, a *normal* person would never even *think* of sucking on a—
THE GUARD *(Gently lays his hands on Bill Plaid)*: All right, that's enough,
quiet down, it's all right . . . *(Leads him off)*
BILL PLAID *(Resisting)*: HEY, WHAT ARE YOU DOING? WHAT
ARE YOU THROWING *ME* OUT FOR? I DIDN'T DO ANY-
THING . . . *(Pointing to the laughing ladies)* They're the ones you
ought to throw out . . . sucking on statues, Jesus! *(And he's gone)*
HARRIET *(Looking at the Moes)*: There's . . . nothing on them!
MAY: They're . . . blank!
HARRIET: BLANK!

*All three go off into a shower of laughter again, falling against each
other, crossing their legs so they don't wet their pants.*

LILLIAN: "*Landscape II*, 1989. Acrylic emulsion and wax on canvas. On
loan from the Sidney Rubin Gallery"!
HARRIET: It looks just like the first one.
MAY: Blank!
LILLIAN: No, I like the first one better!
HARRIET: Me too, the first one's better!

All three go off into gales.

THE GUARD: I just wish this day would end.
LILLIAN *(At* Starscape XIX*)*: Now . . . *this* is really special!
HARRIET: You're right, this one's the best!

They all stand in front of it.

LILLIAN: Guess what the title is?
HARRIET *(Taking her time)*: Let's see . . . SNOWSTORM!

All three laugh like crazy.

LILLIAN: "*Starscape XIX*"!
HARRIET: I don't see any stars!
LILLIAN: I don't see any paint!

All three laugh like crazy again.

LILLIAN *(Reading)*: "Acrylic emulsion and wax on canvas." They're all
acrylic emulsion and wax.
HARRIET: It must be the latest thing.
LILLIAN: I guess they melt the wax right into the acrylic emulsion.
MAY: What is *acrylic emulsion* anyway?

HARRIET: If you ask me, he should have put a wick in with the wax, and lit a match!

All three howl.

THE GUARD: Ladies, please. You're disturbing the other visitors in the gallery.

It's true, with each outbreak of hysteria, the other people in the room are jolted out of their concentration and look at them with annoyance. Lillian, Harriet and May work themselves down to the clothesline. They spot Gilda Norris on the way, furiously sketching from the Moe. They point at her, then at the Moe, and collapse with a fresh shower of giggles. Lillian catches sight of the clothesline, lets out her loudest shriek of all.

LILLIAN: OH, NO!

MAY *(Diving for the basket, enthralled)*: LOOK AT THIS. HE LEFT OUT THE BASKET OF CLOTHESPINS!

THE GUARD *(Strides over to them)*: Please don't handle the artworks!

MAY *(Picks up a clothespin)*: Wait a minute, they don't make this kind of round-headed clothespin anymore.

LILLIAN *(Takes it from her)*: Let me see . . .

HARRIET *(Also taking one)*: I HAVEN'T SEEN A ROUND-HEADED CLOTHESPIN WITHOUT A SPRING FOR YEARS!

MAY: My mother used to use round-headed clothespins like these. I still remember her holding a clothespin just like this and leaning down to show it to me, saying, "Maisie, line-dried wash hung with round-headed clothespins always hangs better, and don't you ever forget it!"

LILLIAN: I didn't think they made them anymore.

HARRIET: They must be old . . .

MAY: The round-headed ones grip much better than the flat-headed ones.

LILLIAN: They do, they do!

THE GUARD *(Trying to get them to put the pins back)*: Ladies . . . *please!*

MAY: Also, the flat-headed ones tend to split in two.

HARRIET: The springs always rusted on the flat-headed ones.

MAY: That's right, and then they'd come shooting off the line like little rockets . . .

TINK SOLHEIM *(Gazing at one of the Vaags, to The Guard with feeling)*: EACH OF HER PIECES IS A SMALL MIRACLE!

THE GUARD (*Moves to Tink, trying to keep an eye on the other ladies*): I know, I know . . .

TINK SOLHEIM: NO YOU DON'T KNOW! NOBODY KNOWS!

Lillian, Harriet and May stealthfully stuff clothespins into their handbags and pockets now that The Guard's busy with Tink. They try hard but unsuccessfully to muffle their giggles.

THE GUARD (*To Tink*): Calm down . . .

TINK SOLHEIM: There's a secret . . .

THE GUARD: Yes, Miss, I believe you.

TINK SOLHEIM: Aggie told me that she hid a special surprise inside each piece . . .

THE GUARD: Yes, I'm sure . . .

TINK SOLHEIM: It's not visible to the naked eye. You can only find it through vibrations of sound or touch . . . (*Laying her hands on the pedestal*)

THE GUARD: Everything's going to be all right . . .

TINK SOLHEIM (*Her movements increasingly manic*): THAT'S THE THING ABOUT AGNES VAAG. SHE ALWAYS TAKES YOU BY SURPRISE!

Lillian, Harriet and May are awash with suppressed laughter.

THE GUARD (*Torn in his duty*): Ladies . . . *please!*

TINK SOLHEIM: She only reveals the surface.

LILLIAN: I've got twelve. How many do you have?

Harriet giggles.

MAY: I've got seven.

LILLIAN: Only seven? Take more.

HARRIET (*Ecstatic*): I HAVEN'T SEEN A ROUND-HEADED CLOTHESPIN WITHOUT A SPRING . . . IN YEARS!

TINK SOLHEIM: She challenged me: FIND THE MIRACLE TINK! FIND IT ON THE LAST DAY!

THE GUARD (*Dashes over to the ladies*): LADIES, LADIES, LADIES! NOW THAT'S ENOUGH. LET'S PUT ALL THE CLOTHESPINS BACK LIKE GOOD GIRLS AND TRY AND REMEMBER THAT YOU'RE IN A MUSEUM! PUT THEM BACK IN THE BASKET . . . EVERY ONE. HURRY UP. . . . DO AS I SAY. . . . THAT'S IT. . . . THAT'S THE WAY . . .

Lillian, Harriet and May, leaking clothespins, lurch out of the room, wobbling with laughter. It's the best time they've had in their lives. The room is very quiet. Nothing happens for some time. Out of nowhere, The Guard sings a long, rather mournful note. Liz, worn out from her search, enters depressed.

LIZ: Carol? Blakey? Guys? . . . Shit! *(She exits)*
TINK SOLHEIM: Aggie told me she hid a special surprise in each piece. She challenged me: Find it on the last day.
THE GUARD *(Dimly)*: Last day . . .

Giorgio and Zoe enter, a polished couple in their forties.

GIORGIO: Today's the last day . . .
ZOE: The last day?
TINK SOLHEIM: The last day . . .
ZOE: I didn't realize it was the last day!
THE GUARD: God in heaven . . .
GIORGIO: Today's the last day!
TINK SOLHEIM: Laaaaaaaaaaaaaast day!

Julie Jenkins, another photographer, enters. A tall, leggy knockout. She carries three times more photographic equipment than the others. She slings it all down in front of the clothesline.

THE GUARD: NOW WAIT JUST ONE MINUTE, IT'S AGAINST MUSEUM REGULATIONS TO PHOTOGRAPH THE ART-WORKS!
GIORGIO *(Looking at* Landscape I): Zachery Moe!
ZOE *(To Giorgio)*: Look at that girl, she's touching one of the statues . . .
JULIE JENKINS: But today's the last day!
ZOE: Giorgio, look!
THE GUARD: I'm sorry, Miss. It's against museum regulations.
GIORGIO: His parents are deaf, I believe.
JULIE JENKINS: But I came to photograph Bill Stevens' clothesline!
THE GUARD: You mean, Steve Williams, not Bill Stevens.
JULIE JENKINS: Steve Stevens?
THE GUARD: STEVE WILLIAMS!
JULIE JENKINS: I thought his name was Bill Stevens.
THE GUARD: Steve Stevens?
JULIE JENKINS *(Desperate)*: WILLIAM STEVENSON!
THE GUARD: Stevenson?
JULIE JENKINS: Williamson?
THE GUARD: Stephen Williamson?
JULIE JENKINS: *WILLIAM* Williamson!

THE GUARD: Steve!

JULIE JENKINS *(Amazed)*: STEVE?

THE GUARD: Williams!

JULIE JENKINS: *Williams?*

THE GUARD: Steve. Williams!

JULIE JENKINS: Artists always have such tricky names . . .

GIORGIO: Or is it Raoul Io's parents who are deaf?

ZOE *(Absorbed with Tink)*: She's not supposed to be doing that.

THE GUARD: You have to get permission from the Director to photograph the artwork!

JULIE JENKINS *(Waving a slip)*: I have permission.

THE GUARD *(Taking it)*: Yes, I see.

JULIE JENKINS: From the Director . . .

THE GUARD: Oh?

JULIE JENKINS: Daddy!

ZOE: She's going to get into trouble . . .

JULIE JENKINS *(Unloading her gear)*: Daddy's the Director!

ZOE: Look at her, Giorgio!

GIORGIO *(Examining* Landscape I *up close)*: Very interesting!

JULIE JENKINS: GOD, I LOVE STEVE STEVENS' WORK!

THE GUARD: The Director's daughter *(Indicating Gilda Norris)* . . . your sister's here too!

ZOE: She's touching them . . .

GIORGIO: Brilliant brushwork!

JULIE JENKINS: All my life I've wanted to photograph a real Bill Stevenson!

GIORGIO *(Nose against the canvas)*: It's extraordinary how much of the detail you miss when you don't take the time to really examine a canvas!

THE GUARD *(Going over to him)*: Please sir, don't *smell* the painting!

GIORGIO: I'm not *smelling* the painting, I'm examining the brushwork!

THE GUARD: Zachery Moe doesn't use a brush!

ZOE: Oh, Giorgio!

GIORGIO: He use a roller?

THE GUARD: Nope.

ZOE: Come on, don't start this again.

GIORGIO: Stain technique?

THE GUARD: Nope.

GIORGIO: Spilling?

THE GUARD: No.

The Guard and Giorgio go faster and faster.

GIORGIO: Pooling?

THE GUARD: No.

GIORGIO: Scumbling?

THE GUARD: No.

ZOE: People are staring . . .

GIORGIO: Blotting?

THE GUARD: No.

GIOᴋGIO: Toweling?

THE GUARD: No.

GIORGIO: Shit!

THE GUARD: No.

GIORGIO: AIR BRUSH?

THE GUARD: You got it!

GIORGIO *(Laughing)*: I knew it all along!

ZOE: Did not . . .

GIORGIO *(To The Guard)*: In air brushing successive layers of paint, Moe stresses the actuality of the surface and limits the distances between the—

ZOE *(Pulling at him)*: Come on, Giorgio, I'm bored. Let's look at something else . . . I'm tired of this. . . . Come on, let's go to another floor . . . Giorgio!

GIORGIO *(To The Guard)*: It's the relationship of the figure to the support and the consequent affirmation of the picture plane that makes it difficult to penetrate the atmosphere space behind it—

Tink Solheim suddenly releases the miracle buried in The Holy Wars of Babylon Rage through the Night. *The lights dim. A floodlight pours down on the statue and Bach's* Dorian *Toccata and Fugue in D Minor, BWV 538 for organ swells from a speaker concealed in the pedestal.*

TINK SOLHEIM: I FOUND IT! I FOUND IT! *The Holy Wars of Babylon Rage through the Night!*

Everyone is thunderstruck. They gaze at Tink and the statue, chills racing up their backs. There's a hush and a slow realization that the music is part of the statue.

TINK SOLHEIM: I found the switch. I found it!

GIORGIO: How beautiful . . .

ZOE: Oh, Giorgio . . .

GILDA NORRIS: I'm going to die . . .

Everyone slowly draws near the statue to worship.

JULIE JENKINS: It's a wave . . . cresting!
GIORGIO: It's a stunning Renaissance landscape . . .
MICHAEL WALL: It's the urban vision of a futurist . . .

Fred Izumi recites some haiku in Japanese.

GILDA NORRIS: "And lo, the angel of the Lord came upon them, and the glory of the Lord shone around about them . . ."
TINK SOLHEIM: She challenged me: Find it on the last day . . .
THE GUARD: It's a self-portrait.
ZOE: Growth!

As the music pours from its source, each viewer improvises on the unique beauty he sees. Their voices frequently overlap, but rich details of observation come through. This lasts for several minutes. The volume of the music slowly decreases.

TINK SOLHEIM: It was worth it . . .
ZOE: Nothing like this has ever happened to me before . . .
TINK SOLHEIM: It was all worth it . . . *everything!*
THE GUARD: The museum had no idea . . .
GIORGIO: Of course there are precedents for *heard* art . . .
ZOE: Giorgio, hold me . . . !
GILDA NORRIS: I'll never forget this day . . . never!
FRED IZUMI: She must have snuck in after the installation of the show and set it all up . . .
THE GUARD: None of the security force was told.
TINK SOLHEIM: *She is vindicated!* Through me! Through me! *(She exits)*

Everyone takes one last look at the statue and then drifts to other Agnes Vaag works in hopes of finding similar wonders. The Guard watches over The Holy Wars, *trying to figure out what triggered the music and lights. He breathes on it in a certain way and the music stops; the lights go back to normal. Baffled, he keeps circling it. First Guard, dressed just like The Guard, enters and joins him.*

FIRST GUARD: Busy?

The Guard, caught actually studying an artwork, is embarrassed and feigns indifference. He whistles.

FIRST GUARD: You look busy.
THE GUARD: This is the last day of my show.
FIRST GUARD: Oh, a closing.

Second Guard, dressed as the others, joins them.

SECOND GUARD: Busy?

THE GUARD: Boy!

FIRST GUARD: I've been swamped!

SECOND GUARD: Colonial Quilts and Weathervanes are slow. I only had three people this morning.

FIRST GUARD: I must have sold a hundred and fifty dollars worth of postcards in the last hour.

THE GUARD: It's been very busy here.

SECOND GUARD: My show still has two more weeks. I don't know how I'm going to make it, it's so slow.

FIRST GUARD: Engagement calendars aren't doing well, but they just can't get enough postcards!

SECOND GUARD: Very slow.

THE GUARD: The Director has given three photographers permission to photograph the artworks.

FIRST AND SECOND GUARD: THREE?

THE GUARD: And a sketcher!

FIRST GUARD: Jesus . . .

SECOND GUARD: Son of a bitch . . .

THE GUARD: I don't know where it will end.

FIRST GUARD (*To the Second Guard*): You busy this morning? I'm swamped!

SECOND GUARD: Very slow. Only three people. (*Looking around*) You look pretty busy.

THE GUARD: This is the last day of my show.

SECOND GUARD: I haven't been busy like this since my American Abstract show last spring.

THE GUARD: They keep stealing my clothespins.

FIRST GUARD: I've just about sold out of your catalogues.

THE GUARD: I'm not surprised.

SECOND GUARD: Thursdays are slow.

FIRST GUARD: Thursdays are slow. But *Tuesdays* . . .

SECOND GUARD: Tuesdays! (*Silence*) Saturdays are pretty bad.

FIRST GUARD: I'd rather work on a Saturday than a Sunday, though.

SECOND GUARD: Sundays aren't so bad.

THE GUARD: I don't mind Sundays.

SECOND GUARD: I like Sundays.

THE GUARD: Sundays are nice . . .   SECOND GUARD: Sunday's a good day.

Silence.

THE GUARD: I just wish people would stop stealing the clothespins.

FIRST GUARD: Hey, did you hear the radio this morning?

SECOND GUARD: THOSE EUROPEAN MUSEUMS HAVE SHIT FOR SECURITY!

Everyone looks up.

SECOND GUARD *(Lowering his voice)*: Any maniac can get away with anything in a European museum. Look what happened to Michelangelo's *Pietà* . . .

FIRST GUARD: And that Rembrandt last year, slashed with a bread knife.

SECOND GUARD: That's right. It could never happen here.

FIRST GUARD: American security is the best.

THE GUARD: You can't beat American security.

FIRST GUARD: NUMBER ONE!

SECOND GUARD: That's right. WE'RE NUMBER ONE ON SECURITY!

Everyone looks up again.

FIRST GUARD: First!

THE GUARD: The best!

FIRST GUARD: American museums have the tightest security of any museum in the whole fucking world!

THE GUARD AND THE SECOND GUARD: Yeah, you said it, that's right, number one. The best. *(Etc.)*

FIRST GUARD: The people over there are nuts!

THE GUARD AND THE SECOND GUARD: You can say that again. Here, here. You ain't just whistling Dixie. *(Etc.)*

FIRST GUARD: Violent bastards. An American would never shoot a painting!

SECOND GUARD: Well, they know they can get away with it over there, so that just encourages them to be violent.

They get more and more worked up.

THE GUARD: That's right, that's right!

FIRST GUARD: The worst that's happened over there is some nut with a can of spray paint that washes right off.

SECOND GUARD: Everyone's nuts these days.

THE GUARD: I just wish they'd stop stealing the clothespins!

FIRST GUARD: Did you hear what the guy kept screaming as he shot the painting? "Cursed is the ground for thy sake."

SECOND GUARD: "Cursed is the *ground* for thy sake"?

THE GUARD: Crazy bastards!

FIRST GUARD: It's what Adam said to Eve after she ate the apple.

SECOND GUARD: Jesus.

THE GUARD: Crazy bastards!

FIRST GUARD: Crazy fuckers always yell out something religious when they attack artworks!

SECOND GUARD: You wouldn't find me working over there for shit!

FIRST GUARD: They're all nuts on religion over there . . .

THE GUARD: Crazy bastards . . .

FIRST GUARD: He pumped eighteen bullets into the damned painting before he was restrained . . . eighteen bullets!

Silence.

SECOND GUARD *(Reaches in his pocket)*: Hey, look what I found this morning. Someone must have dropped it.

THE GUARD: Let's see.

FIRST GUARD: What is it?

SECOND GUARD *(Holding it up to the light)*: A piece of rose quartz.

THE GUARD *(Takes it and holds it up to the light)*: It looks more like pink tourmaline to me. *(Hands it to the First Guard)*

FIRST GUARD *(Looking at it)*: This isn't tourmaline, it's rhodochrosite!

SECOND GUARD *(Snatching it back)*: Rhodochrosite shit, it's rose quartz!

FIRST GUARD: It's too opaque to be rose quartz.

THE GUARD: But it's too dense to be rhodochrosite!

SECOND GUARD: Dense? This isn't dense! It's translucent!

FIRST GUARD *(Holding it up to the light)*: There *are* semitranslucent varieties of rhodochrosite!

THE GUARD: Pink tourmaline can be dense or translucent. It's pink tourmaline.

SECOND GUARD: This can't be pink tourmaline because tourmaline doesn't come in pink!

FIRST GUARD: How could it be rose quartz? It's closer to pink tourmaline . . . even if there's no such animal.

THE GUARD: Rhodochrosite is worth a lot more than rose quartz.

FIRST GUARD: Or pink tourmaline, for that matter.

SECOND GUARD *(Putting the stone back in his pocket and pulling out some papers)*: All right, you guys, I've got our assignments for lunch hour.

The other guards groan.

SECOND GUARD: It's not too bad. *(To The Guard)* Since Lou and George were let go last week, you'll be needed at the register in the Gift Shop because he's *(The First Guard)* got to relieve Otto in the Members' Lounge.

THE GUARD: Son of a—

SECOND GUARD *(To the First Guard)*: You go to the Members' Lounge while I cover for Raoul in the Checkroom since no one's been in the Klein retrospective all week. Colonial Quilts and Weathervanes is closed for the rest of the day.

THE GUARD *(In an urgent whisper)*: But someone has to stay here. It's the last day of the show.

SECOND GUARD: You'll be back in a half-hour. I just need you to cover for him in the Gift Shop so he can relieve Otto.

THE GUARD: I don't think it's a good idea to leave the room . . . unattended . . .

Everyone looks up and then quickly away.

SECOND GUARD: It's orders.

THE GUARD: You know what closings are like. Everyone takes things . . .

Everyone looks up again.

SECOND GUARD: You mean . . . *(Laughs)* clothespins . . . ?

THE GUARD: Yes, clothespins!

Second Guard bursts out laughing.

FIRST GUARD: Clothespins!

THE GUARD *(Picks up a clothespin to show them)*: They can't get enough of them. They're the old-fashioned kind with round heads.

FIRST GUARD *(Takes it)*: You mean the ones without the spring in the middle?

THE GUARD: That's right.

FIRST GUARD: Jeez, we used to have those . . .

Steve Williams, the artist, enters. He radiates charisma. Everyone stares at him; they're not sure who he is, but they know he's someone important and draw back silently. He's come to look at his clothesline and wears the identical clothes as his self-portrait which hangs on the line. He studies the arrangement of the figures from across the room, perplexed. A silence.

SECOND GUARD (*Eyes glued to Steve Williams*): You know, I thought my American Abstract show was busy, but I've got to hand it to you, yours is busier!

THE GUARD (*Also staring at Williams*): Huh?! Huh?!

FIRST GUARD: Come on, we've got to get out of here quietly so no one will notice . . .

THE GUARD: That's right, just slip right out . . .

SECOND GUARD: Sssssshhhhhhh . . .

They exit on tiptoe.

FIRST GUARD: Listen, the Gift Shop isn't as bad as the Members' Lounge, I don't care what you say . . . (*Etc.*)	THE GUARD: Christ, I hate the Gift Shop! The worst shift of all has got to be the goddamned Gift Shop . . . (*Etc.*)	SECOND GUARD: Otto hasn't had lunch for three weeks now, three weeks. His doctor says he's developing incipient ulcers . . . (*Etc.*)

GILDA NORRIS (*The first to realize, her heart in her throat*): That's . . . Steve Williams!

GIORGIO: My God, the artist!

ZOE: Oh, Giorgio!

MICHAEL WALL: I thought he looked familiar!

FRED IZUMI: Steve Williams!

ZOE: He's dressed just like his self-portrait!

GILDA NORRIS (*Swooning*): Steve . . . Williams?

JULIE JENKINS: STEVE STEVENS!

The three photographers quickly take advantage of this media event, and start snapping pictures of Williams and his amazing performance. At times they work independently, and then suddenly strike group poses. Steve Williams ignores everyone and stands engrossed before his work. Something's wrong, the figures aren't positioned correctly. One by one, he unpins the bodies, laying them carefully on the benches and floor until the clothesline is bare. After careful thought he picks up the Mexican boy, cradles him in his arms, and hangs him first on the line. With considerable dash he adds the bride, then his own figure, which he handles with rough good humor, and so on until the lineup is complete. He doesn't make a sound and wields the bodies with such grace that everyone is deeply affected, as Giorgio strides over to the clothesline, and reads Williams' bio from the catalogue.

GIORGIO: "Steven Williams was born October 30, 1943, in Santa Rosa, California. He studied at the Leonardo da Vinci School and had his first one-man show at the Dilexi Gallery, San Francisco, in 1952; an exhibition of animal heads in cement, which in their open framework and pitted surfaces, were a powerful refutation of the prevailing modern traditions of neat forms, clean surfaces, and truth to materials. Williams lived in Paris from 1952 through 1958 where he exhibited in a group show at the Galerie Maeght, visited Giacometti's studio, and was exposed to and impressed by the works of Paul Klee, Dada, and Surrealism. His sculpture thereafter presented anguished images of the anonymity of modern man, using cast-off objects assembled according to an indisputably human framework. Since 1970, Williams' sculpture, although still governed by the principles of assemblages, comprise more simply structured monumental components, incorporated with techno-logical precision into quite different icons of modernity."

Steve Williams, finished with his work, stands back to survey the new lineup. He smiles. Everyone smiles. The photographers pull out all their stops. Julie Jenkins starts using a flash, Michael Wall practically crawls inside Williams' clothing, Fred Izumi photographs from daring new angles. The women in the room reach out their hands towards Williams. Steve Williams is pleased and walks energetically out of the room, flashing one final smile. A silence. The lines that follow should spill over each other.

GILDA NORRIS: I thought I was going to die . . . just sink down to the floor, shut my eyes, and quietly die . . .

JULIE JENKINS: Did you see those hands?

MICHAEL WALL: That was pure . . . once in a lifetime!

FRED IZUMI: Harrison isn't going to believe this!

JULIE JENKINS: And his arms . . . MY GOD, THE TENDERNESS IN HIS ARMS!

GILDA NORRIS: I'll never be the same.

ZOE: But you're not supposed to touch anything once it's been installed, are you?

GIORGIO: His pieces sell for over two hundred thousand dollars! Two hundred thousand dollars!

Everyone is silent again. They gaze at the clothesline for some time.

ZOE: Oh, Giorgio, let's take something . . . as a remembrance.

JULIE JENKINS: Steve Stevens . . .

ZOE: One of the clothespins . . . something he touched.
GILDA NORRIS: Something he touched . . .
JULIE JENKINS: Something he touched . . .
MICHAEL WALL: A clothespin . . .
FRED IZUMI: A clothespin . . .

No one moves. Zoe breaks the spell, walks to the clothesline and brazenly snatches a clothespin. One by one each person approaches the basket, and takes one or more pins. It's not a mad scramble, but a communion, enacted with quiet reverence. Once the first theft has been tasted, they become thirsty for more. The bride's arm is pulled off with an awful rending sound. Julie Jenkins rushes up to the Steve Williams figure and throws her arms around him. Gilda Norris edges past her and kisses his face; his head falls off in her amazed hands. The others move in for their share: half of the Mexican boy is removed; the businessman's legs are severed; arms, legs, and pieces of clothing are snatched. The lights dim as each person scurries out with his booty. The clothesline is almost picked clean. Only a few stray torsos, heads, and veils are left.

Mr. and Mrs. Moe, Zachery Moe's deaf-mute parents, slip in unnoticed during these final moments. Caring only for their son's work, they go directly to his paintings and stand before them, radiant with pride and happiness. The Guard returns from his lunch break, sees the devastation of the clothesline and is horrified. He tries to protect the few scraps that remain and then starts running in terrible confusion. He finally notices the Moes.

THE GUARD: What happened in here? What's been going on? The clothesline! Who did this? Look at it . . . the clothesline . . . it's been picked apart . . . destroyed . . . what . . . happened? WILL YOU PLEASE TELL ME . . . WHAT HAPPENED? WHO DID THIS?

Mr. and Mrs. Moe don't answer. The Guard realizes they're beyond him and kneels by the basket of clothespins, broken. Mr. and Mrs. Moe keep gazing at the paintings, completely unaware of The Guard. They move to their favorite one and stand beneath it, riveted. Mrs. Moe turns to her husband and speaks in sign language.

MRS. MOE: Remember the drawings he used to make as a child?
MR. MOE: The sketches he did of all his toys in his nursery . . .
MRS. MOE: How wonderful they were, bursting with life . . .
MR. MOE: *Noisy* with life!

MRS. MOE: Remember how he'd make the walls shake when he wanted something?

MR. MOE: And how they shook! He shouted with the voice of a thousand men!

The lights fade on their rhapsodic hands as the curtain slowly falls.

THE ART
OF DINING

Coproduced by the New York Shakespeare Festival and the Kennedy Center, *The Art of Dining* was staged in New York and then in Washington, D.C. in 1979, under the direction of A.J. Antoon.

Characters

ELLEN, co-owner and chef extraordinaire of The Golden Carousel, mid-thirties

CAL, co-owner and supple headwaiter of The Golden Carousel, Ellen's husband, mid-thirties.

HANNAH GALT, beautifully dressed and hungry, mid-forties.

PAUL GALT, beautifuly dressed and hungrier, mid-forties.

ELIZABETH BARROW COLT, exceedingly shy and nearsighted. A writer, in her early thirties, afraid of food.

HERRICK SIMMONS, enthusiastic and a good eater, early thirties.

NESSA VOX, easily upset and a more neurotic eater, early thirties.

TONY STASSIO, perpetually on a diet and miserable, early thirties.

DAVID, OSSLOW, the head of his own publishing company, successful, at ease, son and husband of good cooks, mid-fifties and in top shape.

Time

The present. Early evening.

Place

The Golden Carousel Restaurant, New Jersey.

ACT ONE

Scene 1

The ground floor of a nineteenth-century townhouse on the New Jersey shore which has been converted into a restaurant, The Golden Carousel. It's a wonderfully elegant little place with a high tin ceiling, arched windows and masses of hanging plants. A pair of restored carousel horses with flashing gold manes or hooves prance in a corner. A surreal nostalgia suffuses the room. Things are on the verge of lifting off the, ground or disappearing entirely. Nothing is quite what it seems. Embedded within, behind or to one side of this magical dining area is a full working kitchen. Though many of its features are old—sink, lighting fixtures, ornate molding, for example—it's equipped with all the most up-to-date appliances. It's late November, unusually cold, and a month after the restaurant's grand opening. Four tables are set for dinner, and the fragrance of the evening's offerings fills the air.

Ellen and Cal are sitting at one of the tables about to sample two different desserts. They should be mistaken for customers.

Ellen, tense with expectancy, dips her spoon into her glass of Floating Island, tastes it and holds her breath.

Cal stabs his spoon into his dish of Pears and Cointreau with Frozen Cream and croons with delight.

Ellen savors her mouthful and exhales with relief.

Cal very rapidly takes another taste, sighs.

Ellen takes a cautious second taste and makes a humming sound.

Cal takes three rapid-fire tastes, making little whimpering sounds after each one.

Ellen licks her lips and pauses.

Cal, scraping his spoon against the sides of his dish with fervor, takes a heaping mouthful and groans with pleasure.

Ellen takes another apprehensive taste. Yes, it's excellent; she purrs.

Cal overcome, drops his head in his hands.

Ellen puts her spoon down and nods her head yes. Silence. She shoves her dessert over to Cal to try. He dips his spoon in, takes a slow loving taste. It's even better than his! He moans helplessly and pushes his dessert over to her. Ellen takes a swift taste of the pears, making little lip-smacking noises.

Cal takes a huge spoonful of Floating Island and is mute.

A silence.

Ellen exhales with pleasure. She takes another taste, inhales, stares into space, puts her spoon down, and clicks her tongue, exhilarated. A silence.

Cal takes a smaller taste, then makes a low sob and takes five very fast spoonfuls grunting during each one.

Ellen reaches across the table and takes back her Floating Island and returns the pears to Cal. She scrapes the sides of her glass.

Cal fiercely attacks what's left of his pears.

They finish, breathing heavily.

CAL *(Weakly)*: Pears . . .

ELLEN *(Undone)*: Meringues . . .

CAL: Cointreau . . .

ELLEN: Vanilla . . .

CAL: Heavy cream . . .

ELLEN: Caramel . . .

CAL: Chilled . . .

ELLEN: Poached . . .

CAL: Cool . . .

ELLEN: Quivering . . .

CAL: . . . to perfection!

ELLEN: In English Cream!

CAL: Pure sin!

ELLEN: Real joy.

CAL: A person could die . . .

ELLEN: Which did you like better?

CAL: What a way to go!

ELLEN: The pears . . .

CAL: Christ!

ELLEN: . . . or the Floating Island?

Cal frantically scrapes at his dish, nothing is left.

ELLEN: I preferred the pears, didn't you?

CAL *(Reaching for her dish)*: Do you have any left?

ELLEN: They're more challenging.

Ellen picks up Cal's empty dish and rises. She wipes invisible crumbs from the table, straightens the tablecloth as Cal scrapes his spoon in Ellen's dish for the last bits of Floating Island, then plunges his finger in and starts scraping the sides.

Ellen goes into the kitchen. She puts Cal's dish in the sink and starts stirring the soup on the stove as Cal, scraping the sides of Ellen's dish with alternate fingers and sucking them clean, rises and follows Ellen into the kitchen. He looks around, finds the saucepan of warm Floating Island and pours more into his empty dish, gets a new spoon and takes slow loving mouthfuls as he watches Ellen work on her soup.

These are the various works in progress:
Belgian Oxtail Soup
Billi Bi on a low flame
Several ducks browning in a heavy frying pan
Veal
Wild rice

Set aside on the counters are the beginnings of:
The stuffing for the veal
The shrimp mousse for the bass
A huge tossed salad
A saucepan full of Floating Island

Hidden in the refrigerator are:
The Pears in Cointreau with Frozen Cream
The uncooked bass
Basic ingredients for the sauces, Hollandaise and Velouté
Celery
A bowl of grapes for the duck

ELLEN *(Stirring and tasting her soup)*: They were firm enough, weren't they?
CAL *(Involved with his Floating Island)*: Oh . . . so smooth!
ELLEN: Nothing is worse than limp pears!
CAL: So light . . .
ELLEN: What time is it?
CAL: . . . perfect!
ELLEN: They were all right, weren't they?
CAL *(Referring to the Floating Island)*: You added something.
ELLEN *(Referring to the pears)*: I added something.
CAL: What is it? I can't tell.
ELLEN: A touch of . . . ginger.
CAL *(Smacking his lips)*: It tastes more like . . . cinnamon . . .
ELLEN: And a hint of almond.
CAL: No wait, I've got it . . .
ELLEN: Did you notice?
CAL: NUTMEG!
ELLEN *(Tasting the soup)*: I'll bet you didn't even notice the almond.

CAL: It's nutmeg.

ELLEN: The ginger flavor is much stronger.

CAL: It's wonderful.

ELLEN: How much time do we have?

CAL: Really delicious.

ELLEN *(Offering him a taste of soup)*: What do you think? I don't know, the bouquet's a little weak . . .

CAL *(Referring to the Floating Island)*: You should make it more often, everyone loves it.

ELLEN: It needs more thyme for one thing.

CAL *(Gobbling up the rest of the Floating Island)*: I can't stop eating this Floating Island! I don't know what you do to your desserts, this is irresistible!

ELLEN *(Holding out a spoonful of soup)*: I need you to taste. How is it?

CAL: It tastes like Floating Island.

ELLEN: Come on Cal, they'll be here soon. Try again.

CAL: Oh, I forgot to tell you, Table Four canceled because of the bad weather.

ELLEN: They'll come back . . . *(Holding out a fresh taste of soup)* Now tell me; how is it?

CAL *(Takes his time, savors it)*: Good.

ELLEN: *Good?* Is that all?

CAL *(Helps himself to another spoonful)*: Very good.

ELLEN: Damn! *(She has another taste)* The bouquet's still weak . . .

Cal strides over to her with his spoon, starts dipping it into the soup and slurping.

ELLEN *(Tastes in a much more exacting way)*: Wait a minute!

CAL: VERY GOOD!

ELLEN: I FORGOT THE WATERCRESS!

CAL: And this is without the added touches of smoked ham and Madeira.

ELLEN *(Laughing, gets the watercress from the refrigerator)*: I forgot the watercress.

CAL: It's perfect, it doesn't need watercress!

ELLEN: What do you mean, it doesn't need watercress?

CAL: It's delicious without watercress.

ELLEN: It's incomplete without watercress! *(She adds some)*

CAL: Watercress is overrated.

ELLEN: Watercress is *essential*!

CAL: Watercress is a pain in the ass!

ELLEN: Watercress is one of the staples of French and Chinese cuisine!

CAL: It's overrated.
ELLEN: It's piquant . . .
CAL: It's soggy . . .
ELLEN: It's refreshing . . .
CAL: It's overpriced . . .

The telephone rings. There are two phones in the kitchen. Depending on where he's standing, Cal alternates between them.

ELLEN: Oh God! *(She works faster on her soup)*
CAL: I've got it! *(On the phone)* Good evening, The Golden Carousel, may I help you?
ELLEN: God, God, God!
CAL: Reservations for two this Friday night at eight? . . . Hold on a sec, let me check our calendar. *(To Ellen)* Reservations for two this Friday at eight.
ELLEN: We're filled for the rest of the week!
CAL *(Back on the phone, eyeing the calendar)*: Yes, I see a space.
ELLEN: We're filled!
CAL: Could I have your name, please? . . . I'm sorry, would you mind spelling that for me?
ELLEN *(In an urgent whisper)*: I'm making apricot brandy souffles on Friday!
CAL: K.A.S.T.F.S.
ELLEN: I have to prepare a fresh apricot puree for each one.
CAL *(Slower)*: K.A.S.T.O.F.S.K. . . . WHAT?
ELLEN: It makes all the difference.
CAL: O.F.S.K.*Y*!
ELLEN: That way, the full apricot aroma is retained until the very last.
CAL: *Kas*tofsky.
ELLEN: If you make the puree beforehand and let it sit until the souffle is ready to pour then . . .
CAL: Oh, Kas*tof*sky, I'm sorry!
ELLEN: Apricot is very delicate.
CAL *(Pleased)*: KasTOFsky!
ELLEN: Much more so than lemon or orange, a lemon souffle . . .
CAL: Yes, Kas*tof*sky. I've got it now!
ELLEN: Or even a strawberry souffle would be . . .
CAL: Well, thank you for calling, Mr. Kastofsky. We'll see you on Friday night then at eight. Good-bye. *(He hangs up. To Ellen, radiant)* WHAT DID I TELL YOU?
ELLEN: Apricot is tricky.
CAL *(Adding the Kastofskys to their calendar, which is already black with*

reservations): The word is spreading! We've only been open four weeks and we're already booked into next month!

ELLEN: I can't cook for more than two sittings a night.

CAL: They're breaking down the doors . . .

ELLEN: We've been over this before.

CAL: Jamming the phones . . .

ELLEN: If you rush me, the food will suffer.

Cal goes to the second pot of soup on the stove, the Billi Bi, and helps himself to a huge spoonful. He burns his tongue and yowls in pain, jumping up and down.

ELLEN *(Rushing over to him)*: What happened?

Cal keeps yowling, his tongue hanging out.

ELLEN: I can't understand you . . .

CAL *(Completely garbled since his tongue is out)*: I burned my tongue!

ELLEN: Oh baby!

CAL *(Jumping up and down)*: Get me the boric acid!

The telephone starts to ring.

ELLEN *(Rushes to the refrigerator)*: I'm getting the butter! *(She returns with a stick of butter)*

CAL *(Garbled)*: Not butter, boric acid!

ELLEN: What?

CAL *(Garbled)*: I SAID, *BORIC ACID!*

ELLEN: Hold still, this will numb the pain . . .

CAL: Answer the phone!

ELLEN: What?

CAL *(Waving towards the ringing phone)*: The phone, the phone, the phone!

ELLEN: Hold still, or I can't get it on.

CAL *(Garbled)*: Will you answer the goddamned phone???!

ELLEN: I know it hurts, honey, just hang on one minute! *(She starts smearing butter on his flapping tongue)*

CAL *(More garbled than ever)*: I DON'T WANT BUTTER! I WANT BORIC ACID. BORIC ACID!

ELLEN *(Imitates the way he says it to try and understand him)*: Boric acid?

CAL: Will you please answer the phone before they hang up.

ELLEN *(Says "boric acid" as before, completely confused)*: Boric acid??

CAL *(Lunges for the phone, tongue still out and incomprehensible)*: Good evening, The Golden Carousel, may I help you?

ELLEN *(Takes the phone from him)*: Oh! The telephone!

CAL *(Puts his tongue back in his mouth, as clear as day)*: The telephone.

ELLEN: Well, why didn't you say so? *(Into the phone)* Good evening, The Golden Carousel, could you hold on for just a moment please? *(She puts the receiver aside. To Cal)* Now, what is it that you want?

CAL *(His tongue in his mouth, clearly)*: Boric acid.

ELLEN *(Amazed)*: Ohhhh! Boric acid! You mean, *baking soda!*

Cal sticks out his tongue and says it all queer again. Ellen copies him.

ELLEN *(Keeping her tongue out, garbled)*: Coming right up. *(She gets the baking soda from a cupboard)*

CAL *(His tongue out)*: I think I burned off all the skin.

ELLEN *(Laughing, imitates him again)*: I think I burned off all the skin!

CAL *(His tongue back in, clear)*: I burned off all the skin.

ELLEN *(Gently fingering his tongue)*: No you didn't. It's just a bit red. Now hold still so I can get this butter off.

CAL *(Garbled again)*: At least you could have used sweet butter!

Ellen, tongue out, imitates what he said.

CAL *(Tongue back in)*: Sweet butter.

ELLEN: Sweet butter! *(Puts some baking soda on his tongue)* How does that feel?

CAL: It hurts.

ELLEN: I'm sorry. Did you enjoy the soup at least?

CAL: I couldn't taste it.

ELLEN: I haven't added the egg yolks yet.

CAL *(In pain)*: Son of a bitch.

ELLEN: They make all the difference . . .

CAL *(Touching his tongue)*: I burned off all my damned taste buds!

ELLEN *(Gently blowing on his tongue)*: No you didn't, it's just red.

CAL: That feels good.

ELLEN *(Keeps blowing on it)*: Poor baby.

CAL: They're so fragile.

ELLEN: What are?

CAL: Taste buds.

ELLEN: That's because they're nerves.

CAL: Millions of tiny fragile pink dots. They have roots, you know. Long roots that extend all the way through your tongue . . . they're like the fingers on a hand . . . long sensitive fingers, touching and feeling . . . and now I've burned them all off . . . OH JESUS, THE TELEPHONE! *(He rushes to the telephone)* Hello? Are you still there? Hello? Hello? *(He slams the receiver down)* They hung up! *(Ellen laughs)* It's not funny.

ELLEN: They'll call back.

CAL: How do you know? *(He goes to the refrigerator and starts looking for something to eat)*

ELLEN: We've got to hurry!

CAL *(Making a racket moving things about)*: We might have lost a customer just now.

ELLEN: It's getting late.

CAL: They probably won't call back.

ELLEN *(Holding out a spoonful of soup to him)*: Come on, open.

Cal pulls out a bowl of green grapes set aside to garnish the duckling in wine, fitfully starts eating them.

CAL: Ellen, we've borrowed seventy-five thousand dollars to open this place, and if we don't come up with twenty thousand next month, the whole thing will go under. Good-bye. Gone. We can't afford to lose any phone calls.

ELLEN *(The spoon still extended)*: Please.

CAL *(Wolfing down the grapes)*: We've got to clear nine hundred dollars a night!

ELLEN: Taste!

CAL: And if we don't serve a minimum of thirty-six customers a night—

ELLEN: No!

CAL: —at approximately thirty-five dollars each—

ELLEN: Cal!

CAL: —we won't clear that nine hundred dollars!

ELLEN: Please . . .

CAL: We're so close!

ELLEN *(Offers him a fresh spoonful, blows on it)*: Taste . . .

CAL *(Eating the grapes with more relish)*: We could really do it!

ELLEN: Do you like it?

CAL: Serve outstanding food *and* make money at the same time!

ELLEN: Is it all right?

The telephone rings. Cal pushes past Ellen and grabs the phone.

CAL: There they are!

ELLEN *(Working on her soup)*: I'm falling behind.

CAL *(On the phone while popping grapes in his mouth)*: Good evening, The Golden Carousel. Did you just call us? *(To Ellen) It's them!* *(On the phone)* I'm sorry, we had a slight . . . may I help you? Three for next Tuesday? Let me check our calendar.

ELLEN: We're filled.

CAL (*Looking at the calendar*): What time was that again? Nine o'clock? Just one moment, please.

ELLEN: We're filled for the entire week. Hey, don't eat all those grapes. I need them for the Duckling in Wine with Green Grapes!

CAL: Yes, I see a space. We could fit you in at nine.

ELLEN: I'm never going to make it.

CAL: Your name, please?

ELLEN: Never!

CAL: Canelli? . . . Thank you very much for calling, Mr. Canelli. We'll be expecting you next Tuesday at nine, then.

ELLEN: Cal, we're booked!

CAL: Your friends said it was the best restaurant in the United States? (*To Ellen*) The best restaurant in the United States! (*Back on the phone*) And they've eaten everywhere? (*To Ellen*) They've eaten *everywhere*!

ELLEN: I haven't even started the celery or begun the Sauce Velouté . . .

CAL (*On the phone*): You've already sent five couples here? (*To Ellen*) *Five* couples!

ELLEN (*Snapping off the tops of the celery*): Don't panic.

CAL: They loved it!

ELLEN: You see, they loved it!

CAL (*On the phone*): Thank you very much for your kind words. I hope we'll be able to live up to them for you next Tuesday. Good-bye. (*He hangs up, pops more grapes in his mouth*) They can't get enough!

ELLEN (*Feeling overwhelmed*): Oh boy!

CAL: They're coming back! A second time, a third time!

ELLEN: Oh boy, oh boy!

CAL: They're telling their friends!

ELLEN (*Frantically washing, scraping and cutting the celery*): Oh boy oh boy oh boy *oh boy*!

CAL: And those friends are telling other friends!

ELLEN (*Faster and faster*): OH BOY OH BOY OH BOY!

CAL (*Lunges back into the bowl of grapes*): This is just the beginning!

Ellen makes a small strangled sound.

CAL: We can't lose!

Ellen makes another sound.

CAL: The chance of a lifetime!

The doorbell rings.

ELLEN *(Whispers)*: They're here!   CAL *(Whispers)*: The door!

ELLEN *(Grabs an onion, starts chopping it)*: Help!

CAL: Relax! *(He reaches for a black bow tie and starts putting it on)*

ELLEN: They're here.

Cal sings his favorite show tune under his breath.

ELLEN: I'm not ready . . . nowhere *near* ready! There's still the wine sauce for the duck and the Hollandaise, not to mention the shrimp mousse for the bass . . .

Cal sings on, preening.

ELLEN: Oh well, it's just par for the course, right? RIGHT???! *(Notices the empty bowl)* Where did all the Floating Island go?

The doorbell rings again.

CAL: Just a minute . . .

ELLEN: You ate all the Floating Island!

Cal, still singing, bolts upstairs to get his tuxedo jacket.

ELLEN *(Gazing into the empty bowl)*: He ate all the Floating Island. Our first customers of the evening have arrived . . . and he's eaten half the desserts . . .

Cal bounds back into the kitchen, splendid in his tuxedo. He salutes Ellen.

CAL: We're off! *(Addressing the door)* Coming . . .

Ellen goes to the sink, angrily turns on the faucet to wash the celery.

ELLEN: I don't believe this!

The lights fade on Ellen and rise on Cal advancing to the front door.

Scene 2

Cal is a changed person in his tuxedo jacket. He glitters with charm, elegance and the desire to please. He opens the door.

Paul and Hannah Galt are literally blown in. They're in their middle forties and are sumptuously dressed: he in a hand-tailored suit under a cashmere coat, she in a floating crepe dress under a mink coat.

CAL *(Bowing slightly)*: Good evening. The Galt party? Won't you come in?

HANNAH *(Shivering so violently she totters)*: Ooooooooh, it's soooooooooo cold!

PAUL *(Slapping his gloved hands together)*: That wind is . . .

HANNAH: I've never been so . . .

PAUL: WICKED!

CAL *(Reaching for Hannah's coat)*: May I?

HANNAH: Cold!

PAUL: It's got to be forty below out there!

CAL *(Reaching for Paul's coat)*: Sir?

HANNAH: Unbearable!

PAUL: And with the windchill factor, it's more like sixty below.

HANNAH: And only *November*!

CAL: They say the worst is yet to come.

HANNAH *(Hands over her ears)*: Don't . . .

PAUL *(To Cal)*: Yes, I heard that too. Arctic storms are due down from Canada sometime in mid-January . . .

CAL *(To Paul)*: In February we're supposed to have the worst blizzard this country has ever seen! The National Guard's being prepared for this one.

HANNAH *(Looking around the room)*: Oh Paul, look! It's charming!

CAL: Please, won't you follow me to your table? We'll warm you up in no time. *(He pulls out the chair for Hannah)* Madame?

HANNAH *(Enthralled with one of the horses)*: Ooooooh, merry-go-round horses!

Paul unwittingly sits down in the chair meant for Hannah.

CAL: *Monsieur!*

HANNAH: I love them!

PAUL *(To Cal, sitting down)*: Thank you.

HANNAH: I WANT THEM!

PAUL: I haven't felt wind like that since . . .

HANNAH: Aren't they wonderful?

CAL: Could I warm you up with something from the bar?

PAUL *(Sighs, looking around)*: This is very nice.

CAL: A cocktail?

PAUL: Oh look, Hannah. They have your merry-go-round horses!

HANNAH: They're almost impossible to find these days.

CAL: Some sherry?

PAUL: Those are old!

HANNAH: Aren't they wonderful? I wonder where they got them?

CAL *(To Hannah)*: Would you care for something from the bar?

HANNAH: I'll bet you've gotten plenty of offers for those . . .

PAUL: I don't know about you, but I am starved!

HANNAH *(To Cal)*: A word of advice: Don't sell them!

CAL: A glass of white wine . . . ?

PAUL: I could eat a horse!

HANNAH: No matter what they offer you!

PAUL: I need a drink!

CAL: Yes Sir?

HANNAH *(To Cal)*: Every year, they triple in value!

PAUL: Give me a double Scotch, straight up.

CAL: Very good, and you Madame?

HANNAH *(Comes to the table and sits down)*: *You hang on to them!*

PAUL: I don't know why I should be so hungry, I had a perfectly good lunch!

HANNAH *(To Paul, under her breath)*: God, I'd love to get my hands on those!

CAL: And for you, Madame?

PAUL: Tartar steak and salad . . .

HANNAH: Let's see, I guess I'll have a vodka gimlet.

CAL: Thank you. *(He retires to the bar area to mix their drinks)*

PAUL: I even had a pastry for dessert.

HANNAH: I'm hungry.

PAUL: A plum tart . . .

HANNAH: I only had a small omelette for lunch.

PAUL: . . . with an apricot glaze.

HANNAH: Mushroom . . .

PAUL: It was . . . incredible!

HANNAH: . . . with a hint of dill.

PAUL: Melt . . . in . . . your . . . mouth.

HANNAH: I behaved myself and skipped dessert.

PAUL: I almost ordered a second.

HANNAH: What did you have for lunch today?

PAUL: *Almost* . . .

HANNAH: I hardly had anything . . .

PAUL: You should have seen the plum tart I had for dessert . . .

HANNAH: Just an omelette.

PAUL: The pastry shell alone . . .

HANNAH: I thought of having a muffin with it . . .

PAUL: . . . *was* unbelievable!

HANNAH: Only a half, of course . . .

PAUL: It could have been served on its own.

HANNAH: But I didn't.

PAUL: I almost broke down and had a second.

HANNAH: Paul!

PAUL: I know, I know!

HANNAH: You shouldn't even *think* of having a second dessert!

PAUL: Well, did I have it? Did I?

HANNAH: I don't know. How would I know?

PAUL: I JUST SAID THAT I DIDN'T. JESUS!

A silence.

HANNAH: I only had an omelette . . .

A silence.

PAUL: I didn't have a second dessert, all right???!

HANNAH: . . . a small mushroom omelette . . .

PAUL: All right????

HANNAH *(Patting her stomach)*: Uuuuh, it was so filling!

A silence. Paul, depressed, sighs.

HANNAH: It's amazing how filling a small mushroom omelette is . . . but then again mushrooms are very . . . starchy . . .

A silence. Cal returns from the bar, puts down Hannah's drink with a flourish.

CAL: A vodka gimlet for Madame!

HANNAH: Thank you very much.

CAL *(Sensing the tension between them, sets down Paul's drink with even more flair)*: And a double Scotch for you, Sir. I hope you enjoy it.

Hannah leans back, takes a long sip of her drink, sighs. Paul mutters and takes a gulp.

CAL: Would you be interested in seeing the menu now, or would you rather wait?

PAUL: Yes, now please.   HANNAH: Oh, let's wait!

CAL *(More and more flashy in his gestures)*: Very good, I'll bring them right over. *(He fetches them and hands one to Hannah)* Madame?

HANNAH: Now, what was it that Ken and Diva said was so good?

CAL *(Handing one to Paul)*: Monsieur?

HANNAH: Sole Veronique?

PAUL *(Under his breath)*: You know I'd never have two desserts for lunch on a day we were going out for dinner!

HANNAH: Or was it Sole Meunière?

PAUL: I'm not that stupid!

HANNAH: No wait, I think it was Sole Florentine!

PAUL: And in case you've forgotten, I jogged three miles after I got home from the office.

HANNAH: I'VE GOT IT! IT WAS SOLE BONNE FEMME!

PAUL: In fact, it was closer to four and a half.

HANNAH: Ken had Poulet Farci . . . and Diva had Sole Bonne Femme!

PAUL: I've never been in such good shape!

HANNAH: Or was it the other way around?

PAUL *(Punching his stomach)*: See that? Hard as a rock!

HANNAH: Ken had the Sole Bonne Femme, and Diva had the Poulet Farci!

PAUL: Go on, hit me in the stomach, I won't even feel it!

HANNAH: No, wait a minute . . .

PAUL *(Thrusting out his stomach)*: Come on!

HANNAH: Diva had Poulet Bonne Femme . . .

PAUL: Hit me!

HANNAH: . . . and Ken had Sole Farci!

PAUL *(Slugs himself)*: See, I didn't feel a thing!

HANNAH: No, that can't be right. There's no such dish as Sole Farci.

PAUL: I'll do it harder. *(He does)* Nothing . . . !

HANNAH: Anyway, both of them said it was the most delicious Sole Bonne Femme they'd ever had!

PAUL *(Really socks himself)*: See that? Didn't even feel it.

A silence.

PAUL: Want me to do it again?

Paul repeatedly socks himself in the stomach. A silence.

PAUL *(Cheerful)*: What was it that Ken and Diva said was so good?

HANNAH: I'm in the mood for veal.

PAUL: Sole Almondine?

HANNAH: You know how on some days you wake up with a craving for something?

CAL *(Hovering nearby)*: We change our menus every day.

PAUL: Oh?

HANNAH: Friends of ours had your Sole Bonne Femme last week. They said it was out of this world!

CAL: Yes, my wife is a remarkable cook.

HANNAH: Oh, it's your wife who's the chef. I didn't know that.

PAUL: Remember that Chicken Bonne Femme we had at the Pavillion years ago?

HANNAH: It's very rare to come across a woman who's a paid chef.
PAUL: Remember the sauce . . . ?
HANNAH: There are only a handful in this country.
PAUL: . . . with white wine and truffles . . .
CAL: Julia Child . . .
HANNAH: Dionne Lucas.
CAL: She's been dead for several years.
HANNAH: She died? I didn't know that!
PAUL: . . . salt pork and meat glaze . . .
CAL: There aren't many.
PAUL: . . . and remember the baby potatoes served with it?
HANNAH *(To Cal)*: Do you cook too?
CAL: No, I'm afraid I just eat.
HANNAH: We both cook.
CAL: How nice!
HANNAH *(Nodding towards Paul)*: He's very good.
PAUL *(Fingering his menu)*: Well, shall we begin?
CAL: I'm sure.
HANNAH: He does much better soups than me.
CAL: Soups are tricky.
PAUL *(Holding up his menu)*: Are you ready?
HANNAH: You should taste his gazpacho!
CAL: I love gazpacho!
HANNAH: Well you should taste his . . . ! *(She purrs, remembering the taste)*
PAUL *(Holding out her menu for her)*: Hannah!
HANNAH: Out . . . of . . . this . . . world!
PAUL: Are you ready?

Hannah sighs again.

PAUL: I'm opening mine . . . *(He looks at her and waits)*
CAL: If I can assist you in any way, just—
PAUL: Hannah, I'm hungry!

Cal goes to the rear of the room and flicks on the opening movement of J. S. Bach's Sonata No. 3 in E major for violin and harpischord. The opening measures sound before the Galts begin.
Paul flicks open his menu with a meaingful look.
Hannah follows suit.
Paul glances down the length of it, sighs.
Hannah also glances but in tense silence.
Paul inhales, takes a deep breath.

Hannah pushes a strand of hair up off her forehead.
Paul exhales.
Hannah tosses her head in bewilderment.
Paul sighs again, louder.
Silence.
Hannah, overcome, shuts her menu and puts it face down on the table.
Paul gently picks it up and hands it back to her, smiling.
Hannah scans it again. It's such a feast of choices, she can't decide. She moans.
Paul pushes back in his chair, eyeing the menu; he narrows his eyes, inhales.

HANNAH: Oh Paul!

Paul, still looking at his menu, covers her hand with his.

HANNAH: It's . . .
PAUL: Sssssssh!

Hannah makes a helpless little sound.

PAUL: I know. I know.
HANNAH: Help me.
PAUL: Sweetheart!
HANNAH: Oh Paul!
PAUL: Take your time . . .
HANNAH: I . . .
PAUL: There's no rush . . .
HANNAH: I'm so . . .
PAUL: Relax.
HANNAH *(With a sob)*: I can't!
PAUL: Of course you can!
HANNAH *(Her head in her hands)*: I'm scared.
PAUL *(Lifting her head up, cupping it in his hands)*: Trust me.

Cal turns up the volume of the music.

PAUL *(Under his breath, to Cal)*: Not so loud.
CAL: Sorry! *(Lowers the volume)*
PAUL *(Leans close to Hannah and points to something on her menu)*: To start . . .
HANNAH *(Melting)*: Oh Paul . . . !

Paul points to something else. A low sexy giggle comes from Hannah.

PAUL *(Points again)*: And maybe . . .

Hannah kisses him lightly and coos.

PAUL *(Pointing to something else)*: Or, how about . . . ?

Hannah goes off into a shower of giggles.

PAUL *(Pointing)*: With a side order of . . .
HANNAH *(Horrified, closes her menu on his hand)*: Paul!
PAUL *(Reaches over and kisses her)*: Forgive me!

A silence. Hannah, suddenly aggressive, leans over Paul until she's almost in his lap. She points.

HANNAH: Okay. . . . How about . . . ?
PAUL *(Shocked)*: Hannah?
HANNAH *(Pointing elsewhere)*: Plus some . . .

They both go off into gales. Cal watches them with amusement and laughs to himself.

PAUL *(Out of breath)*: Stop it!
HANNAH *(Points again)*: And . . .
PAUL *(Reaches over and kisses her)*: Darling! You're being obscene and you know it!
HANNAH *(Laughing, points again)*: And . . . for dessert!
PAUL *(Noticing that Cal is watching them)*: People are staring . . .

Cal quickly looks the other way as Hannah shoots him a dirty look. The doorbell rings. Cal, saved, heads for the door. The lights fade on the Galts. The music stops.

Scene 3

CAL *(Opens the door)*: Yes?

Elizabeth Barrow Colt staggers in. She's terribly shy and nervous and very nearsighted. A writer, in her early thirties, she's almost paralyzed with awkwardness. When she speaks she's completely inaudible.

CAL: Good evening, you're with the uh . . . which party?
ELIZABETH BARROW COLT *(Inaudible)*: I'm meeting David Osslow.
CAL: Pardon me?
ELIZABETH BARROW COLT *(Inaudible)*: Mr. Osslow.
CAL *(Straining to hear)*: I'm sorry . . .

ELIZABETH BARROW COLT *(In a terrified whisper, looks around the room)*: David Osslow.

CAL *(Looking at his reservations list)*: Ah yes, David Osslow! *(Elizabeth cringes)* He hasn't come yet. May I take your coat and show you to your table?

ELIZABETH BARROW COLT *(Panic-stricken)*: I'm early?

CAL: I beg your pardon?

ELIZABETH BARROW COLT: Oh dear.

CAL: Let me take your coat and I'll show you to your table.

Elizabeth clutches her coat around her and stands rooted to the spot.

CAL: Wouldn't you like me to show you to your table? I'm sure Mr. Osslow will be here any minute.

Elizabeth looks around the room furtively, opens her pocketbook and, head lowered, takes out a comb and starts combing her hair. As she does, several things fall out of her pocketbook. She dives for them, bumping into Cal as he tries to help her retrieve them.

| CAL: I'm sorry. Excuse me, I was just trying to . . . I'm sorry . . . wanted to help you get that . . . here's your toothbrush. | ELIZABETH BARROW COLT: Oh dear, I dropped my . . . I'm sorry, I didn't mean to . . . my lipstick and diary . . . oh dear! |

CAL *(Hands her a few things)*: Here, I hope I didn't . . .

ELIZABETH BARROW COLT *(Very softly)*: I'm not wearing my glasses.

CAL *(Jovial)*: It sure is cold out there!

ELIZABETH BARROW COLT *(Dumping everything back into her pocketbook)*: I can't see very well . . .

CAL *(Gently)*: May I take your coat?

ELIZABETH BARROW COLT *(With a sudden wild giggle)*: I can't see anything at all! *(She sneaks her glasses out of her pocketbook and quickly holds them up to her eyes to get her bearings)* OH LOOK AT THOSE MERRY-GO-ROUND HORSES! GRACIOUS!

Elizabeth bumps into the serving cart, which careens towards Hannah, who screams.

CAL *(To the Galts)*: I'm terribly sorry, I'll have her seated in just one moment . . .

Elizabeth opens her pocketbook again and, head lowered, sneaks on a smear of bright lipstick.

CAL: I heard it's thirty below with the windchill factor.

Elizabeth drops the lipstick back in her bag, reaches for her comb and combs her hair again.

ELIZABETH BARROW COLT: I look a mess.

CAL: And next year, if you can believe it, we're supposed to get hit even harder!

Elizabeth takes out her glasses again, puts them on for a second, lowers her head and makes several strange low sobs.

CAL *(Touching her)*: Could I take your coat for you?

ELIZABETH BARROW COLT *(Her wild giggle again)*: OH . . . MY COAT!!! *(She fumbles with the buttons)*

CAL: It's all right, take your time. *(Pause)* We're supposed to get some relief over the weekend.

As Elizabeth struggles with her coat buttons, she drops her bag again and everything spills out.

ELIZABETH BARROW COLT: Oh dear.

CAL: Here, I'll get it . . . *(He dives for the floor and scoops it all back into her bag, which he finally hands to her)* Here you go.

ELIZABETH BARROW COLT *(Barely audible)*: I can't see very well.

CAL: I beg your pardon?

ELIZABETH BARROW COLT: I can't see very well.

CAL *(Helping her off with her coat, which becomes a great muddle as she can't get her arms out of the sleeves properly)*: Here, let me help you.

ELIZABETH BARROW COLT *(Struggling between Cal and the coat)*: I'M AS BLIND AS A BAT!

CAL *(Gets the coat off, sighs)*: Please . . . follow me.

And Cal leads Elizabeth to her table, pulling her chair way way out to give her plenty of leeway. Elizabeth, rigid with panic, muddles the timing of when to sit down, plops awkwardly. She sneaks out her glasses for another look, drops them back in her bag.

CAL *(Pushing her the long distance to her table)*: Could I get you something to drink while you wait? *(Elizabeth sobs again)* Something from the bar?

ELIZABETH BARROW COLT *(Inaudible)*: What time is it?

CAL: I beg your pardon?

ELIZABETH BARROW COLT *(Very shrill)*: TIME?

CAL *(Startled, jumps, looks at his watch)*: 7:15.

ELIZABETH BARROW COLT *(Faintly)*: I don't know what he looks like.
CAL *(Leaning down close to her)*: I'm sorry . . .
ELIZABETH BARROW COLT: I've only talked to him on the phone.
CAL *(Mystified)*: Could I get you something from the bar?
ELIZABETH BARROW COLT: How will I know him? *(Sobs)*
CAL: Are you all right?

> *Elizabeth fishes in her pocketbook, hauls out a paperback edition of Thomas Mann's* The Magic Mountain, *opens it in the middle and starts reading, holding the book very close to her face.*

ELIZABETH BARROW COLT: I brought my book . . .
CAL: How about a little appetizer or something while you wait?

> *Elizabeth keeps reading, making her little sob every now and then. She twists a strand of her hair.*

CAL: He should be here any minute now . . . it's this awful weather . . . slows everyone down . . . cars won't start . . . batteries frozen up . . . he should be here any time now . . . worst winter we've had since I can remember . . .
PAUL: Waiter? Waiter, we're ready to order.
CAL: Would you excuse me, Mademoiselle? *(He heads towards the Galts' table)*

> *The light slowly fades on Elizabeth Barrow Colt.*

Scene 4

And rises on Ellen, who is holding a beautiful fresh bass.

ELLEN: Just look at you, you sad beauty, you prehistoric fluke . . . where do you come from, anyway? All silver and slippery, with such a mournful face . . . *(She holds its face up to hers and imitates its pout)* You don't even know you're a fish, do you? Aaaaaahhh, but *we* do . . . and we know how good you taste . . . oh yes . . . we know all about that . . .

> *Ellen starts sharpening her knife. The light fades on her busy hands.*

Scene 5

And rises on Cal hovering over the Galts.

PAUL: Hannah?
HANNAH: Oh Paul, I'm not ready!

PAUL: Take your time.

HANNAH: I keep changing my mind.

PAUL: There's no rush.

HANNAH: I'm so . . . tense.

PAUL: We have all the time in the world.

HANNAH *(Motioning to Cal)*: The Belgian Oxtail Soup is . . .

CAL: A hearty beef broth with winter vegetables, smoked ham, and Madeira.

HANNAH: Madeira . . .

CAL: Madeira . . .

HANNAH: And the Billi Bi is . . .

CAL: A cream of mussel soup seasoned with fresh herbs, shallots, white wine, and a thread of saffron.

HANNAH *(Impressed)*: A thread of saffron . . .

CAL: Saffron . . .

HANNAH: And the Veal Prince Orloff is . . .

CAL: Roast veal stuffed with onions and wild mushrooms, served with Sauce Mornay . . .

HANNAH *(Rolling it on her tongue)*: Sauce Mornay . . .

CAL: Sauce Velouté with Gruyère cheese added . . .

HANNAH: Sauce Velouté . . .

PAUL: Mornay!

HANNAH: And the Roast Duckling in Wine with Green Grapes is . . .

CAL: Fresh.

HANNAH: Fresh! And the Striped Bass with Shrimp Mousse . . . is . . .

CAL: In season!

HANNAH: In season!

Paul grunts with anticipation.

HANNAH: Your vegetable of the day?

CAL: Braised celery.

PAUL *(Kissing his fingers)*: My favorite!

A silence.

HANNAH: Oh Paul!

PAUL *(Reaching for her hand)*: Sssssshhhhh . . .

HANNAH: I'm just so . . .

PAUL: I know, I know . . .

HANNAH: I love roast duck!

CAL: The duck is—

PAUL: I'm having the bass!

HANNAH: But I woke up with a craving for veal.

PAUL: I don't care for duck . . .

CAL: The veal is—

HANNAH: You know how I love veal!

PAUL: I had veal last week . . .

HANNAH: But I haven't had fresh roast duckling in . . .

CAL: You might like the bass . . .

PAUL: My rule of thumb: always order fish that's in season.

HANNAH: I only had an omelette for lunch.

CAL: The duckling is—

PAUL: I don't know about you, but I am starving!

HANNAH: I've been good all week.

PAUL: I can almost taste that mussel soup!

Faster and faster.

HANNAH: I've got to decide!

PAUL: I can't wait much longer . . .

HANNAH: I always have veal . . .

PAUL: I don't care for duck . . .

HANNAH: I could have the bass . . .

PAUL: I just want to start . . .

HANNAH: I need some more time . . .

PAUL: I can't wait much more . . .

HANNAH: I think I can go . . .

PAUL: I just want to . . .

HANNAH: I know I can . . .

PAUL: I . . .

HANNAH: I . . .

PAUL *(In a burst)*: I'll have the Belgian Oxtail Soup to start, the bass with shrimp, and Floating Island for dessert! *(He pants slightly)*

CAL *(Writing it down)*: Very good, Sir . . . and you, Madame?

HANNAH *(Takes a deep breath, shuts her eyes, clenches her hands, pauses, then very fast)*: Billi Bi, Duckling in Wine with Green Grapes, and Pears in Cointreau with Frozen Cream.

PAUL *(Applauds her)*: Nice going, Hannah! Very nice! Good work! *(He leans over the table and kisses her)*

CAL *(Writing it down)*: Yes, you did very well. *(He shakes her hand)* Congratulations.

HANNAH *(Eyes still shut, murmurs)*: Oh thank you, thank you, thank you so much . . .

Cal puts the last flourish on his pad and glides into the kitchen. The light fades on the rhapsodic Galts.

Scene 6

Ellen is more frantic than ever. She has several bass out and is dressing them.

CAL *(Bursting in)*: One oxtail . . . one billi, one bass, one duck, one Floating Island, and one pears!

ELLEN *(Eyes closed, reciting)*: One oxtail, one billi, one bass, one duck, one Floating Island, and one pears.	CAL: One oxtail, one billi, one bass, one duck, one Floating Island, and one pears!

ELLEN: You do the shrimp and I'll do the eggs!

Ellen starts whipping egg whites with an automatic mixer as Cal removes the shrimp from the refrigerator and dumps them into the Cuisinart. He turns it on. Both appliances make a fearful clatter.

ELLEN *(Over the din)*: Heavy cream!
CAL: How much?
ELLEN: Half a cup.
CAL *(Starts pouring it into the Cuisinart)*: Watch . . .
ELLEN: That's enough.

They finish their chores simultaneously.

ELLEN: You slice the mushrooms and I'll finish the mousse!

Ellen pours the mousse out of the Cuisinart and carefully folds in the egg whites she's just whipped as Cal slices the mushrooms with lightning speed and precision.

ELLEN: You cut the grapes and I'll do the soups. *(She returns to her soups on the stove)*
CAL: I'll cut the grapes . . .
ELLEN: While I do the soups.
CAL: Where are the grapes?
ELLEN *(Muttering as she works on the soup)*: One oxtail . . . one billi, one bass, and one duck . . .
CAL: Where are the grapes?
ELLEN: Second shelf of the refrigerator.
CAL: Of course. *(Starts rooting around in the refrigerator)*
ELLEN: One oxtail . . . one billi, one bass, and one duck . . .
CAL: Second shelf.
ELLEN: That's right. *(Tastes the soup)*

CAL: It's not there.

ELLEN: Then look in the bin.

CAL *(Thumping around)*: Nope.

ELLEN: Try in the door.

CAL *(Making more and more noise)*: Nothing.

ELLEN: Check the top shelf.

CAL: I already did.

ELLEN: They're not with the pears?

CAL: Not with the pears.

ELLEN: Not in the bin?

CAL: Not in the bin.

ELLEN: Start taking things out.

CAL *(Does)*: I am!

ELLEN: They're not in the back?

CAL: Not . . . in . . . the back!

ELLEN: Under the bass?

CAL: Nowhere in sight!

ELLEN: Try by the cream.

CAL: I already have. *(He's now spread a great arc of food around the refrigerator)*

ELLEN: They've got to be there.

CAL: Ellen, I'm looking!

ELLEN: Next to the stock.

CAL: Nowhere in sight!

ELLEN: Oh honey, I need them!

CAL: Yes, I know . . .

ELLEN: Should I come and help?

CAL: Son of a bitch!

ELLEN: I can't do the duck— *(Reaches for the salt and notices the bowl of empty grape stems)* OH NO!

CAL *(Picking over the mess strewn on the floor)*: They've got to be here!

ELLEN: *I DON'T BELIEVE THIS! (She lifts up the bowl to show Cal)*

CAL *(His back to her)*: I remember seeing them . . .

ELLEN: CAL, YOU ATE THEM!

CAL *(His back to her, finds something tempting, starts eating it)*: Mmmmmmmm . . .

ELLEN *(Holding up an empty branch)*: There's nothing left but the stems!

CAL: What *is* this?

ELLEN: LOOK!

CAL *(Facing her)*: What?

ELLEN: You ate all the grapes.

CAL: No, I didn't. I didn't eat those.

ELLEN *(Waving the branch)*: CAL!

CAL: I didn't eat any grapes.

ELLEN: I saw you!

CAL: Why would I eat those grapes?

ELLEN: I don't know, but I saw you!

CAL: I don't even like grapes.

ELLEN: I asked you to stop, don't you remember?

CAL: I'd never eat grapes.

ELLEN: CAL, YOU ATE THOSE GRAPES, I SAW YOU!

CAL *(In a whisper)*: Not so loud, they'll hear you out front.

ELLEN *(Whispering)*: How are we going to serve Duckling in Wine with Green Grapes?

CAL: I didn't do it.

ELLEN: You've ruined the dish.

CAL: You've made a mistake.

ELLEN: I can't go on like this . . .

CAL: Serve it with something else.

ELLEN: What's scary is, you don't even know you're doing it.

CAL: Peaches or cherries.

ELLEN: It's like a disease . . .

CAL: Roast duck with Bing cherries is a classic!

ELLEN: YOU ATE THE BING CHERRIES THIS MORNING! *(She starts to cry)*

CAL: Well, we have peaches don't we? Substitute peaches!

ELLEN: Cal, I can cook. I can *really* cook!

CAL: It's even better with peaches!

ELLEN: I could win us three stars, maybe even four!

CAL *(Starts opening cupboard doors)*: Now where are those peaches?

ELLEN: I've trained with the best . . .

CAL *(Thumping in one of the cupboards)*: I know they're in here somewhere . . .

ELLEN: . . . cooked with the best!

CAL *(Finds a can of peaches)*: You see!

ELLEN: But I can't do this alone. I need you to help.

CAL *(Starts opening the can)*: You golden babies . . .

ELLEN: You've always had such a keen palate.

The lid off, Cal inhales the fragrance, then reaches down for a peach, lifts it up, dripping and bright yellow. He pops it in his mouth.

ELLEN: A razor-sharp instinct. I need it, Cal!

CAL: There's nothing wrong with canned peaches, they're just as good as fresh. *(He takes a swig of the juice)* I don't know when I've tasted such a delicious peach . . .

ELLEN: Do you still have it? *(She rushes to a cupboard and sweeps down an armful of spice tins)* SHOW ME IT'S THERE, SHOW ME YOUR TALENT! *(Concealing its identity, she pours out a heaping teaspoon of mustard and offers it to him)* Taste this!

CAL *(Offering her a large syrupy peach, his words garbled)*: I really wish you'd try this, it's—

ELLEN *(Fierce, forces the teaspoon of mustard into his mouth)*: Taste!

CAL *(Spitting)*: What you are doing?

ELLEN *(Shoveling in another batch)*: I SAID, TASTE IT!

CAL *(Sputtering)*: Jesus, what is this?

ELLEN: You tell me, Cal!

CAL *(Gagging)*: It's poison.

ELLEN: Try again!

Cal is certainly strong enough to overpower her, but it is food and he can't resist anything that's put into his mouth. He coughs.

ELLEN: What is it?

CAL: How am I supposed to tell, my mouth is on fire?!

ELLEN: Well, you'd better be able to tell if you want to stay in business, my dear! *(Forces in another spoonful)*

CAL *(Weakly)*: It's . . . curry powder!

ELLEN: Wrong!

CAL: Paprika . . .

ELLEN: Wrong!

CAL: Clove . . .

ELLEN: Wrong!

CAL *(In pain)*: . . . Horseradish.

ELLEN: Think, Cal. Think!

CAL: Soy sauce?

ELLEN: Wrong!

CAL: Saffron?

ELLEN: Wrong!

CAL: Ginger?

ELLEN: Wrong!

CAL *(With a sob)*: I don't know!

ELLEN: IT'S MUSTARD, CAL. SIMPLE MUSTARD! *(She pours out another teaspoon of spice and puts it in his mouth)* And this?

CAL *(Spits it out)*: Uuugh! You've gone crazy.

ELLEN: You don't know, do you!

CAL: Dill . . .

ELLEN: You're so glutted, you can't even tell . . . !

CAL: Cinnamon.

ELLEN: You can't even tell bitter from sweet.

CAL: Coffee?

ELLEN: It could be dirt for all you know! *(Shoves in another taste)*

CAL: Nutmeg?

ELLEN: Unbelievable!

CAL: Anise? . . . Brown sugar? . . . Oregano? . . . Coriander? . . . Tarragon?

ELLEN: It's salt, Cal.

The doorbell rings.

CAL: No!

ELLEN: What are we doing to do?

CAL: It didn't taste anything like—

ELLEN: *Salt!*

CAL *(Pouring some in his hand)*: Salt . . .

ELLEN: You drank all the Floating Island.

CAL: It didn't taste anything like salt!

ELLEN: You ate all the grapes.

CAL *(Tastes the bit in his palm)*: Son of a bitch . . .

ELLEN: And now, canned peaches . . . *canned!*

CAL: You know, that is amazing. I never would have guessed it was . . . salt . . .

ELLEN: It makes no difference to you anymore. You'd eat *anything* and like it.

The doorbell rings again. Ellen goes back to stirring her oxtail soup, tastes it, pours the remaining beaten egg yolk into the Billi Bi, tastes that, adding spices. She starts to cry.

ELLEN: There's someone at the door, you'd better get it.

CAL: I'm sorry, El . . . I'll watch it from now on . . . I didn't realize . . .

ELLEN *(Crying softly as she stirs the soup)*: I can't do it all by myself, I just can't . . . it's too hard . . . so much to do . . . I get lost sometimes, afraid I've done something wrong . . . I need you to help me . . .

CAL *(Wraps his arms around her, rocks her)*: Sssshhhh, come on El . . . it will be all right . . . we can still do it . . . we'll work it out . . . I'll watch the eating . . . they love you out there . . . they're breaking the

reassure me, Cal . . . tell me
it's good . . . tell me it's fine
. . . give me that strength . . .
tell me it's fine . . .

doors down . . . listen to
them . . . baby . . . baby . . .
please . . .

The doorbell rings with strident insistence as the curtain slowly falls.

ACT TWO

Scene 1

One hour later. A general view of the restaurant. Hannah and Paul Galt are lingering over their desserts. David Osslow has finally arrived and is eating his soup as Elizabeth Barrow Colt stares at hers. The lights settle on the latest arrivals, a trio of lively women in their thirties: Herrick Simmons, a hearty eater, Nessa Vox, a guilty eater, and Tony Stassio, a noneater who's on a perpetual diet. A Telemann trio sonata plays softly, then fades.

HERRICK SIMMONS *(Looking at the wine list, trying to make up her mind)*: Puligny-Montrachet! *(Hands the list to Nessa)*

NESSA VOX *(Scanning it, considering)*: Puligny-Montrachet . . . ?

TONY STASSIO *(Takes the list from Nessa and points)*: Pinot Chardonnay!

HERRICK SIMMONS: Pinot Chardonnay?

NESSA VOX *(Takes the list from Tony and announces)*: Chateau de Lascombes!

HERRICK SIMMONS: Spare me!

A pause. Cal, sensing trouble, comes to their table.

CAL: Could I be of any assistance?

Tony, taking the list back from Nessa, makes another choice. She knows nothing about wine.

TONY STASSIO: Côtes-du-Rhône!

CAL: Would you like a red wine or white?

TONY STASSIO *(Pointing to another selection, mispronouncing it)*: Châteauneuf-du-Papé!

CAL: A Burgundy or Beaujolais?

NESSA VOX: I'd like a chateau-bottled red Bordeaux!

CAL *(Making suggestions for her)*: Château Belgrave . . . Château La Lagune . . .

HERRICK SIMMONS: I think a white Burgundy would serve us much better.

CAL *(Now to Herrick)*: Pouilly Fuissé . . . Puligny-Montrachet . . .

TONY STASSIO *(Stubborn)*: Nuits St. Georges!

CAL *(Suggesting more Burgundies to Herrick)*: Corton-Charlemagne . . .

TONY STASSIO: Pinot Chardonnay!

HERRICK SIMMONS *(A tremendous sigh)*: Corton-Charlemagne, that's more like it!

TONY STASSIO *(Has made up her mind, with stunning authority)*: PU-LIGNY-FUISSÉ!

CAL *(Bewildered, as no such brand exists)*: Puligny-Fuissé?

HERRICK SIMMONS *(Trying to correct Tony)*: Puligny-*Montrachet*!

NESSA VOX *(Likewise)*: *Pouilly*-Fuissé!

TONY STASSIO *(More and more stubborn, more and more incorrect)*: Montrachet-Fuissé!

CAL: Montrachet-*Puligny*!

NESSA VOX: Puligny . . . Pouilly!

HERRICK SIMMONS: Pouilly-Fuissé!

CAL: Pouilly-Montrachet!

HERRICK SIMMONS: Pouilly-Montrachet?

NESSA VOX: Montrachet-Puligné *(Pronounced "Pulignay")*

CAL *(Repeating after her)*: Montrachet-Puligné!

HERRICK SIMMONS *(Correcting his pronunciation)*: Nee!

CAL *(Quickly, embarrassed)*: Nee!

TONY STASSIO: Montrachet-Romanee!

CAL *(Correcting her pronunciation)*: Montrachet-Romané, nay!

TONY STASSIO *(Triumphant in her ignorance)*: MONTRACHET-PU-LIGNAY!

CAL, HERRICK AND NESSA: Nee, nee!

A pause.

HERRICK SIMMONS *(Turns to Cal and gives him their order)*: Montrachet-Puligny!

CAL *(Dutifully repeats after her)*: Montrachet-Puligny!

TONY STASSIO *(Realizes they've reversed the order)*: Puligny-*Montrachet*!

CAL, HERRICK AND NESSA *(All realize she's right and start laughing, repeating after her)*: Puligny-Montrachet!

The lights fade on them.

Scene 2

And rise on Elizabeth Barrow Colt and David Osslow. Elizabeth is staring at her soup, motionless. David Osslow, the successful head of his own publishing company, a man with a glowing appetite and glowing literary taste, is happily eating his. He's in his fifties, is dapper, at ease and ready for anything.

DAVID OSSLOW: I like your work very much.

Elizabeth drops her head and murmurs.

DAVID OSSLOW: We all like it . . .

Elizabeth shuts her eyes, murmurs again.

DAVID OSSLOW: I beg your pardon? *(Elizabeth flinches)* Are you all right?

ELIZABETH BARROW COLT *(Nodding, eyes closed)*: Fine, fine, fine, fine, fine . . .

A silence.

DAVID OSSLOW: For some reason I imagined you very differently. *(A silence)* I thought you'd have a very large head.

Elizabeth starts laughing, wishing she could stop.

DAVID OSSLOW: No, really I did. I thought you'd have this . . . *(Indicating the size with his hands)* huge head!

Elizabeth finds this hysterical, and trying not to laugh, makes peculiar squeaking sounds.

DAVID OSSLOW: You know how you form an image of someone you haven't met? *(Elizabeth keeps laughing)* I also pictured you as having very bushy eyebrows. You know, the kind that almost meet over the bridge of the nose . . .

Elizabeth, helpless with laughter and embarrassment, tries to hide her face in her napkin and accidentally knocks over her bowl of soup, spilling the entire contents into her lap. She leaps to her feet, flapping like a wet puppy.

ELIZABETH BARROW COLT: Oh dear!

DAVID OSSLOW *(Bolts out of his seat to help her)*: Are you all right?

ELIZABETH BARROW COLT *(Frantically wiping at her dress with her napkin)*: I spilled . . .

DAVID OSSLOW *(Lifting his napkin to help)*: Did you burn yourself?

ELIZABETH BARROW COLT *(Shrinking from him)*: I spilled all my soup . . .

DAVID OSSLOW *(Starts wiping at her dress with his napkin)*: Here, let me help . . .

ELIZABETH BARROW COLT *(Turning her back to him)*: No, no, I can . . .

DAVID OSSLOW: Are you sure you're . . .

ELIZABETH BARROW COLT: I'm sorry . . .

DAVID OSSLOW: Let me get the waiter. Waiter!

Her back turned, Elizabeth hunches over the stain as if the most secret part of her body had suddenly sprung a leak.

ELIZABETH BARROW COLT: I can . . .

CAL *(Striding over)*: Yes?

DAVID OSSLOW: I'm afraid we've had a slight spill. Could you please bring us some water and extra napkins?

ELIZABETH BARROW COLT: It's fine . . . it's coming right out . . . it's nothing . . . really nothing . . . *(Showing her dress)* See, I got it all out . . .

CAL: Yes, right away, I'll get you some fresh napkins and we'll clean it up in no time!

Cal produces several napkins from his pocket and joins David in wiping Elizabeth off.

ELIZABETH BARROW COLT *(Dying of embarrassment since the spill hit her squarely in her crotch)*: No really I can . . . let me . . .

CAL: It shouldn't stain. A good dry cleaner should be able to get this right out . . . *(Feeling the material)* What is the material, anyway? Cotton?

ELIZABETH BARROW COLT: It isn't my dress . . . *(She keeps fussing over it)*

CAL *(To David, feeling the fabric)*: Wouldn't you say this was cotton?

DAVID OSSLOW *(Feels it)*: No, that isn't cotton, it feels more like . . . rayon to me . . .

ELIZABETH BARROW COLT *(Still wiping away)*: A friend lent it to me.

CAL *(Feeling another section of it)*: Rayon? It's too lightweight to be rayon . . .

DAVID OSSLOW: It could be a wool challis . . .

CAL: I say it's either cotton or a cotton blend.

ELIZABETH BARROW COLT: I don't have a proper dress . . .

DAVID OSSLOW: As long as it's a synthetic, she should have no problems . . .

CAL *(Feeling it again)*: You know, it might just be . . . silk!

DAVID OSSLOW *(Feels)*: Silk?

CAL: That's right: silk!

DAVID OSSLOW *(Still feeling)*: It certainly has the weight of silk . . .

CAL: It's silk! That's what it is!

ELIZABETH BARROW COLT: She'll kill me.

CAL: Don't worry, this will come right out. Silk sheds stains like water! *(Pushes into the kitchen with the soiled napkins)*

DAVID OSSLOW: It's a nice dress.

ELIZABETH BARROW COLT *(Trying to hide the immense stain with her napkin, heads back towards her chair)*: I'm sorry . . .

DAVID OSSLOW *(Pulls out her chair for her)*: These kinds of things happen all the . . .

ELIZABETH BARROW COLT *(Collapses in the chair before he's pulled it out all the way, making a loud plop)*: Oh dear, I . . .

DAVID OSSLOW *(Strains to push the chair, with her in it, closer to the table)*: There we go . . .

David returns to his seat, looks at Elizabeth, reaches across the table and picks up her hand, squeezes it and then lets it go.

DAVID OSSLOW: Are you all right?

ELIZABETH BARROW COLT *(Head down)*: Fine, fine, fine, fine fine . . .

A silence. Cal returns with a brand-new bowl of steaming soup, which he sets down before Elizabeth.

CAL: There we go! *(And he turns on his heel)*

ELIZABETH BARROW COLT *(Her shoulders giving way, looks at it)*: Oh dear.

A slight pause.

DAVID OSSLOW: Elizabeth, I'd like to publish your short stories.

ELIZABETH BARROW COLT *(Looking into the soup, stunned)*: Oh my.

DAVID OSSLOW: They're wonderful.

ELIZABETH BARROW COLT: Mercy!

DAVID OSSLOW: What did you say?

ELIZABETH BARROW COLT *(Softly)*: I don't know what to say . . .

DAVID OSSLOW: Really wonderful!

ELIZABETH BARROW COLT: I never imagined . . . *(Starts fishing around in her pocketbook)*

DAVID OSSLOW: You're incredibly gifted . . .

ELIZABETH BARROW COLT: Oh no, I'm . . . *(Pulls out her lipstick, lowers her head and sneaks on a smear, hands shaking. Suddenly she drops the lipstick. It falls into her soup with a splash)* Oh no!

DAVID OSSLOW: What was that?

ELIZABETH BARROW COLT *(Dives for it)*: Oh nothing, I just dropped my lipstick . . .

Elizabeth repeatedly tries to retrieve her lipstick with her spoon, but it keeps splashing back down into her soup. She finally gives up, fishes it out with her hands and drops it into her purse.

DAVID OSSLOW: Don't you like the soup?

ELIZABETH BARROW COLT *(Hunched over her pocketbook)*: Oh yes, it's . . .

DAVID OSSLOW: It looks delicious.
ELIZABETH BARROW COLT *(Staring at it)*: Yes, it's very nice.

DAVID OSSLOW: I've always loved French Provincial . . . I'm sorry . . . I . . .

ELIZABETH BARROW COLT: Would you like it?

A pause.

ELIZABETH BARROW COLT: OH, YOU HAVE IT!
DAVID OSSLOW: No, really, I . . .
ELIZABETH BARROW COLT *(Picks up the bowl with trembling hands and starts lifting it across the table to him, her spoon still in it)*: I want you to have it!
DAVID OSSLOW: *Careful!*
ELIZABETH BARROW COLT *(Giddy, the soup sloshing wildly)*: I never have soup!
DAVID OSSLOW: *LOOK OUT!*
ELIZABETH BARROW COLT: In fact, I hardly ever have dinner, either!
DAVID OSSLOW: Really, I . . .
ELIZABETH BARROW COLT *(Sets it down in front of him, spilling some)*: THERE!
DAVID OSSLOW *(Looks at it. Weakly)*: Well, thank you.

Incredibly relieved, Elizabeth looks at David and sighs. He picks up her spoon and dips it into the soup.

ELIZABETH BARROW COLT: This is nice. . . . How is it?
DAVID OSSLOW: Very good. Would you like a taste?
ELIZABETH BARROW COLT: Oh, no thank you!

A silence.

DAVID OSSLOW: Do you cook at all?
ELIZABETH BARROW COLT: Oh no.
DAVID OSSLOW *(Reaches a spoonful of soup across the table to her)*: Come on, try some.
ELIZABETH BARROW COLT *(She tastes it)*: My mother didn't cook either.
DAVID OSSLOW: Now isn't that good? *(Gives her another taste)*
ELIZABETH BARROW COLT: Mmmmmmmm . . . *(Quickly wipes her mouth with her napkin)*
DAVID OSSLOW *(Takes a taste himself)*: My mother was a great cook.
ELIZABETH BARROW COLT: She didn't know how. She grew up with servants.

DAVID OSSLOW: Her Thanksgiving dinners . . . !

ELIZABETH BARROW COLT: We had a cook. Lacey. She was awful and she smelled.

DAVID OSSLOW: I cook every once in a while.

ELIZABETH BARROW COLT: We all hated her. Especially my mother.

DAVID OSSLOW: My wife is a great cook! Some night you'll have to come over for dinner! *(He settles into the soup, eating with less and less relish as her story progresses)*

ELIZABETH BARROW COLT: In fact, when I was young I never even saw my mother in the kitchen. The food just appeared at mealtime as if by magic, all steaming and ready to eat. Lacey would carry it in on these big white serving platters that had a rim of raised china acorns. Our plates had the same rim. Twenty-two acorns per plate, each one about the size of a lump of chewed gum. When I was very young I used to try and pry them off with my knife. . . . We ate every night at eight o'clock sharp because my parents didn't start their cocktail hour until seven, but since dinnertime was meant for exchanging news of the day, the emphasis was always on talking . . . and not on eating. My father bolted his food, and my mother played with hers: sculpting it up into hills and then mashing it back down through her fork. To make things worse, before we sat down at the table she'd always put on a fresh smear of lipstick. I still remember the shade. It was called "Fire and Ice" . . . a dark throbbing red that rubbed off on her fork in waxy clumps that stained her food pink, so that by the end of the first course she'd have rended everything into a kind of . . . rosy puree. As my father wolfed down his meat and vegetables, I'd watch my mother thread this puree through the raised acorns on her plate, fanning it out into long runny pink ribbons . . . I could never eat a thing . . . "WAKE UP, AMERICA!" she'd trumpet to me. "You're not being excused from this table until you clean up that plate!" So, I'd take several mouthfuls and then when no one was looking, would spit them out into my napkin. Each night I systematically transferred everything on my plate into that lifesaving napkin . . .

DAVID OSSLOW: Jesus Christ.

ELIZABETH BARROW COLT: It's amazing they never caught on.

David lights a cigarette and takes a deep drag.

ELIZABETH BARROW COLT: I mean, you'd think Lacey would have noticed the huge bundles of half-chewed food I left in my chair . . .

DAVID OSSLOW: I have never had trouble eating!

ELIZABETH BARROW COLT: We used cloth napkins, after all. They were collected after each meal.

DAVID OSSLOW: I can always eat, no matter where I am!

ELIZABETH BARROW COLT: We had a fresh one each evening.

DAVID OSSLOW: Believe me, I could use a little of your problem . . .

ELIZABETH BARROW COLT: Lacey washed and ironed them.

DAVID OSSLOW: That is, if you call not eating a problem.

ELIZABETH BARROW COLT: To launder them, she had to dump the food out.

DAVID OSSLOW *(Patting his stomach)*: I should have such problems!

ELIZABETH BARROW COLT: She must have noticed I left so much, at least a pound . . .

DAVID OSSLOW: I'm so bad, I start thinking about my next meal before I've even finished the one I'm eating!

ELIZABETH BARROW COLT: I wonder what she thought? If she was hurt that I could never get it down . . .

DAVID OSSLOW: Now *that's* serious . . . !

ELIZABETH BARROW COLT: I lived in constant fear that she'd tell my parents. You see I was terribly underweight.

DAVID OSSLOW: I love to eat!

ELIZABETH BARROW COLT: Or worse, that she'd sneak into my room some night, lugging all those bulging napkins . . . and spill everything out . . . from one end of my bed to the other . . . and *force* me to eat it . . .

DAVID OSSLOW: I've always loved to eat. . . . It will be the death of me. . . . Every time I see my doctor, he says the same thing. He says, "David, you've got to lose some of that weight!"

A silence.

ELIZABETH BARROW COLT: I used to bite my nails. I think it was because I was so hungry all the time.

DAVID OSSLOW *(Hands her back her empty soup bowl)*: Thank you, it was delicious.

ELIZABETH BARROW COLT *(Hiding her hands)*: I still bite them sometimes. *(A silence. She looks around the room, a sigh)* This is wonderful.

Another silence.

DAVID OSSLOW: Oh! I forgot to return your spoon!

David hands the spoon to Elizabeth, covering her hand with both of his. She grasps it, turns it gently in her hands, sneaks it up against her cheek for a moment . . . and then drops it into her pocketbook.

ELIZABETH BARROW COLT: I can't believe this is happening.

The lights fade.

Scene 3

And rise on the entire restaurant and kitchen.

CAL *(Pouring the wine for Herrick)*: Puligny-Montrachet.

ELLEN *(Fussing over her entrees)*: Oooooooohhhhhhh!

HERRICK SIMMONS *(Tasting the wine)*: Mmmmmmmmmmm . . .

ELLEN *(Inhaling the fragrance)*: Aaaaaaaahhhhhhh!

HERRICK SIMMONS *(Crooning over her wine in a different register)*:
Uuuuuuuuhhhhhh!

NESSA VOX *(Eagerly, to Herrick)*: How is it?

HANNAH: Oh Paul, that was . . .

ELLEN: Arrange the peach slices on the duck . . .

HERRICK SIMMONS: Symphonic!

HANNAH: . . . divine!

DAVID OSSLOW *(To Elizabeth)*: That . . . was an outstanding soup!

ELLEN *(Gazing at the veal)*: Beautiful!

PAUL: Better than the Pavillion, better than the Tour d'Argent . . .

CAL *(Pouring wine for Nessa)*: Mademoiselle . . .

TONY STASSIO: I can hardly wait.

ELIZABETH BARROW COLT: I wasn't sure how to get here . . .

ELLEN: Ladle the Mornay on the veal . . .

Nessa Vox tastes her wine and makes little mewing sounds.

HANNAH: Better than *any* meal I've had anywhere . . .

ELLEN *(Handling the duck)*: Inspired!

PAUL: Here, here . . .

TONY STASSIO *(Grabs Nessa's hand)*: I'm going to have a heart attack!

ELLEN *(Fussing over the bass)*: Yes, my little bass . . .

PAUL: The best . . . !

TONY STASSIO *(Her hand on her heart)*: No, really, I am!

HANNAH: Well, Ken and Diva did rave, remember?

NESSA VOX *(To Tony)*: Just don't keel over until the food comes!

DAVID OSSLOW: In fact, *both* soups were outstanding!

ELLEN *(Inhaling the bass)*: Devastating . . .

ELIZABETH BARROW COLT *(To David)*: I almost got on the wrong bus.

HERRICK SIMMONS *(Raises her glass to her friends)*: To the meal!

NESSA VOX: To the meal!

TONY STASSIO: To the meal!

CAL *(Dives back into the kitchen, to Ellen)*: They can hardly wait!

ELLEN *(Has put the final touches on her entrees)*: All set . . .

CAL *(Hoists the tray over his head)*: So far . . . so good . . . *(And plunges back into the dining room)*

ELLEN *(As he disappears)*: So far . . . so good.

Cal glides towards the women's table with his tray.

HERRICK SIMMONS *(Catching sight of the food)*: Oooooooohhhhhh!

NESSA VOX: Aaaaaaaahhhhhhhhhhhh!

TONY STASSIO: Mmmmmmmmmmmmmmmmmmm!

Cal sets his tray down on a folding waiter's table. He picks up the duckling and sets it down before Herrick.

CAL: Duckling in Wine with . . . Sliced Peaches!

TONY STASSIO: Ohhhh, look!

NESSA VOX: It's a masterpiece! Look at the color of those peaches . . . pure Cezanne!

TONY STASSIO: Sir, I think you made a mistake, *I* was the one who ordered . . .

Tony starts to reach for the duck but is stopped as Cal sets down the veal at her place. Each dish he presents is more spectacular than the last one.

CAL: And for Mademoiselle, Veal Prince Orloff!

TONY STASSIO *(Stops her hand's flight towards the duck and gasps)*: Yessss!

NESSA VOX *(Staring at it)*: My God!

HERRICK SIMMONS *(Weakly)*: Do you see that . . . stuffing?

NESSA VOX: It's . . . overwhelming! Absolutely . . .

TONY STASSIO *(Looking down at it, very pleased)*: Perfect!

HERRICK SIMMONS: Do you smell that sauce? That's Sauce Velouté! . . . Phillip's favorite!

NESSA VOX: I think I'm going to die!

HERRICK SIMMONS: I'd know it anywhere!

NESSA VOX *(To Tony)*: I thought you wanted the duck.

HERRICK SIMMONS: No, she ordered the bass. He made a mistake, the veal is mine!

TONY STASSIO: I didn't order bass!

NESSA VOX *(To Cal)*: Excuse me, Sir, but I believe that veal belongs to *me*!

HERRICK SIMMONS *(Holding out her plate of duck)*: Who ordered this duck?

TONY STASSIO: I'd never order bass with shrimp, I'm on a diet!

HERRICK SIMMONS: That veal is mine!

TONY STASSIO *(To Herrick)*: The *duck* is yours!
NESSA VOX *(To Tony)*: I thought the duck was *yours*!
HERRICK SIMMONS: No, it's *hers*! *(Indicating Nessa)* The veal is mine.
NESSA VOX: Then who ordered the bass?
HERRICK SIMMONS *(To Tony)*: You did.
TONY STASSIO *(Indicating Nessa)*: She did!

Cal sets the bass down before Nessa. It's the triumph of the three dishes. They all want it. Cal exits.

NESSA VOX *(Gasps)*: My God!
TONY STASSIO *(Reaches for the bass)*: No, no, *that's* mine! *I* ordered the bass!

Herrick snatches the bass out from under Nessa and gives Nessa her duck in exchange.

HERRICK SIMMONS *(To Tony)*: Oh no you didn't!
NESSA VOX *(Looking at the duck)*: Hey, where's my bass?
TONY STASSIO *(Grabs the bass away from Herrick and gives her the veal in exchange)*: Now, wait just one minute!
NESSA VOX: I didn't order duck!
HERRICK SIMMONS: And I didn't order veal!
TONY STASSIO *(Starts to eat the bass)*: Mmmmmmmmmmmm . . .
NESSA VOX *(Pulls the bass away from Tony and gives her the duck)*: HEY, YOU CAN'T EAT THAT BASS. IT'S MINE!
HERRICK SIMMONS *(To Tony)*: You ordered the duck, don't you remember?
TONY STASSIO *(Handing Nessa Herrick's veal)*: *She* ordered the veal . . . *(Handing Herrick Nessa's duck) You* ordered the duck . . . and *(Taking Nessa's bass)* I ordered the bass!
NESSA VOX: I would never order veal!
HERRICK SIMMONS: You think I'd order . . . *duck*?
TONY STASSIO: Of course you'd order duck!

This entree-snatching speeds up into a whirlwind.

HERRICK SIMMONS *(Taking the bass from Tony and giving her the duck in exchange)*: That is, if *you* hadn't ordered it first!
NESSA VOX *(Totally confused, to Herrick)*: I thought you wanted the veal.
TONY STASSIO *(Takes Nessa's veal and gives it to Herrick, then takes Herrick's bass and gives Nessa the duck)* Yes! *(To Herrick)* You did!
NESSA VOX: Then who ordered the bass?
HERRICK SIMMONS *(Grabs the bass back from Tony and gives her the veal in exchange)*: I did!

NESSA VOX: Oh, no, you didn't . . . this bass is *mine!* (*She takes the bass from Herrick and gives her the duck*)

TONY STASSIO: NO, THE VEAL IS YOURS! (*She gives Nessa the veal and snatches the bass*) IT'S MY BIRTHDAY, SO THE BASS IS MINE!

Tony starts eating the bass. Silence.

HERRICK SIMMONS (*To Nessa*): She's eating all my bass!

NESSA VOX: Well, you're eating all her duck! (*Raises her glass to Tony*) Happy Birthday!

HERRICK SIMMONS (*Likewise*): Happy Birthday!

DAVID OSSLOW: Waiter, the wine list please.

Herrick and Nessa start eating with gusto. Tony takes tiny bites. As Cal passes, he croons in shared delight.

TONY STASSIO (*To Nessa*): How's the veal, it looks delicious.

They continue to eat.

TONY STASSIO (*Suddenly pushes her bass away*): I don't know about you two, but I am stuffed!

NESSA VOX: But we've hardly started . . .

TONY STASSIO: Can't . . . eat . . . another . . . bite!

HERRICK SIMMONS: You ought to taste this duck, it's heaven!

TONY STASSIO: I think I'm going to burst.

NESSA VOX: Tony, you haven't eaten anything!

HERRICK SIMMONS (*Offering Tony a forkful of duck*): Come on, try it.

TONY STASSIO (*Shaking her head*): Really, I'm—

NESSA VOX (*Lays down her fork*): I don't believe this!

HERRICK SIMMONS (*Plows into her duck with renewed vigor*): Well, you're missing something fabulous!

NESSA VOX (*To Herrick*): She says she's finished.

HERRICK SIMMONS: Mmmmmmmm!

NESSA VOX: Look at her plate!

TONY STASSIO: Don't let me spoil your dinner just because I'm dieting . . .

HERRICK SIMMONS: Aaaaaaahhhhhh!

NESSA VOX: She hasn't touched it.

HERRICK SIMMONS: Nessa, you've got to try some of this duck. (*Offers her a forkful*)

TONY STASSIO: You two just go right ahead . . .

NESSA VOX: Well if she's not going to eat, then neither am I!

HERRICK SIMMONS *(Offering Nessa the duck more forcefully)*: Come on, it's sensational!
NESSA VOX *(Tastes it)*: Mmmmmmmmmmmm!
HERRICK SIMMONS: Isn't that something?
TONY STASSIO *(Lifting up her plate)*: Would anyone like my bass?
HERRICK SIMMONS *(Giving Nessa another bite)*: And now taste it with some of the peaches . . .
NESSA VOX *(Does)*: MY GOD!
HERRICK SIMMONS: Hmmm?

Nessa flutters.

TONY STASSIO: I've already lost four pounds this week!
NESSA VOX: TONY, YOU'VE GOT TO TRY THIS DUCK, YOU'LL DIE!
HERRICK SIMMONS *(Reaching a forkful over to Tony)*: It's unbelievable . . .
NESSA VOX: It's the best duck I've ever—
HERRICK SIMMONS: Here, let me get you more sauce. *(She offers Tony a heaping spoonful)*
NESSA VOX: You won't know what hit you!
TONY STASSIO *(Shielding her mouth with her hand)*: No really, I couldn't . . .
NESSA VOX *(To Herrick)*: Wouldn't you say that was the best duck you've ever—
TONY STASSIO *(Trying to ward them off)*: Please . . .
HERRICK SIMMONS *(More threatening with her fork)*: Just a little taste . . . !
NESSA VOX: Come on, it won't kill you!
HERRICK SIMMONS: Open!
NESSA VOX *(Scoops some up with her fork and also menaces Tony with it)*: We insist!
HERRICK SIMMONS: It really is—
NESSA VOX: Quite—
TONY STASSIO: Please!
NESSA VOX: Wonderful.
TONY STASSIO: Don't—
HERRICK SIMMONS: You should—
TONY STASSIO: —force me!
HERRICK SIMMONS: —try it!
NESSA VOX: Come on, Tony! You promised—
HERRICK SIMMONS: Eat the duck!

NESSA VOX: You've hardly eaten anything.

TONY STASSIO: I've got to lose ten more pounds!

NESSA VOX *(Dumps the duck off her fork and threatens Tony with some of her veal)*: At least try the veal!

TONY STASSIO *(Shielding her face with both hands)*: Only ten pounds! *(She starts to cry)*

NESSA VOX *(Slams down her fork)*: FUCK IT THEN. JUST FUCK IT!

Silence.

HERRICK SIMMONS *(Resumes eating her duck)*: Ignore her.

NESSA VOX: HOW CAN I IGNORE HER WHEN WE'RE SITTING AT THE SAME TABLE AND SHE REFUSES TO EAT?!

HERRICK SIMMONS: It's her problem. *(Offering Nessa another forkful of duck)* Come on, help me with this duck.

TONY STASSIO: I'm fat.

NESSA VOX: She says she's fat!

HERRICK SIMMONS *(Reaching across for a taste of Nessa's veal)*: How's your veal?

TONY STASSIO *(Lifts up her arm, pulls the underpart of it)*: Look at that!

NESSA VOX: That isn't fat! That's your arm!

HERRICK SIMMONS *(Eating Nessa's veal)*: Mmmmmmm! Very nice!

TONY STASSIO: It's fat.

NESSA VOX *(Lifts up her plate of veal and gives it to Herrick)*: Here, have it all, I don't want any.

HERRICK SMITH: Don't give it all to me!

TONY STASSIO *(Gives Herrick her bass)*: You can have my bass too.

NESSA VOX: She ruined the whole meal.

HERRICK SIMMONS: I can't eat all of this! *(As she starts to do just that)*

TONY STASSIO *(Smiling, to Nessa)*: How was the veal?

NESSA VOX: You'd think I'd learn . . .

HERRICK SIMMONS: What's going on here?

TONY STASSIO *(To Nessa, referring to the veal)*: It looks good.

NESSA VOX: She does it every time!

TONY STASSIO *(To Herrick)*: And your bass looks really—

NESSA VOX: IT'S NOT AS IF SHE EVER STICKS TO ANY OF HER DIETS! AS SOON AS SHE GETS HOME, SHE'LL OPEN UP THE REFRIGERATOR AND HAVE HERSELF ONE WALLOPING ORGY!

HERRICK SIMMONS: Take it easy . . .

NESSA VOX: SHE DENIES HERSELF IN FRONT OF US, BUT OH, WHEN SHE GETS INTO THE PRIVACY OF HER OWN REFRIGERATOR—

TONY STASSIO *(Hands over her ears)*: I don't know what she's talking about . . .

HERRICK SIMMONS *(To Nessa)*: Come on . . .

NESSA VOX: —DOES SHE EVER GO AT IT! I know her. *(To Herrick)* Would you like to hear?

HERRICK SIMMONS: Nessa, don't—

NESSA VOX: First . . . just to warm up, she wolfs down a Twin Pack of Golden Ridges Potato Chips followed by a fistful of Nabisco Nilla Wafers. Then, it's on to the freezer for the real stuff: Hungry Man TV dinners flash frozen by Swanson's, Howard Johnson's, Stouffer's, Morton's, Mrs. Paul, Ronzoni, and Chun King! . . . But . . . can she wait for them to heat up? . . . God knows, it's a long wait for a Hungry Man TV Dinner when you're languishing for it . . . the piquant steak in onion gravy, the hashed brown potato nuggets, the peas and carrots in seasoned sauce, and the delectable little serving of apple cake cobbler, pristine and golden in its tidy aluminum compartment. . . . So, while its warming at four hundred degrees, she'll help herself to some Pepperidge Farm corn muffins, fully baked and ready to serve. Still frozen, mind you . . . still frosted with a thin sheen of ice, but there's nothing wrong with eating frozen corn muffins . . . especially if you turn out the lights and eat them in the dark . . . lift them up to your mouth . . . in the dark . . . roll your tongue over them . . . in the—

HERRICK SIMMONS: NESSA, THAT'S ENOUGH!

A silence.

TONY STASSIO *(Trying to recover, in a quavering voice)*: Well, I wonder if it's warmed up at all outside . . .

Tony wets her finger and rubs it around the rim of her glass making eerie music. Another silence.

HERRICK SIMMONS *(Pushing her bass away)*: Well, I guess I'm done. Anyone want the rest of this food?

TONY STASSIO: It's actually dangerous to go out on a night like this . . .

A silence.

NESSA VOX: Well, if you two are finished, then so am I . . . *(Pushes her veal towards the center of the table)*

HERRICK SIMMONS: Can't eat another bite!

TONY STASSIO: I don't know when I've been so full!

NESSA VOX: If I have one more taste, I'm going to explode!

HERRICK SIMMONS: You're going to explode! What about me? I won't be able to fit behind the wheel of the car to drive us home!

This gets slower and slower.

TONY STASSIO: I can't go on . . .
NESSA VOX: I've had it . . .
HERRICK SIMMONS: I am stuffed!
TONY STASSIO: I can't move . . .
NESSA VOX: I'm in pain!
HERRICK SIMMONS: I feel sick . . .
TONY STASSIO: I'm . . . dying . . .

The lights fade around them.

Scene 4

And rise on Paul and Hannah Galt. They have just been presented with snifters of after-dinner brandy. Paul picks his up and sloshes it around, inhaling the fragrance. Hannah does the same, then holds out her glass to Paul.

HANNAH: A toast!
PAUL *(Offering her his glass)*: Oh good, I love toasts!
HANNAH *(Clinking his glass)*: To . . . us! *(She drinks)*
PAUL *(Drinks)*: That's very sweet, Hannah.
HANNAH *(Reaches out her glass and clinks his again)*: You and me all the way. *(She drinks)*
PAUL *(Drinks again)*: Here, here!

A silence.

HANNAH *(Lifts up her glass again)*: I want to make another toast!
PAUL: You're on!
HANNAH *(Clinking his glass)*: To our wonderful children . . . Brian and Michelle! *(She drinks)*
PAUL: Brian and Michelle . . . super kids! *(He drinks)*
HANNAH: Gee, I'm having a good time.

Hannah kicks off her shoes. A silence.

PAUL *(Leans back in his chair, swirling his brandy)*: This is very pleasant . . . very pleasant indeed.
HANNAH *(Leaning forward)*: Another toast!
PAUL: Not again!

HANNAH *(Clinking his glass)*: Oh come on, Paul . . . toast!

PAUL *(Clinks with her)*: Toast.

HANNAH: Guess.

PAUL: What do you mean, "guess"?

HANNAH: Guess what I'm going to toast.

PAUL: Hannah, I couldn't possibly *guess* . . .

HANNAH: Of course you can, just try . . .

PAUL *(Raising his glass)*: To . . . oh, Hannah, we could sit here all night, there's no way I could *guess* what you're—

HANNAH: All right, all right! I thought you could guess, but if you can't . . . you can't! *(A pause, she lifts her glass, clinks it to his)* To your long and curly eyelashes!

PAUL *(Pulls back his glass)*: To my . . . long and curly *eyelashes*???!

HANNAH: Yes, they're gorgeous! *(She drinks again)*

PAUL *(In a whisper)*: Hannah, I can't drink to my . . . *eyelashes!*

HANNAH: Well, I can . . . and I'm going to because they're gorgeous!

PAUL: They are?

HANNAH: Very long . . . and very curly!

PAUL: You never told me that before.

HANNAH: Well, I'm telling you now . . .

PAUL *(Studies his reflection in his brandy glass)*: Son of a bitch!

HANNAH *(Getting tipsy, clinking his glass again)*: Toast . . . toast!

PAUL: Not so loud.

HANNAH *(Clinks softer)*: Sorry . . .

PAUL *(Still peering at his reflection in his glass)*: They're really long and curly?

HANNAH *(Touching his glass)*: Toast, toast! . . . To your kneecaps! You have fabulous kneecaps! *(She drinks)*

PAUL *(Looks around the room, embarrassed)*: Hannah!

HANNAH: Come on, drink!! *(She drinks again)*

PAUL *(In a whisper)*: Not to my *kneecaps,* for Christsakes!

HANNAH *(Raps his glass again)*: TO ONE . . . STUNNING PAIR OF KNEECAPS! *(She drinks)*

PAUL *(Embarrassed, laughs)*: Hannah, stop it!

HANNAH: Really . . . *stunning!*

A few of the diners look over at them.

PAUL: Okay . . . if that's the way you want to play . . . *(He holds out his glass to her)* I would like to propose a toast!

HANNAH *(Sitting back in her chair)*: Oh goody! *(She offers her glass)*

PAUL: To your snowy white thighs! *(He clinks and drinks)*

HANNAH *(Snatches her glass away, embarrassed)*: Paul!

PAUL *(Clinking her glass again)*: May they continue to bewitch and excite . . . *(He drinks)*

HANNAH *(In a hiss)*: Paul, stop it, it's not funny! . . . People are looking!

Herrick, Nessa and Tony stare openly and try not to laugh.

PAUL *(Directly to them)*: Well, it's true, she's got one terrific pair of snowy white thighs!

HANNAH *(Dying of embarrassment)*: I don't believe this . . .

PAUL: Would I lie?

HANNAH *(In a dry whisper)*: Paul, stop it! Just . . . stop it!

PAUL *(Stands and toasts everyone in the room)*: Well, bon appetit to one and all. *(He drinks, then sits back down)*

HANNAH: I've never been so embarrassed . . .

PAUL: Oh, come on Hannah, we're just fooling around.

HANNAH: Maybe *you're* fooling around, but *I'm* not . . . !

PAUL: So, all of a sudden *I'm* fooling around, is that it . . . ?

HANNAH: You brought it up, not me!

PAUL: You think I'm fooling around, is that what you're saying?

HANNAH: I never said you were fooling around . . . *you* said *we* were just fooling around.

PAUL: Are you fooling around?

HANNAH: What do you mean, am *I* fooling around? What kind of a question is that?

PAUL: *Are* you fooling around?

HANNAH *(After a pause)*: Well, I'm not telling.

PAUL: You mean you are fooling around?

HANNAH: What do you think?

PAUL: Frankly, I don't know what to think!

HANNAH: Well, neither do I . . . I mean, what a thing to ask me after a nice dinner and everything . . .

PAUL *(Putting his hand over hers)*: I'm sorry.

HANNAH *(Sulking)*: So am I . . .

PAUL *(After a pause)*: Forgive me?

HANNAH: I have to think about it.

A silence as they both sip their brandies.

PAUL: Have you thought about it yet?

HANNAH: Maybe.

PAUL: Would you care to tell me what you decided?

HANNAH: That depends . . .

PAUL: Yes?

HANNAH: Do you promise never to embarrass me in public again?

PAUL: I promise.

HANNAH: Cross your heart?

PAUL *(Crosses his heart)*: Cross my heart! *(Then lifts his glass to hers)* I'll never embarrass you in public again! *(He drinks)*

HANNAH *(She drinks, mournful)*: I'm not fooling around.

A silence.

PAUL *(Eager, reaches his glass forward)*: A toast, another toast!

HANNAH *(Offering her glass)*: Yes?

PAUL: To our next meal! *(He clinks)*

HANNAH: Oh, I like that!

Paul drinks.

HANNAH: That's more like it. *(She drinks)* To our next meal. *(And leans over and kisses him)*

The lights fade.

Scene 5

And rise on Ellen and Cal in the kitchen. The food that Ellen was working with in the first act has multiplied, tenfold. It's tumbling off the counters and overflowing on the stove. Ellen and Cal race in the midst of it like figures in a speeded-up old-time movie.

Ellen is adding raw mushrooms and spices to a salad. She then tosses it, all the while talking on the telephone which she has tucked under her chin.

Cal prepares a tray of coffee, cups, sugar, cream and silverware for the Galts, all the while talking on the other telephone which he has tucked under his chin.

ELLEN: COULD YOU SPEAK INTO THE PHONE A LITTLE LOUDER PLEASE? I'M HAVING TROUBLE HEARING YOU. YES . . . THAT'S MUCH BETTER. Now, you were saying, you'd like reservations for how many? Three for Thursday the ninth . . . I'm sorry, we're completely filled the ninth. Could I suggest Tuesday the

CAL: No, nothing pleases us more than hearing from satisfied customers, you're not bothering us in the least. . . . You've never tasted such inspired Chicken Kiev in your life? ELLEN, THEY'VE NEVER TASTED SUCH INSPIRED CHICKEN KIEV IN THEIR LIVES! And you'd like to come back for more? We change our

fourteenth? I SAID, TUES-DAY THE FOURTEENTH! Yes, that's right, you could choose any time you like. I BEG YOUR PARDON? SOFT-SHELLED CRABS? Yes, I agree with you, they are delicious. . . . Yes . . . yes . . . NO, I WOULDN'T DREAM OF DEEP-FRY-ING THEM, I NEVER DEEP-FRY ANYTHING. . . . Yes, yes . . . you'd like to call me back after you've talked it over with your husband? Fine . . . I SAID, THAT WOULD BE FINE. THANK YOU FOR CALLING. Good-bye. *(She hangs up)*

menu every day, you realize, so I couldn't guarantee you that same Chicken Kiev again. . . . Now, which evening were you thinking of coming back? Thursday the ninth at 7:30? Yes, that would be fine . . . your name please? Kipner? . . . OH YES, OF COURSE, I REMEM-BER YOU FROM LAST WEEK. YOU WERE THE PARTY OF FOUR WHO ORDERED EXTRA SA-LADS. Well, thank you for calling. We'll see you on the ninth. Good-bye. *(He hangs up)*

ELLEN: That was three for the fourteenth . . . maybe.

CAL: Six for the ninth . . . ?

ELLEN: Six for the ninth? We're filled on the ninth!

CAL: You said, fourteen on the third?

ELLEN: You should have made it for the eighteenth. The salads are ready to go.

Cal exits to the dining room with the salads.

ELLEN: We have plenty of room on the eighteenth. He could have made it for the twenty-first which is a holiday . . . *(Turning towards her sauce and picking up three eggs)* And now for my Hollandaise, my thick and rich Hollandaise for the bass! *(She separates the eggs for the Hollandaise sauce)*

CAL *(Careening back into the kitchen)*: Fourteen on the third is fantastic. That's what I like to hear: *big numbers.* Fourteen on the third . . . nineteen on the tenth . . . twenty-five on the sixteenth!

ELLEN *(Beating the yolks)*: Slow down. It's not fourteen on the third. It's three on the fourteenth, but we're talking about the ninth, and we're filled on the ninth!

CAL *(Fussing with his coffee tray)*: We can divide them up into two tables of seven . . .

ELLEN: We have plenty of room on the eighteenth! Vinegar . . . *(She adds a drop)*

CAL: . . . or three tables of five minus one . . .

ELLEN: I could handle four on the eighteenth . . .

CAL: How about one table of six and two tables of four?

ELLEN: Or even five on the nineteenth . . . salt . . . *(She adds a pinch)*

CAL: Or . . . four tables of three . . .

ELLEN: . . . but six on the ninth? . . . Impossible!

CAL *(As he plunges into the dining room with his tray of coffees)*: No problem!

ELLEN: Pepper! MY BASS! *(She rushes to the oven and pulls out her bass, takes the lid off)* Oh, just look how lovely you are! And how delicious you smell . . . a garden full of herbs . . . perfect! *(She puts the bass on a countertop)*

CAL *(Popping back into the kitchen)*: Baby, we are going to expand!

ELLEN: OH NO WE'RE NOT! Fish juices. *(She pours off the fish juices into her Hollandaise)*

CAL: We are going to build onto the side of the house . . .

ELLEN: Over my dead body! Heavy cream. *(She beats in the heavy cream)*

CAL: Enclose the back yard . . .

ELLEN: Just try it . . . twelve tablespoons of melted butter. Smooth and easy. Come on baby . . .

CAL *(Refilling the water pitcher)*: Break through the bedroom . . .

Ellen beats and grunts.

CAL: Knock out those back walls.

ELLEN: Cal, you're losing your mind! Raving like a madman.

CAL: Add a good two hundred feet.

ELLEN: NO!

CAL: If we use our heads, Ellen, we can fit fifty more tables in there! *(He rushes back to the dining room to pour the ladies their wine and deposit his water pitcher)*

ELLEN: The next time he comes through that door, he'll announce we're opening a franchise! *(She returns to her sauce with a joyous fury)* Oh yes . . . you little yellow sweetheart . . . you thick and creamy love of mine . . . you luscious baby . . . thicken! . . . Break through the bedroom . . . ?! Thaaaaat's the way . . . you're doing fine . . . oh yes . . . just fine . . . you tangy heartbreaker, you zesty tease . . . fifty more tables? . . . NEVER! *(She dances around the kitchen whipping her sauce)*

CAL *(Comes careening back)*: With a little planning, we could be feeding two hundred people a night!

ELLEN: Not in this house! Not in *my* restaurant! *(She gives the sauce one more stroke and sets it aside on the counter)* EVERYTHING'S GOING TO BE FINE! Lemon juice . . . *(She adds a final drop of lemon juice)*

CAL: That's over five thousand dollars! *(He eyes the Hollandaise she's just made)*

ELLEN: Just . . . fine!

CAL *(Reaches for a spoon and unconsciously scoops out a taste of the Hollandaise)*: Five thousand dollars a night, comes to thirty thousand dollars a week!

ELLEN *(Turns to the wild rice simmering on another burner, stirs it, adjusting the seasoning)*: They'll love it!

CAL: At that rate we could pay back our loan within six months!

ELLEN: They'll die over it!

CAL: We'd be in the clear . . . *(He takes another taste of the sauce)*

ELLEN: Oh Cal, I want them to die over it!

CAL: If we could just pay off that loan . . . *(He picks up the saucepan of Hollandaise and starts drinking it)*

ELLEN *(Her back to him as she dishes out the rice)*: I am a cook who takes chances!

CAL *(Gulping it down)*: Ellen, I gave up my law practice for this!

ELLEN *(Transferring the bass to a serving platter)*: A cook . . . who delivers!

CAL: Eight years of a successful business!

ELLEN *(Smells the bass, tastes the drippings)*: And I keep getting better!

CAL *(Starts to spill the sauce down his front)*: A lot of people told me I was crazy . . . *you* even told me I was crazy . . . give up an assured annual income of ninety thousand and go seventy-five thousand into debt . . . for what?

ELLEN *(One more taste)*: It's . . . perfect!

CAL: To open a restaurant in our living room!

Ellen croons over the bass.

CAL: Insanity!

ELLEN *(Reaches for her sauce)*: And now for the crowning glory . . . my sauce . . . my Hollandaise . . .

CAL: A wonderful little restaurant that would serve out-of-this-world food . . . an old dream of ours . . .

ELLEN *(Her back to him, scans the countertop)*: Now where did I put it? I just had it . . .

CAL: You could cook to your heart's content . . .

ELLEN: Damn!

CAL: I could run the place, show off my entrepreneurial skills . . .

ELLEN: Where's my sauce?

CAL: *But we'd have to be serious about it and make some money!* I'm having trouble sleeping at night!

ELLEN *(Finally sees him with the pan)*: Oh Cal! You . . . *can't* . . . you . . . *didn't! (She staggers to the stove)*

Cal stops drinking, unaware of his action. Ellen blindly rushes to him and tries to wrest the pan from his hands.

ELLEN: HOW . . . COULD . . . YOU . . . *DRINK* . . . HOLLANDAISE SAUCE???? . . . THE *TASTE*, CAL . . .

CAL *(Trying to ward her off)*: Hey, take it easy . . .

ELLEN: How could you just take it off the burner . . . pick up the pan . . . and drink out of it? *(She starts swatting him with a towel)*

CAL: Watch it!

ELLEN: You're like some animal . . . an animal drinking out of its trough . . .

CAL *(As the sauce sloshes wildly)*: Look out!

Ellen finally wrenches the pan from him, holds it aloft and, with deadly calm, pours the sauce on the floor.

ELLEN: Go on, Cal, drop down to the floor and lap it up! Lower your muzzle into it . . . *and drink!*

Ellen pushes Cal from behind. Cal loses his balance and sprawls on his hands and knees into the sauce. He backs away from it, horrified.

ELLEN *(In a towering rage)*: THAT DOES IT, I'M SORRY, BUT . . . *THAT DOES IT!!!*

Ellen starts hurling pots and pans into the sink. She picks up whatever is big and makes noise and throws it across the room. She then pulls out all the cords to her appliances, turns off the burners on the stove and switches off the overhead lights. The whole room goes black.

ELLEN: No more cooking. I'm through!

CAL *(Still on his knees, starts cleaning up the sauce with some towels)*: Ellen, what are you doing? There are people out there waiting for their food.

ELLEN *(In a whisper)*: Too bad.

CAL: Half of them still haven't had their main course.

ELLEN: Go on, finish up the sauce on the floor. No one can see you.

CAL: Table One is still waiting for its entrees.

ELLEN: It's kind of nice like this . . .

CAL: Table Three may order second desserts . . .

ELLEN: . . . cozy . . .

CAL: Table Two can't make up its mind . . .

ELLEN: . . . comforting . . .

CAL: The next sitting will be here soon . . .

ELLEN: It's so quiet. *(She sits on one of the counters and hugs her legs to her chest)*

CAL: A party of five is coming at nine.

ELLEN: Look at the stove Cal, it's moving.

CAL: We've got to keep ahead of them.

ELLEN: It's like some wonderful dark ocean liner . . .

CAL: ELLEN, LISTEN TO ME! All hell is going to break loose out there!

ELLEN: Cut free from its anchor . . .

CAL: I'm the one on the spot.

ELLEN: . . . pushing through the night . . .

CAL: What am I going to do?

ELLEN: No one can stop it.

CAL *(In a panicky whisper)*: What am I going to do?

ELLEN: It's broken free and is heading out into places unknown.

Scene 6

Lights up on David Osslow and Elizabeth Barrow Colt, who are waiting for their entrees.

DAVID OSSLOW: Most publishing houses shy away from short-story collections.

ELIZABETH BARROW COLT *(Murmurs)*: Oh well, I didn't really . . .

DAVID OSSLOW: They just don't sell . . .

ELIZABETH BARROW COLT *(Murmurs)*: Yes, I suppose when the chips are down . . .

DAVID OSSLOW: But yours are so remarkable. I'm sure people have told you that before.

ELIZABETH BARROW COLT: Actually, I don't see that many . . .

DAVID OSSLOW: I really appreciate you meeting me like this on such a cold—

ELIZABETH BARROW COLT *(Giddy)*: I HAD NO IDEA WHAT YOU LOOKED LIKE. I COULDN'T IMAGINE HOW WE'D EVER . . .

Upset and rushed, Cal plunges into the restaurant and up to their table with the bass.

CAL *(Under his breath)*: Please God, don't let them notice there's no Hollandaise sauce on the bass . . . Bar au Mousse de Crevettes. *(He places it on the table with a flourish)*

DAVID OSSLOW: Aaaahhhh, here comes our entree!

ELIZABETH BARROW COLT: Oh.

CAL *(With very elaborate gestures)*: And would you like me to divide it for you?

DAVID OSSLOW: Please.

Cal does a spectacular job preparing the fish.

DAVID OSSLOW *(In a whisper as Cal works)*: Look at that bass! It's a masterpiece!

Elizabeth peers at Cal nearsightedly, then sneaks on her glasses to see better.

DAVID OSSLOW: I didn't know you wore glasses.

ELIZABETH BARROW COLT *(Quickly takes them off)*: Oh, I don't! These are someone else's.

DAVID OSSLOW: You wear someone else's glasses?

ELIZABETH BARROW COLT: Sylvia Tussman, she works downtown at Hyde and Johnson's . . .

DAVID OSSLOW: You could ruin your eyes wearing someone else's glasses . . .

ELIZABETH BARROW COLT: . . . in the typing pool, she's also good at steno.

DAVID OSSLOW: You should get your own prescription.

ELIZABETH BARROW COLT: She has several different pairs of glasses, so she said—

DAVID OSSLOW *(Looking at her closely)*: You know, you have very beautiful eyes.

ELIZABETH BARROW COLT: Oh no . . .

DAVID OSSLOW: You do. They're so pale, transparent almost . . .

Blazing with embarrassment, Elizabeth drops her head, murmurs.

DAVID OSSLOW *(Cups her face in his hands)*: Let me see them again . . .

ELIZABETH BARROW COLT: It's nothing, they're just . . . eyes . . .

DAVID OSSLOW *(Drawing her head closer)*: No really, they're . . . extraordinary.

ELIZABETH BARROW COLT: I don't know, I . . .

DAVID OSSLOW: I bet they glow in the dark. . . . They do, don't they?

ELIZABETH BARROW COLT *(Has fallen in love with David)*: Not really, I . . .

Cal, finished with his handiwork, tries to set Elizabeth's plate down, but she's all over the place. Just as he's about to put it down, she moves, blocking him. They play a dreadful kind of hesitation dance.

CAL: Sorry, I was just trying to . . . excuse me, I just wanted . . . *I'm sorry!* . . . Hold it right there . . . *if you could just steady her.*

ELIZABETH BARROW COLT: I'm sorry, I'm sorry, I'm sorry, I'm sorry, I'm sorry, I'm sorry.

David holds Elizabeth still with both hands. Cal finally sets the plate down.

CAL: There we are!

ELIZABETH BARROW COLT *(Looks down at it)*: Gosh.

CAL *(Sets down David's plate with ease)*: And for Monsieur . . .

ELIZABETH BARROW COLT *(Looking at her bass, unable to face David)*: Gosh.

DAVID OSSLOW *(Lifts his fork to her)*: Bon appetit! *(And dives in)*

ELIZABETH BARROW COLT *(Paralyzed by shyness)*: Gosh . . . beautiful eyes!

DAVID OSSLOW: Are you all right?

ELIZABETH BARROW COLT: Oh dear.

DAVID OSSLOW: What's wrong?

Elizabeth starts to laugh breathlessly.

DAVID OSSLOW: Don't you like the bass?

ELIZABETH BARROW COLT *(Trying to stop laughing)*: Oh dear, oh dear, oh dear.

David laughs tentatively with Elizabeth, who puts her napkin over her face in an effort to stop, snorts and gasps under it.

ELIZABETH BARROW COLT: No one ever said I had beautiful . . .

David watches her with amusement and then returns to his bass. Elizabeth suddenly rises, pushes her chair back almost knocking it over, and with the napkin partially over her head, lurches towards the rear of the room.

DAVID OSSLOW *(Stands)*: Are you all right?

CAL: The Ladies Room is to the left.

Elizabeth, great peals of laughter erupting from her, careens into the kitchen.

CAL: She went into the kitchen . . .
DAVID OSSLOW: She's been wearing someone else's glasses.
CAL: Oh.

Elizabeth wanders nearsightedly through the dark kitchen amazed at the confusion of food and pots.

DAVID OSSLOW: May we have our wine now please?

He keeps eating.

CAL: Certainly, Sir.
DAVID OSSLOW: She's a writer.
CAL: Yes?
DAVID OSSLOW: And a very good one.
CAL: She looks like a writer.
DAVID OSSLOW: Mmmmm . . .
CAL: Strange eyes . . .
DAVID OSSLOW: I don't think she's been out to restaurants very often.
ELIZABETH BARROW COLT *(Bursts back into the room, laughing)*: I was in the . . . kitchen . . .

Elizabeth twirls around, confused, still looking for the Ladies Room— and following another route, ends up in the kitchen again.

DAVID OSSLOW *(Eating)*: This bass is delicious!
CAL: I'm so glad you like it! *(He puts down the bottle of wine)* Puligny-Montrachet.

As David continues to eat, he nods that Cal should pour the wine. Cal uncorks the bottle and begins the ritual of pouring it. He gives David the cork to smell, pours him a tiny taste, waits for his approval, fills Elizabeth's glass, and then returns to David's as Elizabeth continues to wander through the dark kitchen. She eventually comes upon Ellen— who's sitting on the counter—peers nearsightedly at her, and is unable to make any sense of what's happening. More embarrassed than ever, she lunges back out into the restaurant.

ELIZABETH BARROW COLT: I was in the kitchen . . . again . . . *(She helplessly tries to get her moorings)*
CAL: *Upstairs* . . . the Ladies Room is *upstairs* . . . to the left . . .

Almost on all fours, Elizabeth creeps out of the room.

CAL *(As he watches her)*: Maybe she needs her glasses, she was wearing them earlier.

DAVID OSSLOW: No, I don't think so.

CAL: She seems lost . . .

DAVID OSSLOW *(Drinking his wine)*: She'll be all right.

A silence. Elizabeth gingerly reenters the room. She waves to David from afar.

ELIZABETH BARROW COLT: Oh, dear . . .

DAVID OSSLOW *(Rises, waves back)*: Hi.

ELIZABETH BARROW COLT *(Softly)*: Hi.

DAVID OSSLOW: Are you feeling better? *(He pulls out her chair)*

ELIZABETH BARROW COLT *(Collapses into it)*: I'm sorry . . .

DAVID OSSLOW: Don't be sorry . . . *(He starts pushing her back to the table)*

ELIZABETH BARROW COLT: I'm so embarrassed . . .

DAVID OSSLOW: Your bass is getting cold.

ELIZABETH BARROW COLT *(Is overcome by embarrassment and starts to cry)*: I'm sorry . . .

CAL: Can I get you anything else?

DAVID OSSLOW: No, we're fine, thank you.

CAL: Then I'll be getting back to the kitchen. *(He rushes back to Ellen, angry)* ELLEN, PLEASE!

ELIZABETH BARROW COLT: Oh dear.

DAVID OSSLOW *(Moving closer to her)*: Calm down.

ELIZABETH BARROW COLT *(Can't stop crying)*: Oh dear, oh dear, oh dear . . .

DAVID OSSLOW: Elizabeth, it happens all the time.

ELIZABETH BARROW COLT: No.

DAVID OSSLOW: Yes. All the time. Now dry your eyes and eat your bass.

ELIZABETH BARROW COLT *(Doesn't move)*: Yes.

DAVID OSSLOW: I've seen writers fall to the floor in a dead faint.

ELIZABETH BARROW COLT: Oh.

DAVID OSSLOW: I've seen it all, believe me!

ELIZABETH BARROW COLT *(Looks at her bass)*: Oh my . . .

DAVID OSSLOW: Now try some of that bass.

ELIZABETH BARROW COLT: Yes.

DAVID OSSLOW: It's superb. You'll love it.

Elizabeth looks at her bass again, helpless. She sighs. A silence.

ELIZABETH BARROW COLT (*Very loud and intense*): ONE AFTER-
NOON WHEN I CAME HOME FROM SCHOOL MOTHER
WAS IN TEARS BECAUSE LACEY HAD QUIT, WALKED
OUT IN A TORRENT OF INSULTS. "NEVER AGAIN!"
MOTHER SOBBED. "FROM NOW ON, I'LL DO THE
COOKING MYSELF!" . . . IT WAS A BIG MISTAKE. SHE
DIDN'T KNOW HOW AND SHE WAS IN THE MIDST OF
MENOPAUSE. SHE KEPT BREAKING DISHES AND CUT-
TING HER FINGERS WITH THE CARVING KNIFE. ONE
NIGHT SHE SLICED OFF THE TIP OF HER THUMB AND
GROUND IT UP IN THE GARBAGE DISPOSAL!

*Hannah Galt lurches towards the Ladies Room. The lights rise a little
to reveal the other diners. They're startled by Elizabeth's sudden
outburst and stare, then turn away feigning indifference, but hanging
on every word.*

ELIZABETH BARROW COLT: Mealtime was much the same as it had
always been . . . Father still talked a blue streak, Mother still
mashed her food into a pink soup . . . and I still spit everything
out into my napkin. But they were paper napkins now, and since I
cleared the table, there was no chance of discovery. I breathed
easier. What changed then, was the violence that went into the
cooking beforehand . . . I never saw such bloodletting over meals!
If she didn't nick herself while cutting the tomatoes, she'd delib-
erately slice a finger while waiting for the rice to boil. "Why bother
cooking?" she'd cry, holding her bleeding hands under the faucet.
"We'll all be dead soon enough!" . . . It was around this time that
Mother was starting to get . . . suicidal . . . *(She starts to laugh)* Oh
dear, I shouldn't laugh . . . it was just so . . . comical! You see,
Mother was very comical. She wore hats all the time, great turban-
type creations piled high with artificial flowers and papier-mâché
fruits. She wore them outside and she wore them in the house.
She wore them when she cooked and when she ate . . . great
teetering crowns that bobbed and jingled with every move . . .
poor Mother . . . I don't know what it was that made her so
unhappy . . . her menopause, her cocktails before dinner, some
private anguish . . . but during this period, she used to threaten to
kill herself. After another bloodstained dinner, she'd throw herself
face down on our driveway and beg my father to put the car in
reverse and drive over her. "Don't be ridiculous, dear," he'd say.

But she meant it and would lie there sobbing, "PLEASE . . . DO IT!" It was a ritual we went through every night . . .

DAVID OSSLOW *(Does his best to eat his dinner, stopping only when he's too shaken to swallow)*: And did she ever . . . ? I mean . . . succeed?

ELIZABETH BARROW COLT *(Sighs)*: Oh dear.

DAVID OSSLOW: She did . . .

ELIZABETH BARROW COLT: Poor Mother.

DAVID OSSLOW: How . . . awful . . . *(Elizabeth sighs)* Your father finally gave in and ran over her . . .

ELIZABETH BARROW COLT: Not that.

DAVID OSSLOW: Sleeping pills . . .

ELIZABETH BARROW COLT: If only it had been . . .

DAVID OSSLOW: Poor thing . . .

ELIZABETH BARROW COLT: Yes . . .

DAVID OSSLOW: She shot herself . . . ?

ELIZABETH BARROW COLT: Can't you guess?

DAVID OSSLOW: How could I guess . . . with someone like . . . *that*?

ELIZABETH BARROW COLT: Think! It's so in character!

DAVID OSSLOW: She slit her throat with a carving knife?

ELIZABETH BARROW COLT *(A bit bloodthirsty)*: Better . . .

DAVID OSSLOW *(After a pause)*: Of course . . . I know . . .

DAVID OSSLOW: She turned on the gas . . .   ELIZABETH BARROW COLT: She turned on the gas . . .

ELIZABETH BARROW COLT: She turned on the gas and opened that big mouth of an oven door and stuck her head in . . . with her hat firmly in place . . .

DAVID OSSLOW: Yes, of course . . . the hat!

ELIZABETH BARROW COLT *(Starts laughing)*: It must have been quite a sight . . . Mother down on all fours, trying to fit her head in without knocking her hat off . . .

DAVID OSSLOW: And . . . ?

ELIZABETH BARROW COLT: Oh dear, I shouldn't laugh . . .

DAVID OSSLOW: No, go on . . .

ELIZABETH BARROW COLT: Well, after she'd been in there for ten minutes or so, getting groggier and groggier, something went wrong. The papier-mâché trinkets on her hat began to sizzle and explode like little firecrackers. Within moments the entire hat was in flames. She came to like a shot and raced to the sink . . . her head actually . . . *cooking*! She turned on the water full blast . . . her hat and all of her hair was consumed . . . but she survived.

(Pause) She joked about it afterwards . . . after the hospital stay and plastic surgery . . . about almost having barbecued herself like some amazing delicacy . . . some exotic . . . roast! "I BET I WOULD HAVE TASTED DAMNED GOOD!" she used to say, smacking her lips. *(Long pause)* My mother is very beautiful, you know . . . she's so beautiful . . . people turn around.

Hannah Galt reenters the room and sits down. A silence.

DAVID OSSLOW: You haven't eaten any of your bass.

ELIZABETH BARROW COLT *(Looking at it)*: Oh yes, my bass . . .

DAVID OSSLOW *(With great tenderness)*: You haven't touched it.

ELIZABETH BARROW COLT: I'm sorry, I . . .

DAVID OSSLOW *(Touching her cheek)*: It's getting cold . . .

ELIZABETH BARROW COLT: Yes, I guess it is . . .

DAVID OSSLOW *(Dips her fork into her bass and holds it out to her like a father feeding his child)*: Come . . . just try it . . . one taste . . .

Elizabeth looks at him helplessly, unable to take it. Neither of them moves, and the lights fade around them.

Scene 7

The kitchen. Still in a blackout.

CAL *(Softly)*: Ellen, I beg of you. Don't do this to me . . . to us!

Scene 8

The lights rise on Herrick Simmons, Nessa Vox and Tony Stassio.

HERRICK SIMMONS *(In a whisper)*: The things you overhear in restaurants . . .

Nessa whistles her disbelief.

TONY STASSIO: I don't know . . .

HERRICK SIMMONS: Very strange . . . *(Nessa whistles again)* Poor thing . . .

NESSA VOX: She has such . . . beautiful eyes.

Silence.

HERRICK SIMMONS: Guess what happened to me today?

TONY STASSIO: What?

HERRICK SIMMONS *(Starts to laugh)*: You'll die!

NESSA VOX: Tell us!

HERRICK SIMMONS: I was . . . flashed.

TONY STASSIO: So . . . ?

HERRICK SIMMONS: By a . . . woman!

TONY STASSIO: Gee!

NESSA VOX: What did she flash?

HERRICK SIMMONS: A breast!

NESSA VOX: How wonderful!

TONY STASSIO: How sick!

HERRICK SIMMONS: It wasn't sick at all, it was really quite beautiful. I mean, it was so unexpected. I'd just had lunch with Phillip and was looking in Tiffany's windows. I turned to cross 57th Street, and this very pretty blond woman was crossing towards me. As we passed each other, she smiled at me, lowered one side of her blouse, and flashed a gleaming breast . . .

TONY STASSIO: Sick . . .

NESSA VOX: I love it!

TONY STASSIO: What did you do?

HERRICK SIMMONS: Nothing. I just looked at it.

TONY STASSIO *(Starts sneaking tastes of her bass)*: God! Did she say anything?

HERRICK SIMMONS: Not a word.

NESSA VOX *(Also lighting into her veal)*: I love it! Women finally getting up enough nerve to be flashers!

Herrick starts gobbling her duck. This sneaking of food begins as innocent picking, but gets uglier and uglier as their real hunger and shame sets in.

TONY STASSIO: But imagine . . . doing that . . . showing your breast to a stranger . . .

NESSA VOX: What was it like?

TONY STASSIO: It's really kind of . . .

HERRICK SIMMONS: What was *what* like?

NESSA VOX: Her breast . . .

HERRICK SIMMONS: It was nice.

NESSA VOX: Was it round . . . or pendulous?

Tony sneaks more bass.

HERRICK SIMMONS: Round.

NESSA VOX *(Sneaks more veal)*: I think I'd die if I had pendulous breasts!

At times only one woman is sneaking her food, at times they sneak in concert.

HERRICK SMITH: *Why?*

NESSA VOX: They're so . . . *ugly!*

TONY STASSIO *(In a small voice)*: Mine are pendulous.

NESSA VOX: They are not!

TONY STASSIO: They are so!

HERRICK SIMMONS *(To Tony)*: You have lovely breasts!

TONY STASSIO *(Softly)*: I have shitty breasts.

HERRICK SIMMONS: NO WOMAN HAS SHITTY BREASTS!

NESSA VOX: Listen, mine are dappled.

HERRICK SIMMONS: I'M SORRY, BUT BREASTS ARE LIFE-GIV-ING!

TONY STASSIO: Dappled?

NESSA VOX *(Her head lowered)*: Spotted. You know how sometimes they get all—

HERRICK SIMMONS: I've never heard of spotted breasts!

NESSA VOX: Whenever I'm upset, they get . . . mottled.

HERRICK SIMMONS: Listen, a lot of women—

TONY STASSIO *(In a low voice)*: When I gain weight, mine get *really* pendulous! "Old Bananas," my brother used to call me!

HERRICK SIMMONS: A lot of women are ashamed of their breasts, it's ridiculous!

NESSA VOX: There's some imbalance in my hormones.

TONY STASSIO: In front of his friends.

HERRICK SIMMONS: They should be proud of them!

NESSA VOX *(To Tony)*: At least you're not . . . spotted.

HERRICK SIMMONS *(To Tony)*: One of mine is bigger than the other, but they're still terrific!

TONY STASSIO: I have trouble finding clothes that fit.

NESSA VOX: And don't think it isn't painful!

HERRICK SIMMONS: What the hell . . .

TONY STASSIO: It's a real problem.

NESSA VOX: It's not fair.

TONY STASSIO: Of course when I diet, they do deflate somewhat . . .

NESSA VOX *(To Herrick)*: How would you like a blotchy bosom?

HERRICK SIMMONS: I MEAN, WHAT CAN WE DO ABOUT IT? WHAT CAN WE POSSIBLY DO?

The lights fade on their ravenous and unhappy faces as they openly plunge into their food.

Scene 9

But they don't rise in the kitchen because Ellen is still sitting in the dark. Cal paces nervously. All is stillness for several moments. Then Cal turns on the speaker connected with the tape that plays in the restaurant. The third movement from J. S. Bach's Sonata No. 3 in E major for violin and harpsichord goes on.

CAL: Ellen . . .

ELLEN: Oh, that's nice . . .

CAL: I can't even see you.

ELLEN: Nice to stop and rest . . .

CAL: Could I light a candle at least?

A long sigh from Ellen. Cal gets a candle and sets it into a head of lettuce or some other unlikely object and then lights it.

ELLEN: How pretty . . .

CAL: That's better . . .

Silence.

CAL: Remember when you used to prepare us dinner when we were first married? How I loved it! Watching you cook in the dark . . . it was so romantic. I could hear your heart race as you tended your filets, stirred your sauces. . . . I could never quite see what you were adding, rending, sautéing . . .

ELLEN: You'd never get too close, but would watch from a distance, give me my room . . . and all the time in the world. So much time and so much love . . .

CAL: Yes, I could feel it thickening all around us. I'd sneak glances at you in the darkness and reel at your grace. . . . We were so happy! My God! That newlywed cooking, those honeymoon suppers that lasted and lasted . . .

ELLEN: And here we are again except now you've eaten everything before I could get started . . . *why Cal?*

CAL: Because it's so good.

ELLEN: But it's *not* good! You're eating everything before it's done!

CAL: You're such a good cook . . .

ELLEN: You're eating it raw!

CAL: You have such a gift . . .

ELLEN: Gobbling it up . . .

CAL: . . . an incredible gift!

ELLEN: . . . swallowing it whole!

CAL: It's wonderful.

ELLEN: I can't go on like this.

CAL: Really . . . wonderful!

ELLEN: You've got to give me a chance. . . . LET ME DO MY WORK! PLEASE!

A silence.

CAL *(Starts eating a roll)*: It's this damned not sleeping. I lie awake half the night worrying.

ELLEN: Just let me cook!

CAL: Will we pay off the loan?

ELLEN: I'll go sour without it, you know, soft at the edges, dead at the core!

CAL: Bring in some cash?

ELLEN: I don't care about cash!

CAL: Worrying makes me hungry, you know. Not sleeping makes me hungry.

ELLEN: I can't stop cooking. I've been at it too long.

CAL: It all adds up.

ELLEN: You can still make a choice.

CAL: I know it's a problem.

ELLEN: And you must . . . or we're done for. Totally done for.

A silence.

CAL: I'll try and watch it.

ELLEN: You have to watch it.

CAL: And if for some terrible reason I can't?

ELLEN: It's over.

CAL: The restaurant will close?

ELLEN: No. Everything's over. Finished.

A silence.

CAL: Even me?

ELLEN *(Looks at him, takes her time)*: Even you . . .

CAL: Ellen, don't say that.

ELLEN: It's true.

CAL: I said, *don't*! You don't help matters, you know. . . . "Taste this . . . try that . . . is it good? Oh Cal, will they like it? . . . I want them to die over it!" . . . There's no escaping you and your outstretched spoon, did you ever think about that?

ELLEN: I was just asking you to taste, not eat the ground out from under me.

CAL: I know, I know.

ELLEN: You're out of control.
CAL: I know.

Silence.

ELLEN: Well then, here we sit.
CAL *(In a whisper)*: But there are hungry people out there.
ELLEN: So . . . ?
CAL: Two of the tables are still waiting for their desserts.
ELLEN: So . . . ?
CAL: The next group will be coming soon. *(Ellen sighs contentedly)* This is starting to get scary.
ELLEN: Gee, I'm beginning to enjoy it.
CAL: Can I turn on the light, at least?
ELLEN: Whatever you want.
CAL *(Does)*: Now I can see you, anyway.

Ellen smiles and waves at Cal. He holds out a large wooden spoon to her.

CAL: Come on, baby . . . *(She won't take it)* Please?

Cal tries presenting the spoon to Ellen in a variety of coy ways: hiding it behind his back, trying to press it into her arms like a bouquet of flowers, pressing it up against her cheek, handling it like a baton, a flute, a sword.

CAL: Ellen . . . Ellen! Come on, cook!
ELLEN: Why?
CAL: For us, honey . . . for us! *(He tries more ploys with the spoon)*
ELLEN: I'm just too tired.
CAL: Okay, okay, you want me to change. I'll change . . . WATCH THIS! *(He rushes over to the stove and with great bravura begins melting some butter in a skillet)*
ELLEN: Cal, what are you doing?
CAL *(Performs these actions as he describes them)*: He melts the butter in the pan with nary a lick . . . then he grates a soupçon of orange rind into the butter without touching his fingers to his lips . . .
ELLEN *(Starts to laugh)*: Cal . . .
CAL *(More and more florid)*: Next, he adds a hint of maraschino and a dash of curaçao. . . . Note how he inhales the fragrance of the mixture without taking a taste . . .
ELLEN: You forgot the sugar.
CAL: In a phenomenal display of speed and grace, he manages to add

four tablespoons of sugar before the sauce comes to a boil. . . . And once again, I'd like to draw your attention to the fact that never once does the aromatic spoon approach his lips . . .

ELLEN: Honey, you don't know how to make orange sauce.

Cal blends the ingredients, adding subtle hints of port and cassis.

ELLEN: Not cassis, Cal . . . kirsch!

CAL *(Correcting his error)*: Of course, of course, how stupid of me . . . *(He stirs and inhales with rising intensity)* Please note how he adjusts the flavoring through smell and not taste—how he relies exclusively on the prowess of his olfactory glands . . .

ELLEN *(Goes to him and puts her arms around him)*: Oh, Cal . . .

CAL: Ah-ah, not too close. We don't want anything to spill.

ELLEN: Cal . . . !

CAL *(In one fluid move, he pours the sauce into an appropriate serving bowl)*: And now to find something that looks like Crepes Suzettes . . . *(He roots around in the refrigerator and pulls out a stack of pancakes)* Ahh, here we go . . . the Swedish pancakes you prepared for a rainy day . . . *(He puts them in the oven for a moment and kisses Ellen on the cheek)* You're really amazing you know. *(He turns the heat way up)*

ELLEN: Cal, what *are* you doing?

CAL: Oh, the power of invention . . . !

Cal launches into an exuberant dance while singing an aria to the pancakes. He then removes them from the oven and puts them on a tray along with the sauce.

ELLEN *(Laughing)*: What's going on here?

CAL: It's my treat, my offering to the evening. *(He hands her the tray)*

ELLEN: Wait a minute, why are you giving this to me?

CAL: Because you're going to bring it out when I give you the signal.

ELLEN: But I can't go out there.

CAL: Oh yes you can. We're in this together.

ELLEN *(Protesting)*: Cal . . . !

CAL *(Plunks the tray into Ellen's arms and straightens out her apron, maybe even adding her chef's hat)*: It's a beginning, Ellen. A beginning.

ELLEN *(Teetering under the weight of the tray, laughing)*: You're crazy, you know that? . . . Stark, raving . . .

CAL: And you . . . ? What about you?

Ellen looks at Cal out of brimming eyes as he glides into the dining room.

Scene 10

The lights rise on the diners, who are in considerable agitation.

DAVID OSSLOW: Waiter, could we see the dessert menu, please?

HANNAH: *There* he is!

NESSA VOX *(Hailing Cal)*: Sir?

PAUL: Well, finally! I thought he'd died in there!

NESSA VOX: *Sir??*

CAL *(Fussing with a chafing dish)*: *Okay, Ellen, wait till the count of three!*

HANNAH *(To Paul)*: Ask him if they take MasterCharge?

DAVID OSSLOW: Waiter?

NESSA VOX: Excuse me, Sir. Could you possibly turn up the heat a little more? It's freezing in here!

CAL: One . . .

TONY STASSIO *(Rising to get her coat)*: I'm getting my coat. It must be ninety below out there.

NESSA VOX *(Also rises, stands by the window)*: Get mine too . . .

PAUL: Waiter, the check please!

CAL: Two . . .

DAVID OSSLOW: Anytime you're ready with the dessert menu . . .

HANNAH *(To Cal)*: Excuse me, but do you take MasterCharge?

DAVID OSSLOW: We'd also like a look at the pastry tray.

PAUL: Waiter? It's been half an hour!

CAL: Three!

Ellen steps into the restaurant and puts the sauce and pancakes down on the chafing dish.

TONY STASSIO: What's happening?

HANNAH: What's this?

NESSA VOX: Who's that?

PAUL: What's going on?

TONY STASSIO: Who's she?

DAVID OSSLOW: It must be their dessert . . .

HERRICK SIMMONS *(Returning from the Ladies Room)*: It must be my zabaglione . . .

HANNAH: But we've already—

PAUL: Sssssshhhhhh!

HANNAH: Oh Paul, smell!

HERRICK SIMMONS: I love it!

ELLEN *(To Cal)*: The matches please.

Cal lights a match to the dessert. Orange and blue flames leap up. Hannah gasps.

PAUL: Hannah, hold still!
NESSA VOX: It looks like . . .
DAVID OSSLOW: It must be . . .
HANNAH: Oh, what's that called . . . ?
NESSA VOX: I've got it!

A pause.

NESSA, DAVID AND HANNAH: It's Crepes Suzettes!
HANNAH: Crepes Suzettes!
HERRICK SIMMONS: Crepes Suzettes!
PAUL: I knew it!
CAL *(Stands back and announces)*: CREPES CAROUSELS!

Everyone bursts into applause and sighs, murmurs "Crepes Carousels!"

CAL: On the house!

Even louder cheers and echoes of "On the house!" Ellen starts transferring the crepes into a large serving platter.

TONY STASSIO: I don't believe this!

Herrick sidles over to the platter and looks in. Ellen motions her to help herself. She does and sits back down at her place, smiling.

DAVID OSSLOW *(Advances to take his piece)*: I've been to many restaurants in my day, but this is the first time I've ever seen anything like this!
NESSA VOX: Wait for me! *(She rushes to the platter and takes her share)*
TONY STASSIO: I'm right behind you!
HANNAH *(Helping herself)*: This is extraordinary.
ELIZABETH BARROW COLT: No, not really.

Everyone looks at her, suddenly hushed.

ELIZABETH BARROW COLT: It's like the beginning of time . . .

Nessa and Tony start to laugh.

DAVID OSSLOW: Ssssshhhhh!
HERRICK SIMMONS: Be quiet!
ELIZABETH BARROW COLT *(With great simplicity)*: . . . long, long ago when men ate by a fire . . . crouched close to its warmth . . .

entwined their great arms . . . gave thanks for the kill . . . and shared in the feast.

Elizabeth rises and joins the other diners at the flaming platter. She helps herself to some crepes and for the first time all evening, she eats. She looks at Ellen, who smiles at her.

The diners become more jovial around Ellen and eat with increased gusto, wiping their greasy faces, grunting with pleasure. Ellen throws Cal a backward glance, but he shakes his head indicating he's eaten enough for the evening. Everyone's movements slow down to simple gestures, their language becomes less familiar. The fury of the November wind increases outside and the light from Ellen's bonfire burns brighter and brighter as the diners gather close to its warmth. Ellen stands above them, churning up the flames, her face glowing with a fierce radiance. Purified of their collective civilization and private grief, they feast as the curtain slowly falls.

PAINTING
CHURCHES

ABOUT THE PLAY

Directed by Carole Rothman, *Painting Churches* was initially produced by the Second Stage on New York's Theatre Row in 1983. The play reopened at the Lamb's Theatre in New York the following year, once again under Rothman's direction.

Painting Churches won an Outer Critics Circle Award, a John Gassner Award and a Rosamond Gilder Award. The play was televised on *American Playhouse* in 1986; it was directed by Jack O'Brien.

Characters

FANNY SEDGWICK CHURCH, a Bostonian from a fine old family, in her sixties.

GARDNER CHURCH, her husband, an eminent New England poet from a finer family, in his seventies.

MARGARET CHURCH (MAGS), their daughter, a painter, in her early thirties.

Time

Several years ago.

Place

Boston, Massachusetts.

ACT ONE

Scene 1

The living room of the Churches' townhouse on Beacon Hill one week before everything will be moved to Cape Cod. Empty packing cartons line the room and all the furniture has been tagged with brightly colored markers. At first glance it looks like any discreet Boston interior, but on closer scrutiny one notices a certain flamboyance. Oddities from secondhand stores are mixed in with the fine old furniture, and exotic handmade curios vie with tasteful family objets d'art. What makes the room remarkable, though, is the play of light that pours through three soaring arched windows. At one hour it's hard edged and brilliant; the next, it's dappled and yielding. It transforms whatever it touches, giving the room a distinct feeling of unreality. It's several years ago, a bright spring morning.

Fanny is sitting on the sofa, wrapping a valuable old silver coffee service. She's wearing a worn bathrobe and fashionable hat. As she works, she makes a list of everything on a yellow legal pad. Gardner can be heard typing in his study down the hall.

FANNY *(Picks up a coffee pot)*: God, this is good-looking! I'd forgotten how handsome Mama's old silver was! It's probably worth a fortune. It certainly weighs enough! *(Calling)* GARRRRRRRR-RRRRRRRRRRDNERRRRRRRRRRRRR? . . . Well, it should bring us a pretty penny, that's for sure. *(Wraps it, places it in a carton, and then picks up the tray that goes with it. She holds it up like a mirror and adjusts her hat. Louder in another register)* OH, GARRRRRRRRRRRRRRRRRRDNERRRR?

(Gardner continues typing. She then reaches for a small box and opens it with reverence) Grandma's Paul Revere teaspoons! . . . *(She takes out several and fondles them)* I don't care how desperate things get, these will never go! One has to maintain some standards! *(She writes on her list)* Grandma's Paul Revere teaspoons, Cotuit! . . .WASN'T IT THE AMERICAN WING OF THE METRO-POLITAN MUSEUM OF ART THAT WANTED GRANDMA'S PAUL REVERE TEASPOONS SO BADLY? . . . *(She looks at her reflection in the tray again)* This is a very good-looking hat, if I do say so. I was awfully smart to grab it up. *(Silence)*
DON'T YOU REMEMBER A DISTINGUISHED-LOOK-ING MAN COMING TO THE HOUSE AND OFFERING US FIFTY THOUSAND DOLLARS FOR GRANDMA'S PAUL

REVERE TEASPOONS? . . . HE HAD ON THESE MARVEL-OUS SHOES! THEY WERE SO POINTED AT THE ENDS WE COULDN'T IMAGINE HOW HE EVER GOT THEM ON AND THEY WERE SHINED TO WITHIN AN INCH OF THEIR LIVES AND I REMEMBER HIM SAYING HE CAME FROM THE . . . AMERICAN WING OF THE METROPOLI-TAN MUSEUM OF ART! . . . HELLO? . . . GARDNER? . . . ARE YOU THERE! *(The typing stops)* YOO-HOOOOOOO . . . *(Like a foghorn)* GARRRRRRRRRRRDNERRRRRRR?

GARDNER *(Offstage; from his study)*: YES, DEAR . . . IS THAT YOU?
FANNY: OF COURSE IT'S ME! WHO ELSE COULD IT POSSIBLY BE? . . . DARLING, PLEASE COME HERE FOR A MINUTE. *(The typing resumes)* FOR GOD'S SAKE, WILL YOU STOP THAT DREADFUL TYPING BEFORE YOU SEND ME STRAIGHT TO THE NUT HOUSE? . . . *(In a new register)* GARRRRRRRRRRRRRDNERRRRRR?

He stops.

GARDNER *(Offstage)*: WHAT'S THAT? MAGS IS BACK FROM THE NUT HOUSE?

FANNY: I SAID . . . Lord, I hate this yelling. . . . PLEASE . . . COME . . . HERE!

Brief silence.

GARDNER *(Offstage)*: I'LL BE WITH YOU IN A MO-MENT, I DIDN'T HEAR HER RING. *(Starts singing)* "Nothing could be finer than to be in Carolina."

FANNY: It's a wonder I'm not in a straitjacket already. Actually, it might be rather nice for a change . . . peaceful. DAR-LING . . . I WANT TO SHOW YOU MY NEW HAT!

Silence. Gardner enters, still singing. He's wearing mismatched tweeds and is holding a stack of papers which keep drifting to the floor.

GARDNER: Oh, don't you look nice! Very attractive, very attractive!
FANNY: But I'm still in my bathrobe.
GARDNER *(Looking around the room, leaking more papers)*: Well, where's Mags?
FANNY: Darling, you're dropping your papers all over the floor.
GARDNER *(Spies the silver tray)*: I remember this! Aunt Alice gave it to us, didn't she? *(He picks it up)* Good Lord, it's heavy. What's it made of? Lead?!
FANNY: No, Aunt Alice did *not* give it to us. It was Mama's.

GARDNER: Oh, yes . . . *(He starts to exit with it)*
FANNY: Could I have it back, please?
GARDNER *(Hands it to her, dropping more papers)*: Oh, sure thing. . . .
Where's Mags? I thought you said she was here.
FANNY: I didn't say Mags was here, I asked *you* to come here.
GARDNER *(Papers spilling)*: Damned papers keep falling . . .
FANNY: I wanted to show you my new hat. I bought it in honor of
Mags' visit. Isn't it marvelous?
GARDNER *(Picking up the papers as more drop)*: Yes, yes, very nice . . .
FANNY: Gardner, you're not even looking at it!
GARDNER: Very becoming . . .
FANNY: You don't think it's too bright, do you? I don't want to look
like a traffic light. Guess how much it cost?
GARDNER *(A whole sheaf of papers slides to the floor; he dives for them)*:
OH, SHIT!
FANNY *(Gets to them first)*: It's all right, I've got them, I've got them.
(She hands them to him)
GARDNER: You'd think they had wings on them . . .

FANNY: Here you go . . .   GARDNER: . . . damned things
                                                won't hold still!

FANNY: Gar . . . ?
GARDNER *(Engrossed in one of the pages)*: Mmmmm?
FANNY: HELLO?
GARDNER *(Startled)*: What's that?
FANNY *(In a whisper)*: My hat. Guess how much it cost.
GARDNER: Oh, yes. Let's see . . . ten dollars?
FANNY: Ten dollars . . . IS THAT ALL?
GARDNER: Twenty?
FANNY: GARDNER, THIS HAPPENS TO BE A DESIGNER HAT!
DESIGNER HATS START AT FIFTY DOLLARS . . . SEV-
ENTY-FIVE!
GARDNER *(Jumps)*: Was that the door bell?
FANNY: No, it wasn't the door bell. Though it's high time Mags were
here. She was probably in a train wreck!
GARDNER *(Looking through his papers)*: I'm beginning to get fond of
Wallace Stevens again.
FANNY: This damned move is going to kill me! Send me straight to my
grave!
GARDNER *(Reading from a page)*:
"The mules that angels ride come slowly down
The blazing passes, from beyond the sun.

Descensions of their tinkling bells arrive.
These muleteers are dainty of their way . . ."
(Pause) Don't you love that! "These muleteers are *dainty* of their way"!?

FANNY: Gar, the hat. How much? *(Gardner sighs)* Darling . . . ?

GARDNER: Oh, yes. Let's see . . . fifty dollars? Seventy-five?

FANNY: It's French.

GARDNER: Three hundred!

FANNY *(Triumphant)*: No, eighty-five cents.

GARDNER: Eighty-five cents! . . . I thought you said . . .

FANNY: That's right . . . eighty . . . five . . . *cents!*

GARDNER: Well, you sure had me fooled!

FANNY: I found it at the thrift shop.

GARDNER: I thought it cost at least fifty dollars or seventy-five. You know, designer hats are very expensive!

FANNY: It was on the markdown table. *(She takes it off and shows him the label)* See that? Lily Daché! When I saw that label, I nearly keeled over right into the fur coats!

GARDNER *(Handling it)*: Well, what do you know, that's the same label that's in my bathrobe.

FANNY: Darling, Lily Daché designed hats, not men's bathrobes!

GARDNER: Yup . . . Lily Daché . . . same name . . .

FANNY: If you look again, I'm sure you'll see . . .

GARDNER: . . . same script, same color, same size. I'll show you. *(He exits)*

FANNY: Poor lamb can't keep anything straight anymore. *(Looks at herself in the tray again)* God, this is a good-looking hat!

GARDNER *(Returns with a nondescript plaid bathrobe. He points to the label)*: See that? . . . What does it say?

FANNY *(Refusing to look at it)*: Lily Daché was a *hat* designer! She designed ladies' *hats!*

GARDNER: What . . . does . . . it . . . say?

FANNY: Gardner, you're being ridiculous.

GARDNER *(Forcing it on her)*: Read . . . the label!

FANNY: Lily Daché did *not* design this bathrobe, I don't care what the label says!

GARDNER: READ! *(Fanny reads it)* ALL RIGHT, NOW WHAT DOES IT SAY?

FANNY *(Chagrined)*: Lily Daché.

GARDNER: I told you!

FANNY: Wait a minute, let me look at that again. *(She does; then throws the robe at him in disgust)* Gar, Lily Daché never designed a bathrobe in her life! Someone obviously ripped the label off one of her hats and then sewed it into the robe.

GARDNER *(Puts it on over his jacket)*: It's damned good-looking. I've always loved this robe. I think you gave it to me. . . . Well, I've got to get back to work. *(He abruptly exits)*

FANNY: Where did you get that robe anyway? . . . I didn't give it to you, did I . . . ?

Silence. Gardner resumes typing.

FANNY *(Holding the tray up again and admiring herself)*: You know, I think I *did* give it to him. I remember how excited I was when I' found it at the thrift shop . . . fifty cents and never worn! *I* couldn't have sewn that label in to impress him, could I? . . . I can't be that far gone! . . . The poor lamb wouldn't even notice it, let alone understand its cachet. . . . Uuuuuuh, this damned tray is even heavier than the coffee pot. They must have been amazons in the old days! *(Writes on her pad)* "Empire tray, Parke-Bernet Galleries," and good riddance! *(She wraps it and drops it into the carton with the coffee pot)* Where *is* that wretched Mags? It would be just like her to get into a train wreck! She was supposed to be here hours ago. Well, if she doesn't show up soon, I'm going to drop dead of exhaustion. God, wouldn't that be wonderful? . . . Then they could just cart me off into storage with all the old chandeliers and china . . .

The doorbell rings.

FANNY: IT'S MAGS, IT'S MAGS! *(A pause. Dashing out of the room, colliding into Gardner)* GOOD GOD, LOOK AT ME! I'M STILL IN MY BATHROBE!	GARDNER *(Offstage)*: COMING, COMING . . . I'VE GOT IT . . . COMING! *(Dashing into the room, colliding into Fanny)* I'VE GOT IT . . . HOLD ON . . . COMING . . . COM-ING . . .

FANNY *(Offstage)*: MAGS IS HERE! IT'S MAGS. . . . SHE'S FI-NALLY HERE!

Gardner exits to open the front door. Mags comes staggering in carrying a suitcase and an enormous duffel bag. She wears wonderfully distinctive clothes and has very much her own look. She's extremely out of breath and too wrought up to drop her heavy bags.

MAGS: I'm sorry. . . . I'm sorry I'm so late. . . . Everything went wrong! A passenger had a heart attack outside of New London and we had to stop. . . . It was terrifying! All these medics and policemen came swarming onto the train and the conductor kept running up and down the aisles telling everyone not to leave their seats under any circumstances. . . . Then the New London fire department came screeching down to the tracks, sirens blaring, lights whirling, and all these men in black rubber suits started pouring through the doors. . . . *That* took two hours . . .

FANNY *(Offstage)*: DARLING . . . DARLING . . . WHERE ARE YOU?

MAGS: *Then*, I couldn't get a cab at the station. There just weren't any! I must have circled the block fifteen times. Finally I just stepped out into the traffic with my thumb out, but no one would pick me up . . . so I walked . . .

FANNY *(Offstage)*: Damned zipper's stuck . . .

GARDNER: You walked all the way from the South Station?

MAGS: Well actually, I ran . . .

GARDNER: You had poor Mum scared to death.

MAGS *(Finally puts the bags down with a deep sigh)*: I'm sorry. . . . I'm really sorry. It was a nightmare.

Fanny reenters the room, her dress over her head. The zipper's stuck; she staggers around blindly.

FANNY: Damned zipper! Gar, will you please help me with this?

MAGS: I sprinted all the way up Beacon Hill.

GARDNER *(Opening his arms wide)*: Well come here and let's get a look at you. *(He hugs her)* Mags!

MAGS *(Squeezing him tight)*: Oh, Daddy . . . Daddy!

GARDNER: My Mags!

MAGS: I never thought I'd get here! . . . Oh, you look wonderful!

GARDNER: Well, you don't look so bad yourself!

MAGS: I love your hair. It's gotten so . . . white!

FANNY *(Still lost in her dress, struggling with the zipper)*: This is *so* typical . . . just as Mags arrives, my zipper has to break! *(She grunts and struggles)*

MAGS *(Waves at her)*: Hi, Mum . . .

FANNY: Just a minute, dear, my zipper's . . .

GARDNER *(Picks up Mags' bags)*: Well, sit down and take a load off your feet . . .

MAGS: I was so afraid I'd never make it . . .

GARDNER *(Staggering under the weight of the bags)*: What have you got in here? Lead weights?

MAGS: I can't believe you're finally letting me do you.

Fanny flings her arms around Mags, practically knocking her over.

FANNY: OH, DARLING . . . MY PRECIOUS MAGS, YOU'RE HERE AT LAST.

GARDNER *(Lurching around in circles)*: Now let's see . . . where should I put these . . . ?

FANNY: I was sure your train had derailed and you were lying dead in some ditch!

MAGS *(Pulls away from Fanny to come to Gardner's rescue)*: Daddy, please, let me . . . these are much too heavy.

FANNY *(Finally noticing Mags)*: GOOD LORD, WHAT HAVE YOU DONE TO YOUR HAIR?!

MAGS *(Struggling to take the bags from Gardner)*: Come on, give them to me . . . please? *(She sets them down by the sofa)*

FANNY *(As her dress starts to slide off one shoulder)*: Oh, not again! . . . Gar, would you give me a hand and see what's wrong with this zipper. One minute it's stuck, the next it's falling to pieces.

Gardner goes to her and starts fussing with it.

MAGS *(Pacing)*: I don't know, it's been crazy all week. Monday, I forgot to keep an appointment I'd made with a new model. . . . Tuesday, I overslept and stood up my advanced painting students. . . . Wednesday, the day of my meeting with Max Zoll, I forgot to put on my underpants . . .

FANNY: GODDAMMIT, GAR, CAN'T YOU DO ANYTHING ABOUT THIS ZIPPER?!

MAGS: I mean, there I was, racing down Broome Street in this gauzy Tibetan skirt when I tripped and fell right at his feet . . . SPLATTT! My skirt goes flying over my head and there I am . . . everything staring him in the face . . .

FANNY: COME ON, GAR, USE A LITTLE MUSCLE!

MAGS *(Laughing)*: Oh, well, all that matters is that I finally got here. . . . I mean . . . there you are . . .

GARDNER *(Struggling with the zipper)*: I can't see it, it's too small!

FANNY *(Whirls away from Gardner, pulling her dress off altogether)*: OH, FORGET IT! JUST FORGET IT! The trolley's probably missing half its teeth, just like someone else I know. *(To Mags)* I grind my teeth in my sleep now, I've worn them all down to stubs. Look at that! *(She flings open her mouth and points)* Nothing left but the gums!

GARDNER: I never hear you grind your teeth . . .

FANNY: That's because I'm snoring so loud. How could you hear anything through all that racket? It even wakes me up. It's no wonder poor Daddy has to sleep downstairs.

MAGS *(Looking around)*: Jeez, look at the place! So, you're finally doing it . . . selling the house and moving to Cotuit year round. I don't believe it. I just don't believe it!

GARDNER: Well, how about a drink to celebrate Mags' arrival?

MAGS: You've been here so long. Why move now?

FANNY: Gardner, what are you wearing that bathrobe for?

MAGS: You can't move. I won't let you!

FANNY *(Softly to Gardner)*: Really, darling, you ought to pay more attention to your appearance.

MAGS: You love this house. *I* love this house . . . the room . . . the light.

GARDNER: So, Mags, how about a little . . . *(He drinks from an imaginary glass)* to wet your whistle?

FANNY: We can't start drinking now, it isn't even noon yet!

MAGS: I'm starving. I've got to get something to eat before I collapse! *(She exits towards the kitchen)*

FANNY: What *have* you done to your hair, dear? The color's so queer and all your nice curl is gone.

GARDNER: It looks to me as if she dyed it.

FANNY: Yes, that's it. You're absolutely right! It's a completely different color. She dyed it bright red!

Mags can be heard thumping and thudding through the icebox.

FANNY: NOW, MAGS, I DON'T WANT YOU FILLING UP ON SNACKS. . . . I'VE MADE A PERFECTLY BEAUTIFUL LEG OF LAMB FOR LUNCH! . . . HELLO? . . . DO YOU HEAR ME? . . . *(To Gardner)* No one in our family has *ever* had red hair, it's so common looking.

GARDNER: I like it. It brings out her eyes.

FANNY: WHY ON EARTH DID YOU DYE YOUR HAIR *RED*, OF ALL COLORS?!

MAGS *(Returns, eating Saltines out of the box)*: I didn't dye my hair, I just added some highlight.

FANNY: I suppose that's what your arty friends in New York do . . . dye their hair all the colors of the rainbow!

GARDNER: Well, it's damned attractive if you ask me . . . damned attractive!

Mags unzips her duffel bag and rummages around in it while eating the Saltines.

FANNY: Darling, I told you not to bring a lot of stuff with you. We're trying to get rid of things.

MAGS *(Pulls out a folding easel and starts setting it up)*: AAAAAHHH-HHH, here it is. Isn't it a beauty? I bought it just for you!

FANNY: Please don't get crumbs all over the floor. Crystal was just here yesterday. It was her last time before we move.

MAGS *(At her easel)*: God, I can hardly wait! I can't believe you're finally letting me do you.

FANNY: *Do* us? . . . What *are* you talking about?

GARDNER *(Reaching for the Saltines)*: Hey, Mags, could I have a couple of those?

MAGS *(Tosses him the box)*: Sure! *(To Fanny)* Your portrait.

GARDNER: Thanks. *(He starts munching on a handful)*

FANNY: You're planning to paint our portrait now? While we're trying to move . . . ?

GARDNER *(Sputtering Saltines)*: Mmmmm, I'd forgotten just how delicious Saltines are!

MAGS: It's a perfect opportunity. There'll be no distractions; you'll be completely at my mercy. Also, you promised.

FANNY: I did?

MAGS: Yes, you did.

FANNY: Well, I must have been off my rocker.

MAGS: No, you said, "You can paint us, you can dip us in concrete, you can do anything you want with us just so long as you help us get out of here!"

GARDNER *(Offering the box of Saltines to Fanny)*: You really ought to try some of these, Fan, they're absolutely delicious!

FANNY *(Taking a few)*: Why, thank you.

MAGS: I figure we'll pack in the morning and you'll pose in the afternoons. It'll be a nice diversion.

FANNY: These *are* good!

GARDNER: Here, dig in . . . take some more.

MAGS: I have some wonderful news . . . amazing news! I wanted to wait till I got here to tell you.

Gardner and Fanny eat their Saltines, passing the box back and forth as Mags speaks.

MAGS: You'll die! Just fall over into the packing cartons and die! Are you ready? . . . BRACE YOURSELVES. . . . OKAY, HERE

GOES. . . . I'm being given a one-woman show at one of the most important galleries in New York this fall. Me, Margaret Church, exhibited at Castelli's, 420 West Broadway. . . . Can you believe it?! . . . MY PORTRAITS HANGING IN THE SAME ROOMS THAT HAVE SHOWN RAUSCHENBERG, JOHNS, WARHOL, KELLY, LICHTENSTEIN, STELLA, SERRA, ALL THE HEAVIES. . . . It's incredible, beyond belief . . . I mean, at my age. . . . Do you know how good you have to be to get in there? It's a miracle . . . an honest-to-God, star-spangled miracle!

Pause.

FANNY *(Mouth full)*: Oh, darling, that's wonderful. We're so happy for you!	GARDNER *(Mouth full)*: No one deserves it more, no one deserves it more!

MAGS: Through some fluke, some of Castelli's people showed up at our last faculty show at Pratt and were knocked out . . .

FANNY *(Reaching for the box of Saltines)*: More, more . . .

MAGS: They said they hadn't seen anyone handle light like me since the French Impressionists. They said I was this weird blend of Pierre Bonnard, Mary Cassatt and David Hockney . . .

GARDNER *(Swallowing his mouthful)*: I told you they were good.

MAGS: Also, no one's doing portraits these days. They're considered passé. I'm so out of it, I'm in.

GARDNER: Well, you're loaded with talent and always have been.

FANNY: She gets it all from Mama, you know. Her miniature of Henry James is still one of the main attractions at the Atheneum. Of course no woman of breeding could be a professional artist in her day. It simply wasn't done. But talk about talent . . . that woman had talent to burn!

MAGS: I want to do one of you for the show.

FANNY: Oh, do Daddy, he's the famous one.

MAGS: No, I want to do you both. I've always wanted to do you and now I've finally got a good excuse.

FANNY: It's high time somebody painted Daddy again! I'm sick to death of that dreadful portrait of him in the National Gallery they keep reproducing. He looks like an undertaker!

GARDNER: Well, I think you should just do Mum. She's never looked handsomer.

FANNY: Oh, come on, I'm a perfect fright and you know it.

MAGS: I want to do you both. Side by side. In this room. Something really classy. You look so great. Mum with her crazy hats and everything and you with that face. If I could just get you to hold still long enough and actually pose.

GARDNER *(Walking around, distracted)*: Where are those papers I just had? Goddammit, Fanny . . .

MAGS: I have the feeling it's either now or never.

GARDNER: I can't hold on to anything around here. *(He exits to his study)*

MAGS: I've always wanted to do you. It would be such a challenge.

FANNY *(Pulling Mags onto the sofa next to her)*: I'm so glad you're finally here, Mags. I'm very worried about Daddy.

MAGS: Mummy, please. I just got here.

FANNY: He's getting quite gaga.

MAGS: Mummy . . . !

FANNY: You haven't seen him in almost a year. Two weeks ago he walked through the front door of the Codman's house, kissed Emily on the cheek and settled down in the maid's room, thinking he was home!

MAGS: Oh, come on, you're exaggerating.

FANNY: He's as mad as a hatter and getting worse every day! It's this damned new book of his. He works on it around the clock. I've read some of it, and it doesn't make one word of sense, it's all at sixes and sevens . . .

GARDNER *(Pokes his head back in the room, spies some of his papers on a table and grabs them)*: Ahhh, here they are. *(He exits)*

FANNY *(Voice lowered)*: Ever since this dry spell with his poetry, he's been frantic, absolutely . . . frantic!

MAGS: I hate it when you do this.

FANNY: I'm just trying to get you to face the facts around here.

MAGS: There's nothing wrong with him! He's just as sane as the next man. Even saner, if you ask me.

FANNY: You know what he's doing now? You couldn't guess in a million years! . . . He's writing criticism! Daddy! *(She laughs)* Can you believe it? The man doesn't have one analytic bone in his body. His mind is a complete jumble and always has been!

There's a loud crash from Gardner's study.

GARDNER *(Offstage)*: SHIT!

MAGS: He's abstracted. . . . That's the way he is.

FANNY: He doesn't spend any time with me anymore. He just holes up in that filthy study with Toots. God, I hate that bird! Though actually they're quite cunning together. Daddy's teaching him Gray's *Elegy*. You ought to see them in there, Toots perched on top of Daddy's head, spouting out verse after verse . . . Daddy, tap-tap-tapping away on his typewriter. They're quite a pair.

GARDNER *(Pokes his head back in)*: Have you seen that Stevens' poem I was reading before?

FANNY *(Long-suffering)*: NO, I HAVEN'T SEEN THAT STEVENS' POEM YOU WERE READING BEFORE! . . . Things are getting very tight around here, in case you haven't noticed. Daddy's last Pulitzer didn't even cover our real estate tax, and now that he's too doddery to give readings anymore, that income is gone . . . *(Suddenly handing Mags the sugar bowl she'd been wrapping)* Mags, *do* take this sugar bowl. You can use it to serve tea to your students at that wretched art school of yours . . .

MAGS: It's called Pratt! The Pratt Institute.

FANNY: Pratt, Splatt, whatever . . .

MAGS: And I don't serve tea to my students, I teach them how to paint.

FANNY: Well, I'm sure none of them has ever seen a sugar bowl as handsome as this before.

GARDNER *(Reappearing again)*: You're sure you haven't seen it?

FANNY *(Loud and angry)*: YES, I'M SURE I HAVEN'T SEEN IT! I JUST TOLD YOU I HAVEN'T SEEN IT!

GARDNER *(Retreating)*: Right you are, right you are. *(He exits)*

FANNY: God!

Silence.

MAGS: What do you have to yell at him like that for?

FANNY: Because the poor thing's as deaf as an adder!

Mags sighs deeply; silence. Fanny, suddenly exuberant, leads her over to a lamp.

FANNY: Come, I want to show you something.

MAGS *(Looking at it)*: What is it?

FANNY: Something I made. *(Mags is about to turn it on)* WAIT, DON'T TURN IT ON YET! It's got to be dark to get the full effect. *(She rushes to the windows and pulls down the shades)*

MAGS: What *are* you doing?

FANNY: Hold your horses a minute. You'll see . . . *(As the room gets darker and darker)* Poor me, you wouldn't believe the lengths I go to to amuse myself these days . . .

MAGS *(Touching the lampshade)*: What is this? It looks like a scene of some sort.

FANNY: It's an invention I made . . . a kind of magic lantern.

MAGS: Gee . . . it's amazing . . .

FANNY: What I did was buy an old engraving of the Grand Canal . . .

MAGS: You *made* this?

FANNY: . . . and then color it in with crayons. Next, I got out my sewing scissors and cut out all the street lamps and windows . . . anything that light would shine through. Then I pasted it over a plain lampshade, put the shade on this old horror of a lamp, turned on the switch and . . . *(She turns it on)* VOILÀ . . . VENICE TWINKLING AT DUSK! It's quite effective, don't you think . . . ?

MAGS *(Walking around it)*: Jeeez . . .

FANNY: And see, I poked out all the little lights on the gondolas with a straight pin.

MAGS: Where on earth did you get the idea?

FANNY: Well you know, idle minds . . . *(She spins the shade, making the lights whirl)*

MAGS: It's really amazing. I mean, you could sell this in a store!

GARDNER *(Enters)*: HERE IT IS. IT WAS RIGHT ON TOP OF MY DESK THE WHOLE TIME. *(He crashes into a table)* OOOOOWW-WWW!

FANNY: LOOK OUT, LOOK OUT!

MAGS *(Rushes over to Gardner)*: Oh, Daddy, are you all right?

FANNY: WATCH WHERE YOU'RE GOING, WATCH WHERE YOU'RE GOING!

GARDNER *(Hopping up and down on one leg)*: GODDAMMIT! . . . I HIT MY SHIN.

FANNY: I was just showing Mags my lamp . . .

GARDNER *(Limping over to it)*: Oh, yes, isn't that something? Mum is awfully clever with that kind of thing. . . . It was all her idea. Buying the engraving, coloring it in, cutting out all those little dots.

FANNY: Not "dots" . . . lights and windows, lights and windows!

GARDNER: Right, right . . . lights and windows.

FANNY: Well, we'd better get some light back in here before someone breaks their neck. *(She zaps the shades back up)*

GARDNER *(Puts his arm around Mags)*: Gee, it's good to have you back.

MAGS: It's good to be back.

GARDNER: And I like that new red hair of yours. It's very becoming.

MAGS: But I told you, I hardly touched it . . .

GARDNER: Well, something's different. You've got a glow. So . . . how do you want us to pose for this grand portrait of yours . . . ? *(He poses self-consciously)*

MAGS: Oh, Daddy, setting up a portrait takes a lot of time and thought. You've got to figure out the background, the lighting, what to wear, the sort of mood you want to—

FANNY: OOOOH, LET'S DRESS UP, LET'S DRESS UP! *(She grabs a packing blanket, drapes it around herself and links arms with Gardner, striking an elegant pose)* This *is* going to be fun. She was absolutely right! Come on, Gar, look distinguished!

MAGS: Mummy, please, it's not a game!

FANNY *(More and more excited)*: You still have your tuxedo, don't you? And I'll wear my marvelous long black dress that makes me look like that fascinating woman in the Sargent painting! *(She strikes the famous profile pose)*

MAGS: MUMMY?!

FANNY: I'm sorry, we'll behave, just tell us what to do.

Fanny and Gardner settle down next to each other.

GARDNER: That's right, you're the boss.

FANNY: Yes, you're the boss.

MAGS: But I'm not ready yet; I haven't set anything up.

FANNY: Relax, darling, we just want to get the hang of it . . .

Fanny and Gardner stare straight ahead, trying to look like suitable subjects, but they can't hold still. They keep making faces, lifting an eyebrow, wriggling a nose, twitching a lip. Nothing big and grotesque, just flickering changes; a half-smile here, a self-important frown there. They steal glances at each other every so often.

GARDNER: How am I doing, Fan?

FANNY: Brilliantly, absolutely brilliantly!

MAGS: But you're making faces.

FANNY: *I'm* not making faces. *(Turning to Gardner and making a face)* Are *you* making faces, Gar?

GARDNER *(Instantly making one)*: Certainly not! I'm the picture of restraint!

Without meaning to, Fanny and Gardner get sillier and sillier. They start giggling, then laughing.

MAGS *(Can't help but join in)*: You two are impossible . . . completely impossible! I was crazy to think I could ever pull this off! *(Laughing away)* Look at you . . . just . . . look at you!

Blackout.

Scene 2

Two days later, around five in the afternoon. Half of the Church household has been dragged into the living room for packing. Overflowing cartons are everywhere. They're filled with pots and pans, dishes and glasses, and the entire contents of two linen closets. Mags has placed a stepladder under one of the windows. A pile of tablecloths and curtains is flung beneath it. Two side chairs are in readiness for the eventual pose.

Mags has just pulled a large crimson tablecloth out of a carton. She unfurls it with one shimmering toss.

MAGS: PERFECT . . . PERFECT!

FANNY *(Seated on the sofa, clutches an old pair of galoshes to her chest)*: Look at these old horrors; half the rubber is rotted away and the fasteners are falling to pieces. . . . GARDNER? . . . OH, GARRRRRRRRRRRDNERRRRR?

MAGS *(Rippling out the tablecloth with shorter snapping motions)*: Have you ever seen such a color?

FANNY: I'VE FOUND YOUR OLD SLEDDING GALOSHES IN WITH THE POTS AND PANS. DO YOU STILL WANT THEM?

MAGS: It's like something out of a Rubens!

Mags slings the tablecloth over a chair and then sits on a footstool to finish the Sara Lee banana cake she started. As she eats, she looks at the tablecloth, making happy grunting sounds. Fanny lovingly puts the galoshes on over her shoes and wiggles her feet.

FANNY: God, these bring back memories! There were real snowstorms in the old days. Not these pathetic little two-inch droppings we have now. After a particularly heavy one, Daddy and I used to go sledding on the Common. This was way before you were born. . . . God, it was a hundred years ago! . . . Daddy would stop writing early, put on these galoshes and come looking for me, jingling the fasteners like castanets. It was a kind of mating call, almost . . . *(She jingles them)* The Common was always deserted after a storm; we had the whole place to ourselves. It was so romantic. . . . We'd haul the sled up Beacon Street, stop under the State House, and aim it straight down to the Park Street Church, which was much further away in those days. . . . Then Daddy would lie down on the sled, I'd lower myself on top of him, we'd rock back and forth a few times to gain momentum and then . . . WHOOOOOOOO-OSSSSSSSHHHHH . . . down we'd plunge like a pair of eagles locked in a spasm of lovemaking. God, it was wonderful! . . . The city whizzing past us at ninety miles an hour . . . the cold . . . the darkness . . . Daddy's hair in my mouth . . . GAR . . . REMEMBER HOW WE USED TO GO SLEDDING IN THE OLD DAYS? . . . Sometimes he'd lie on top of me. That was fun. I liked that even more. *(In her foghorn voice)* GARRRRRRRRRD-NERRRRR?

MAGS: Didn't he say he was going out this afternoon?

FANNY: Why, so he did! I completely forgot. *(She takes off the galoshes)* I'm getting just as bad as him. *(She drops them into a different carton—wistful)* Gar's galoshes, Cotuit.

A pause. Mags picks up the tablecloth again, holds it high over her head.

MAGS: Isn't this fabulous? . . . *(She then wraps Fanny in it)* It's the perfect backdrop. Look what it does to your skin.

FANNY: Mags, what *are* you doing?

MAGS: It makes you glow like a pomegranate . . . *(She whips it off her)* Now all I need is a hammer and nails . . . *(She finds them)* YES! *(She climbs up the stepladder and starts hammering a corner of the cloth into the molding of one of the windows)* This is going to look so great! . . . I've never seen such color!

FANNY: Darling, what is going on . . . ?

MAGS: Rembrandt, eat your heart out! You seventeenth-century Dutch has-been, you. *(She hammers more furiously)*

FANNY: MARGARET, THIS IS NOT A CONSTRUCTION SITE. . . . PLEASE . . . STOP IT. . . . YOO-HOOOOO . . . DO YOU HEAR ME?

Gardner suddenly appears, dressed in a raincoat.

GARDNER: YES, DEAR, HERE I AM. I JUST STEPPED OUT FOR A WALK DOWN CHESTNUT STREET. BEAUTIFUL AFTERNOON, ABSOLUTELY BEAUTIFUL! . . . WHY, THAT LOOKS VERY NICE, MAGS, very nice indeed . . .

FANNY *(To Mags)*: YOU'RE GOING TO RUIN THE WALLS TO SAY NOTHING OF MAMA'S BEST TABLECLOTH. . . . MAGS, DO YOU HEAR ME? . . . YOO-HOO! . . . DARLING, I MUST INSIST you stop that dreadful . . .

MAGS (*Steps down; stands back and looks at the tablecloth*): That's it. That's *IT!*

FANNY (*To Gardner, worried*): Where have *you* been?

Mags kisses her fingers at the backdrop and settles back into her banana cake.

GARDNER (*To Fanny*): You'll never guess who I ran into on Chestnut Street . . . Pate Baldwin!

Gardner takes his coat off and drops it on the floor. He sits in one of the posing chairs.

MAGS (*Mouth full of cake*): Oh, Daddy, I'm nowhere near ready for you yet.

FANNY (*Picks up Gardner's coat and hands it to him*): Darling, coats do *not* go on the floor.

GARDNER (*Rises, but forgets where he's supposed to go*): He was in terrible shape. I hardly recognized him. Well, it's the Parkinson's disease . . .

FANNY: You mean, Hodgkin's disease . . .

GARDNER: Hodgkin's disease . . . ?

MAGS (*Leaves her cake and returns to the tablecloth*): Now to figure out exactly how to use this gorgeous light . . .

FANNY: Yes, Pate has Hodgkin's disease, not Parkinson's disease. Sammy Bishop has Parkinson's disease. In the closet . . . your coat goes . . . in the closet!

GARDNER: You're absolutely right! Pate has Hodgkin's disease. (*He stands motionless, the coat over his arm*)

FANNY: And Goat Davis has Addison's disease.

GARDNER: I always get them confused.

FANNY (*Pointing towards the closet*): That way . . .

Gardner exits to the closet; Fanny calls after him.

FANNY: Grace Phelps has it too, I think. Or, it might be Hodgkin's, like Pate. I can't remember.

GARDNER (*Returns with a hanger*): Doesn't The Goat have Parkinson's disease?

FANNY: No, that's Sammy Bishop.

GARDNER: God, I haven't seen The Goat in ages! (*The coat still over his arm, he hands Fanny the hanger*)

FANNY: He hasn't been well.

GARDNER: Didn't Heppy . . . *die?!*

FANNY: What are you giving me this for? . . . Oh, Heppy's been dead for years. She died on the same day as Luster Bright, don't you remember?

GARDNER: I always liked her.

FANNY (*Gives Gardner back the hanger*): Here, I don't want this.

GARDNER: She was awfully attractive.

FANNY: Who?

GARDNER: Heppy!

FANNY: Oh, yes, Heppy had real charm.

MAGS (*Keeps adjusting the tablecloth*): Better . . . better . . .

GARDNER: Which is something The Goat is short on, if you ask me. He has Hodgkin's disease, doesn't he? (*Puts his raincoat back on and sits down*)

FANNY: Darling, what *are* you doing? I thought you wanted to hang up your coat!

GARDNER (*After a pause*): OH, YES, THAT'S RIGHT!

Gardner goes back to the closet; a pause.

FANNY: Where were we?

GARDNER (*Returns with yet another hanger*): Let's see . . .

FANNY (*Takes both hangers from him*): FOR GOD'S SAKE, GAR, PAY ATTENTION!

GARDNER: It was something about The Goat . . .

FANNY (*Takes the coat from Gardner*): HERE, LET ME DO IT! . . . (*Under her breath to Mags*) See what I mean about him? You don't know the half of it!

Fanny hangs the raincoat up in the closet.

FANNY: Not the half.

MAGS (*Still tinkering with the backdrop*): Almost . . . almost . . .

GARDNER (*Sitting back down in one of the posing chairs*): Oh, Fan, did I tell you, I ran into Pate Baldwin just now. I'm afraid he's not long for this world.

FANNY (*Returning*): Well, it's that Hodgkin's disease . . . (*She sits on the posing chair next to him*)

GARDNER: God, I'd hate to see him go. He's one of the great editors of our times. I couldn't have done it without him. He gave me everything, everything!

MAGS (*Makes a final adjustment*): Yes, that's it! (*She stands back and gazes at them*) You look wonderful!

FANNY: Isn't it getting to be . . . (*She taps at an imaginary watch on her wrist and drains an imaginary glass*) cocktail time?!

GARDNER *(Looks at his watch)*: On the button, on the button! *(He rises)*
FANNY: I'll have the usual, please. Do join us, Mags! Daddy bought
  some Dubonnet especially for you!
MAGS: Hey. I was just getting some ideas.
GARDNER *(To Mags, as he exits for the bar)*: How about a little . . .
  Dubonnet to wet your whistle?
FANNY: Oh, Mags, it's like old times having you back with us like this!
GARDNER *(Offstage)*: THE USUAL FOR YOU, FAN?
FANNY: I wish we saw more of you. . . . PLEASE! . . . Isn't he darling?
  Have you ever known anyone more darling than Daddy?
GARDNER *(Offstage; hums Jolson's "You Made Me Love You")*: MAGS,
  HOW ABOUT YOU? . . . A LITTLE . . . DUBONNET?

FANNY: Oh, *do* join us!	MAGS *(To Gardner)*: No, nothing, thanks.

FANNY: Well, what do you think of your aged parents picking up and
  moving to Cotuit year round? Pretty crazy, eh what? . . . Nothing
  but the gulls, oysters and us!
GARDNER *(Returns with Fanny's drink)*: Here you go . . .
FANNY: Why thank you, Gar. *(To Mags)* You sure you won't join us?
GARDNER *(Lifts his glass towards Fanny and Mags)*: Cheers!

Gardner and Fanny take that first lifesaving gulp.

FANNY: Aaaaahhhhh!	GARDNER: Hits the spot, hits the spot!

MAGS: Well, I certainly can't do you like that!
FANNY: Why not? I think we look very . . . *comme il faut!*

Fanny slouches into a rummy pose; Gardner joins her.

FANNY: WAIT . . . I'VE GOT IT! I'VE GOT IT! *(She whispers excitedly
  to Gardner)*
MAGS: Come on, let's not start this again!
GARDNER: What's that? . . . Oh, yes . . . yes, yes . . . I know the one
  you mean. Yes, right, right . . . of course.

A pause.

FANNY: How's . . . *this?!*

*Fanny grabs a large serving fork and she and Gardner fly into an
imitation of Grant Wood's* American Gothic.

MAGS: And I wonder why it's taken me all these years to get you to pose for me. You just don't take me seriously! Poor old Mags and her ridiculous portraits . . .

FANNY: Oh, darling, your portraits aren't *ridiculous*! They may not be all that one *hopes* for, but they're certainly not—

MAGS: Remember how you behaved at my first group show in Soho? . . . Oh, come on, you remember. It was a real circus! Think back. . . . It was about six years ago. . . . Daddy had just been awarded some presidential medal of achievement and you insisted he wear it around his neck on a bright red ribbon, and you wore this . . . *huge* feathered hat to match! I'll never forget it! It was the size of a giant pizza with twenty-inch red turkey feathers shooting straight up into the air. . . . Oh, come on, you remember, don't you?

FANNY *(Leaping to her feet)*: HOLD EVERYTHING! THIS IS IT! THIS IS REALLY IT! Forgive me for interrupting, Mags darling, it'll just take a minute. *(She whispers excitedly to Gardner)*

MAGS: I had about eight portraits in the show, mostly of friends of mine, except for this old one I'd done of Mrs. Crowninshield.

GARDNER: All right, all right . . . let's give it a whirl.

A pause; then they mime Michelangelo's Pietà *with Gardner lying across Fanny's lap as the dead Christ.*

MAGS *(Depressed)*: The *Pietà*. Terrific!

FANNY *(Jabbing Gardner in the ribs)*: Hey, we're getting good at this.

GARDNER: Of course it would help if we didn't have all these modern clothes on.

MAGS: AS I WAS SAYING . . .

FANNY: Sorry, Mags . . . sorry . . .

Huffing and creaking with the physical exertion of it all, Fanny and Gardner return to their seats.

MAGS: As soon as you stepped foot in the gallery you spotted it and cried out, "MY GOD, WHAT'S MILLICENT CROWNIN-SHIELD DOING HERE?" Everyone looked up, what with Daddy's clanking medal and your amazing hat which I was sure would take off and start flying around the room. A crowd gathered. . . . Through some utter fluke, you latched on to *the* most important critic in the city, I mean . . . Mr. Modern Art himself, and you hauled him over to the painting, trumpeting out for all to hear, "THAT'S MILLICENT CROWNINSHIELD! I GREW UP WITH HER. SHE LIVES RIGHT DOWN THE STREET FROM US IN BOSTON. BUT IT'S A VERY POOR LIKE-

NESS, IF YOU ASK ME! HER NOSE ISN'T NEARLY THAT
LARGE AND SHE DOESN'T HAVE SOMETHING QUEER
GROWING OUT OF HER CHIN! THE CROWNINSHIELDS
ARE REALLY QUITE GOOD-LOOKING, STUFFY, BUT
GOOD-LOOKING NONETHELESS!"

GARDNER *(Suddenly jumps up, ablaze)*: WAIT, WAIT . . . IF IT'S
MICHELANGELO YOU WANT . . . I'm sorry, Mags. . . . One
more . . . just one more . . . please?

MAGS: Sure, why not? Be my guest.

GARDNER: *Fanny, prepare yourself!*

More whispering.

FANNY: But I think *you* should be God.

GARDNER: Me? . . . Really?

FANNY: Yes, it's much more appropriate.

GARDNER: Well, if you say so . . .

*Fanny and Gardner ease down to the floor with some difficulty and lie
on their sides, Fanny as Adam, Gardner as God, their fingers inching
closer and closer in the attitude of Michelangelo's* The Creation. *Finally
they touch. Mags cheers, whistles, applauds.*

MAGS: THREE CHEERS . . . VERY GOOD . . . NICELY DONE,
NICELY DONE!

*Fanny and Gardner hold the pose a moment more, flushed with
pleasure; then rise, dust themselves off and grope back to their chairs.*

MAGS: So, there we were . . .

FANNY: Yes, *do* go on!

MAGS: . . . huddled around Millicent Crowninshield, when you
whipped into your pocketbook and suddenly announced, "HOLD
EVERYTHING! I'VE GOT A PHOTOGRAPH OF HER
RIGHT HERE, THEN YOU CAN SEE WHAT SHE REALLY
LOOKS LIKE!" . . . You then proceeded to crouch down to the
floor and dump everything out of your bag, and I mean . . .
everything! . . . leaking packets of sequins and gummed stars,
seashells, odd pieces of fur, crochet hooks, a monarch butterfly
embedded in plastic, dental floss, antique glass buttons, small
jingling bells, lace . . . I thought I'd die! Just sink to the floor and
quietly die! . . . You couldn't find it, you see. I mean, you spent
the rest of the afternoon on your hands and knees crawling
through this ocean of junk, muttering, "It's *got* to be here somewhere; I know I had it with me!" . . . Then Daddy pulled me into

the thick of it all and said, "By the way, have you met our daughter Mags yet? She's the one who did all these pictures . . . paintings . . . portraits . . . whatever you call them." *(She drops to her hands and knees and begins crawling out of the room)* By this time, Mum had somehow crawled out of the gallery and was lost on another floor. She began calling for me . . . "YOO-HOO, MAGS . . . WHERE ARE YOU? . . . OH, MAGS, DARLING . . . HELLO? . . . ARE YOU THERE?" *(She reenters and faces them)* This was at my *first* show.

Blackout.

Scene 3

Twenty-four hours later. The impact of the impending move has struck with hurricane force. Fanny has lugged all their clothing into the room and dumped it in various cartons. There are coats, jackets, shoes, skirts, suits, hats, sweaters, dresses, the works. She and Gardner are seated on the sofa, going through it all. Fanny, wearing a different hat and dress, holds up a ratty overcoat.

FANNY: What about this gruesome old thing?

Gardner is wearing several sweaters and vests, a Hawaiian holiday shirt, and a variety of scarves and ties around his neck. He holds up a pair of shoes.

GARDNER: God . . . remember these shoes? Pound gave them to me when he came back from Italy. I remember it vividly.

FANNY: *Do* let me give it to the thrift shop! *(She stuffs the coat into the appropriate carton)*

GARDNER: He bought them for me in Rome. Said he couldn't resist; bought himself a pair too since we both wore the same size. God, I miss him! *(Pause)* HEY, WHAT ARE YOU DOING WITH MY OVERCOAT?!

FANNY: Darling, it's threadbare!

GARDNER: But that's my overcoat! *(He grabs it out of the carton)* I've been wearing it every day for the past thirty-five years!

FANNY: That's just my point: it's had it.

GARDNER *(Puts it on over everything else)*: There's nothing wrong with this coat!

FANNY: I trust you remember that the cottage is an eighth the size of this place and you simply won't have room for half this stuff! *(She holds up a sports jacket)* This dreary old jacket, for instance. You've had it since Hector was a pup!

GARDNER *(Grabs the jacket and puts it on over his coat)*: Oh, no, you don't . . .

FANNY: And this God-awful hat . . .

GARDNER: Let me see that.

Gardner stands next to Fanny and they fall into a lovely tableau. Mags suddenly pops out from behind a wardrobe carton with a flash camera and takes a picture of them.

MAGS: PERFECT!

FANNY *(Hands flying to her face)*: GOOD GOD, WHAT WAS THAT . . . ?	GARDNER *(Hands flying to his heart)*: JESUS CHRIST, I'VE BEEN SHOT!

MAGS *(Walks to the center of the room, advancing the film)*: That was terrific. See if you can do it again.

FANNY: What *are* you doing . . . ?

GARDNER *(Feeling his chest)*: Is there blood?

FANNY: I see lace everywhere . . .

MAGS: It's all right, I was just taking a picture of you. I often use a Polaroid at this stage.

FANNY *(Rubbing her eyes)*: Really, Mags, you might have given us some warning!

MAGS: But that's the whole point: to catch you unawares!

GARDNER *(Rubbing his eyes)*: It's the damndest thing. . . . I see lace everywhere.

FANNY: Yes, so do I . . .

GARDNER: It's rather nice, actually. It looks as if you're wearing a veil.

FANNY: I *am* wearing a veil!

The camera spits out the photograph.

MAGS: OH GOODY, HERE COMES THE PICTURE!

FANNY *(Grabs the partially developed print out of her hands)*: Let me see, let me see . . .

GARDNER: Yes, let's have a look.

Gardner and Fanny have another quiet moment together looking at the photograph. Mags tiptoes away from them and takes another picture.

MAGS: YES!

FANNY: NOT AGAIN! PLEASE,   GARDNER: WHAT WAS THAT?
DARLING!   . . . WHAT HAPPENED?

Fanny and Gardner stagger towards each other.

MAGS: I'm sorry, I just couldn't resist. You looked so—
FANNY: WHAT ARE YOU TRYING TO DO . . . *BLIND* US?!
GARDNER: Really, Mags, enough is enough . . .

Gardner and Fanny keep stumbling about kiddingly.

FANNY: Are you still there, Gar?
GARDNER: Right as rain, right as rain!
MAGS: I'm sorry; I didn't mean to scare you. It's just a photograph can show you things you weren't aware of. Here, have a look. *(She gives them to Fanny)* Well, I'm going out to the kitchen to get something to eat. Anybody want anything? *(She exits)*
FANNY *(Looking at the photos, half-amused, half-horrified)*: Oh, Gardner, have you ever . . . ?
GARDNER *(Looks at the photos and laughs)*: Good grief . . .
MAGS *(Offstage; from the kitchen)*: IS IT ALL RIGHT IF I TAKE THE REST OF THIS TAPIOCA FROM LAST NIGHT?
FANNY: IT'S ALL RIGHT WITH ME. How about you, Gar?
GARDNER: Sure, go right ahead. I've never been that crazy about tapioca.
FANNY: What are you talking about, tapioca is one of your favorites.
MAGS *(Enters, slurping from a large bowl)*: Mmmmmmmmm . . .
FANNY: Really, Mags, I've never seen anyone eat as much as you.
MAGS *(Takes the photos back)*: It's strange. I only do this when I come home.
FANNY: What's the matter, don't I feed you enough?
GARDNER: Gee, it's hot in here! *(Starts taking off his coat)*
FANNY: God knows, you didn't eat anything as a child! I've never seen such a fussy eater. Gar, what *are* you doing?
GARDNER *(Shedding clothes to the floor)*: Taking off some of these clothes. It's hotter than Tophet in here!
MAGS *(Looking at her photos)*: Yes, I like you looking at each other like that . . .
FANNY *(To Gardner)*: Please watch where you're dropping things; I'm trying to keep some order around here.
GARDNER *(Picks up what he dropped, dropping even more in the process)*: Right, right . . .
MAGS: Now all I've got to do is figure out what you should wear.
FANNY: Well, I'm going to wear my long black dress, and you'd be a

fool not to do Daddy in his tuxedo. He looks so distinguished in it, just like a banker!

MAGS: I haven't really decided yet.

FANNY: Just because you walk around looking like something the cat dragged in, doesn't mean Daddy and I want to, do we Gar?

Gardner is making a worse and worse tangle of his clothes.

FANNY: HELLO . . . ?

GARDNER *(Looks up at Fanny)*: Oh, yes, awfully attractive, awfully attractive!

FANNY *(To Mags)*: If you don't mind me saying so, I've never seen you looking so forlorn. You'll never catch a husband looking that way. Those peculiar clothes, that God-awful hair . . . really, Mags, it's very distressing!

MAGS: I don't think my hair's so bad, not that it's terrific or anything . . .

FANNY: Well, I don't see other girls walking around like you. I mean, girls from your background. What would Lyman Wigglesworth think if he saw you in the street?

MAGS: Lyman Wigglesworth?! . . . Uuuuuuughhhhhhh! *(She shudders)*

FANNY: All right then, that brilliant Cabot boy . . . what *is* his name?

GARDNER: Sammy.

FANNY: No, not Sammy . . .

GARDNER: Stephen . . . Stanley . . . Stuart . . . Sheldon . . . Sherlock . . . Sherlock! It's *Sherlock!*

MAGS: Spence!

FANNY: SPENCE, THAT'S IT! GARDNER: THAT'S IT . . .
HIS NAME IS SPENCE! SPENCE! SPENCE CA-
BOT!

FANNY: Spence Cabot was first in his class at Harvard.

MAGS: Mum, he has no facial hair.

FANNY: He has his own law firm on Arlington Street.

MAGS: Spence Cabot has six fingers on his right hand!

FANNY: So, he isn't the best-looking thing in the world. Looks isn't everything. He can't help it if he has extra fingers. Have a little sympathy!

MAGS: But the extra one has this weird nail on it that looks like a talon. . . . It's long and black and . . . *(She shudders)*

FANNY: No one's perfect, darling. He has lovely handwriting and an absolutely saintly mother. Also, he's as rich as Croesus! He's a lot more promising than some of those creatures you've dragged home. What was the name of that dreadful Frenchman who smelled like sweaty socks? . . . Jean Duke of Scripto?

MAGS *(Laughing)*: Jean-Luc Zichot!

FANNY: And that peculiar little Oriental fellow with all the teeth! Really, Mags, he could have been put on display at the circus!

MAGS: Oh, yes, Tsu Chin. He was strange, but very sexy . . .

FANNY *(Shudders)*: He had such tiny . . . feet! Really, Mags, you've got to bear down. You're not getting any younger. Before you know it, all the nice young men will be taken and then where will you be? . . . All by yourself in that grim little apartment of yours with those peculiar clothes and that bright red hair . . .

MAGS: MY HAIR IS NOT BRIGHT RED!

FANNY: I only want what's best for you, you know that. You seem to go out of your way to look wanting. I don't understand it. . . . Gar, what *are* you putting your coat on for? . . . You look like some derelict out on the street. We don't wear coats in the house. *(She helps him out of it)* That's the way. . . . I'll just put this in the carton along with everything else . . . *(She drops it into the carton, then pauses)* Isn't it about time for . . . *cocktails!*

GARDNER: What's that?

Fanny taps her wrist and mimes drinking.

GARDNER *(Looks at his watch)*: Right you are, right you are! *(Exits to the bar)* THE USUAL . . . ?

FANNY: *Please!*

GARDNER *(Offstage)*: HOW ABOUT SOMETHING FOR YOU, MAGS?

MAGS: SURE, WHY NOT? . . . LET 'ER RIP!

GARDNER *(Offstage)*: WHAT'S THAT . . . ?

FANNY: SHE SAID YES. SHE SAID YES!

MAGS: I'LL HAVE SOME DUBONNET!

GARDNER *(Poking his head back in)*: How about a little Dubonnet?

FANNY: That's just what she said. . . . She'd like some . . . Dubonnet!

GARDNER *(Goes back to the bar and hums another Jolson tune)*: GEE, IT'S GREAT HAVING YOU BACK LIKE THIS, MAGS . . . IT'S JUST GREAT! *(More singing)*

FANNY *(Leaning closer to Mags)*: You have such *potential*, darling! It breaks my heart to see how you've let yourself go. If Lyman Wigglesworth . . .

MAGS: Amazing as it may seem, I don't *care* about Lyman Wigglesworth!

FANNY: From what I've heard, he's quite a lady killer!

MAGS: But with whom? . . . Don't think I haven't heard about his fling with . . . Hopie Stonewall!

FANNY *(Begins to laugh)*: Oh, God, let's not get started on Hopie Stonewall again . . . ten feet tall with spots on her neck . . . *(To Gardner)* OH, DARLING, DO HURRY BACK! WE'RE TALKING ABOUT PATHETIC HOPIE STONEWALL!

MAGS: It's not so much her incredible height and spotted skin; it's those tiny pointed teeth and the size eleven shoes!

FANNY: I love it when you're like this!

Mags starts clomping around the room making tiny pointed-teeth nibbling sounds.

FANNY: GARDNER . . . YOU'RE MISSING EVERYTHING! *(Still laughing)* Why is it Boston girls are always so . . . tall?

MAGS: Hopie Stonewall isn't a Boston girl; she's a giraffe. *(She prances around the room with an imaginary dwarf-sized Lyman)* She's perfect for Lyman Wigglesworth!

GARDNER *(Returns with Fanny's drink, which he hands her)*: Now, where were we . . . ?

FANNY *(Trying not to laugh)*: HOPIE STONEWALL . . . !

GARDNER: Oh, yes, she's the very tall one, isn't she?

Fanny and Mags burst into gales.

MAGS: The only hope for us . . . "Boston girls" is to get as far away from our kind as possible.

FANNY: She always asks after you, darling. She's very fond of you, you know.

MAGS: Please, I don't want to hear!

FANNY: Your old friends are *always* asking after you.

MAGS: It's not so much how creepy they all are, as how much they remind me of myself!

FANNY: But you're not "creepy," darling . . . just . . . shabby!

MAGS: I mean, give me a few more inches and some brown splotches here and there, and Hopie and I could be sisters!

FANNY *(In a whisper to Gardner)*: Don't you love it when Mags is like this? I could listen to her forever!

MAGS: I mean . . . look at me!

FANNY *(Gasping)*: Don't stop, don't stop!

MAGS: Awkward . . . plain . . . I don't know how to dress, I don't know how to talk. When people find out Daddy's my father, they're always amazed. . . . "Gardner Church is YOUR father?! Aw, come on, you're kidding?!"

FANNY *(In a whisper)*: Isn't she divine . . . ?

MAGS: Sometimes I don't even tell them. I pretend I grew up in the Midwest somewhere . . . farming people . . . we work with our hands.

GARDNER *(To Mags)*: Well, how about a little refill . . . ?

MAGS: No, no more thanks.

Pause.

FANNY: What did you have to go and interrupt her for? She was just getting up a head of steam . . .

MAGS *(Walking over to her easel)*: The great thing about being a portrait painter, you see, is it's the *other* guy that's exposed; you're safely hidden behind the canvas and easel. *(Standing behind it)* You can be as plain as a pitchfork, as inarticulate as mud, but it doesn't matter because you're completely concealed: your body, your face, your intentions. Just as you make your most intimate move, throw open your soul . . . they stretch and yawn, remembering the dog has to be let out at five. . . . To be so invisible while so enthralled . . . it takes your breath away!

GARDNER: Well put, Mags. Awfully well put!

MAGS: That's why I've always wanted to paint you, to see if I'm up to it. It's quite a risk. Remember what I went through as a child with my great masterpiece . . . ?

FANNY: You painted a masterpiece when you were a child . . . ?

MAGS: Well, it was a masterpiece to me.

FANNY: I had no idea you were precocious as a child. Gardner, do you remember Mags painting a masterpiece as a child?

MAGS: I didn't paint it. It was something I made!

FANNY: Well, this is all news to me! Gar, *do* get me another drink! I haven't had this much fun in years! *(She hands him her glass and reaches for Mags's)* Come on, darling, join me . . .

MAGS: No, no more, thanks. I don't really like the taste.

FANNY: Oh, come on, kick up your heels for once!

MAGS: No, nothing . . . really.

FANNY: Please? Pretty please? . . . To keep me company?!

MAGS *(Hands Gardner her glass)*: Oh, all right, what the hell . . .

FANNY: That's a good girl!   GARDNER *(Exiting)*: Coming right up, coming right up!

FANNY (*Yelling after Gardner*): DON'T GIVE ME TOO MUCH NOW. THE LAST ONE WAS AWFULLY STRONG . . . AND HURRY BACK SO YOU DON'T MISS ANYTHING! . . . Daddy's so cunning, I don't know what I'd do without him. If anything should happen to him, I'd just . . .

MAGS: Mummy, nothing's going to happen to him . . . !

FANNY: Well, wait till you're our age, it's no garden party. Now . . . where were we . . . ?

MAGS: My first masterpiece . . .

FANNY: Oh, yes, but *do* wait till Daddy gets back so he can hear it too. . . . YOO-HOO . . . GARRRRRRDNERRRRRR? . . . ARE YOU COMING? (*Silence*) Go and check on him, will you?

Gardner enters with both drinks. He's very shaken.

GARDNER: I couldn't find the ice.

FANNY: Well, *finally*!

GARDNER: It just up and disappeared . . . (*Hands Fanny her drink*) There you go. (*Fanny kisses her fingers and takes a hefty swig*) Mags. (*He hands Mags her drink*)

MAGS: Thanks, Daddy.

GARDNER: Sorry about the ice.

MAGS: No problem, no problem.

Gardner sits down; silence.

FANNY (*To Mags*): Well, drink up, drink up! (*Mags downs it in one gulp*) GOOD GIRL! . . . Now, what's all this about a masterpiece . . . ?

MAGS: I did it during that winter you sent me away from the dinner table. I was about nine years old.

FANNY: We sent you from the dinner table?

MAGS: I was banished for six months.

FANNY: You *were*? . . . How extraordinary!

MAGS: Yes, it *was* rather extraordinary!

FANNY: But why?

MAGS: Because I played with my food.

FANNY: You did?

MAGS: I used to squirt it out between my front teeth.

FANNY: Oh, I remember that! God, it used to drive me crazy, absolutely . . . crazy! (*Pause*) "MARGARET, STOP THAT OOZING RIGHT THIS MINUTE, YOU ARE *NOT* A TUBE OF TOOTHPASTE!"

GARDNER: Oh, yes . . .

FANNY: It was perfectly disgusting!

GARDNER: I remember. She used to lean over her plate and squirt it out in long runny ribbons . . .

FANNY: That's enough, dear.

GARDNER: They were quite colorful, actually; decorative almost She made the most intricate designs. They looked rather like small, moist Oriental rugs . . .

FANNY *(To Mags)*: But why, darling? What on earth possessed you to do it?

MAGS: I couldn't swallow anything. My throat just closed up. I don't know, I must have been afraid of choking or something.

GARDNER: I remember one in particular. We'd had chicken fricassee and spinach. . . . She made the most extraordinary—

FANNY *(To Gardner)*: WILL YOU PLEASE SHUT UP?! *(Pause)* Mags, what *are* you talking about? You never choked in your entire life! This is the most distressing conversation I've ever had. Don't you think it's distressing, Gar?

GARDNER: Well, that's not quite the word I'd use.

FANNY: What word *would* you use, then?

GARDNER: I don't know right off the bat, I'd have to think about it.

FANNY: THEN, THINK ABOUT IT!

Silence.

MAGS: I guess I was afraid of making a mess. I don't know; you were awfully strict about table manners. I was always afraid of losing control. What if I started to choke and began spitting up over everything . . . ?

FANNY: All right, dear, that's enough.

MAGS: No, I was really terrified about making a mess; you always got so mad whenever I spilled. If I just got rid of everything in neat little curlicues beforehand, you see . . .

FANNY: I SAID: THAT'S ENOUGH!

Silence.

MAGS: *I* thought it was quite ingenious, but you didn't see it that way. You finally sent me from the table with, "When you're ready to eat like a human being, you can come back and join us!" . . . So, it was off to my room with a tray. But I couldn't seem to eat there either. I mean, it was so strange settling down to dinner in my *bedroom.* . . . So I just flushed everything down the toilet and sat on my bed listening to you: clinkity-clink, clatter clatter, slurp, slurp . . . but that got pretty boring after a while, so I looked around for something to do. It was wintertime, because I noticed I'd left some crayons on top of my radiator and they'd melted down into these beautiful shimmering globs, like spilled jello, trembling and pulsing . . .

GARDNER *(Overlapping; eyes closed)*:
"This luscious and impeccable fruit of life
Falls, it appears, of its own weight to earth . . ."

MAGS: Naturally, I wanted to try it myself, so I grabbed a red one and pressed it down against the hissing lid. It oozed and bubbled like raspberry jam!

GARDNER:
"When you were Eve, its acrid juice was sweet,
Untasted, in its heavenly, orchard air . . ."

MAGS: I mean, that radiator was really hot! It took incredible will power not to let go, but I held on, whispering, "Mags, if you let go of this crayon, you'll be run over by a truck on Newberry Street, so help you God!" . . . So I pressed down harder, my fingers steaming and blistering . . .

FANNY: I had no idea about any of this, did you, Gar?

MAGS: Once I'd melted one, I was hooked! I finished off my entire supply in one night, mixing color over color until my head swam! . . . The heat, the smell, the brilliance that sank and rose . . . I'd never felt such exhilaration! . . . Every week I spent my allowance on crayons. I must have cleared out every box of Crayolas in the city!

GARDNER *(Gazing at Mags)*: You know, I don't think I've ever seen you looking prettier! You're awfully attractive when you get going!

FANNY: Why, what a lovely thing to say.

MAGS: AFTER THREE MONTHS THAT RADIATOR WAS . . . SPECTACULAR! I MEAN, IT LOOKED LIKE SOME CO-LOSSAL FRUITCAKE, FIVE FEET TALL . . . !

FANNY: It sounds perfectly hideous.

MAGS: It was a knockout; shimmering with pinks and blues, lavenders and maroons, turquoise and golds, oranges and creams. . . . For every color, I imagined a taste . . . YELLOW: lemon curls dipped in sugar . . . RED: glazed cherries laced with rum . . . GREEN: tiny peppermint leaves veined with chocolate . . . PURPLE: —

FANNY: That's quite enough!

MAGS: And then the frosting . . . ahhhh, the frosting! A satiny mix of white and silver . . . I kept it hidden under blankets during the day. . . . My huge . . . *(She starts laughing)* looming . . . teetering sweet—

FANNY: I ASKED YOU TO STOP! GARDNER, WILL YOU PLEASE GET HER TO STOP!

GARDNER: See here, Mags, Mum asked you to—

MAGS: I was so . . . *hungry* . . . losing weight every week. I looked like a scarecrow what with the bags under my eyes and bits of crayon wrapper leaking out of my clothes. It's a wonder you didn't notice. But finally you came to my rescue . . . if you could call what happened a rescue. It was more like a rout!

FANNY: Darling . . . *please!*   GARDNER: Now, look, young lady—

MAGS: The winter was almost over. . . . It was very late at night. . . . I must have been having a nightmare because suddenly you and Daddy werc at my bed, shaking me. . . . I quickly glanced towards the radiator to see if it was covered. . . . *It wasn't!* It glittered and towered in the moonlight like some . . . gigantic Viennese pastry! You followed my gaze and saw it. Mummy screamed . . . "WHAT HAVE YOU GOT IN HERE? . . . MAGS, WHAT HAVE YOU BEEN DOING?" . . . She crept forward and touched it, and then jumped back. "IT'S FOOD!" she cried . . . "IT'S ALL THE FOOD SHE'S BEEN SPITTING OUT! OH, GARDNER, IT'S A MOUNTAIN OF ROTTING GARBAGE!"

FANNY *(Softly)*: Yes . . . it's coming back . . . it's coming back . . .

MAGS: Daddy exited as usual; left the premises. He fainted, just keeled over onto the floor . . .

GARDNER: Gosh, I don't remember any of this . . .

MAGS: My heart stopped! I mean, I knew it was all over. My lovely creation didn't have a chance. Sure enough . . . out came the blowtorch. Well, it couldn't have *really* been a blowtorch, I mean, where would you have ever gotten a blowtorch? . . . I just have this very strong memory of you standing over my bed, your hair streaming around your face, aiming this . . . flamethrower at my confection . . . my cake . . . my tart . . . my strudel. . . . "IT'S GOT TO BE DESTROYED IMMEDIATELY! THE THING'S ALIVE WITH VERMIN! . . . JUST LOOK AT IT! . . . IT'S PRACTI-CALLY CRAWLING ACROSS THE ROOM!" . . . Of course in a sense you were right. It *was* a monument of my castoff dinners, only I hadn't built it with food. . . . I found my own materials. I was languishing with hunger, but oh, dear Mother . . . I FOUND MY OWN MATERIALS . . . !

FANNY: Darling . . . *please?!*

MAGS: I tried to stop you, but you wouldn't listen. . . . OUT SHOT THE FLAME! . . . I remember these waves of wax rolling across the room and Daddy coming to, wondering what on earth was going on. . . . Well, what did you know about my abilities? . . . You see, I had . . . I mean, I *have* abilities . . . *(Struggling to say it)* I have abilities. I have . . . strong abilities. I have . . . very strong abilities. They are very strong . . . very, very strong . . .

Mags rises and runs out of the room overcome as Fanny and Gardner watch, speechless. The curtain falls.

ACT TWO

Scene 1

Three days later. Miracles have been accomplished. Almost all of the Churches' furniture has been moved out, and the cartons of dishes and clothing are gone. All that remains are odds and ends. Mags's tableau looms, impregnable. Fanny and Gardner are dressed in their formal evening clothes, frozen in their pose. They hold absolutely still. Mags stands at her easel, her hands covering her eyes.

FANNY: All right, you can look now.

MAGS *(Removes her hands)*: Yes! . . . I told you you could trust me on the pose.

FANNY: Well, thank God you let us dress up. It makes all the difference. Now we really look like something.

MAGS *(Starts to sketch them)*: I'll say . . .

A silence as she sketches.

GARDNER *(Recites Yeats's "The Song of Wandering Aengus" in a wonderfully resonant voice as they pose)*:
"I went out to the hazel wood,
Because a fire was in my head,
And cut and peeled a hazel wand,
And hooked a berry to a thread,
And when white moths were on the wing,
And moth-like stars were flickering out,
I dropped the berry in a stream
And caught a little silver trout.

When I had laid it on the floor
I went to blow the fire a-flame,
But something rustled on the floor,
And someone called me by my name:
It had become a glimmering girl
With apple blossoms in her hair
Who called me by my name and ran
And faded through the brightening air.

Though I am old with wandering
Through hollow lands and hilly lands,
I will find out where she has gone,
And kiss her lips and take her hands;

And walk among long dappled grass,
And pluck till time and times are done,
The silver apples of the moon,
The golden apples of the sun."
FANNY: That's lovely, dear. Just lovely. Is it one of yours?
GARDNER: No, no, it's Yeats. I'm using it in my book.
FANNY: Well, you recited it beautifully, but then you've always recited beautifully. That's how you wooed me, in case you've forgotten. . . . You must have memorized every love poem in the English language! There was no stopping you when you got going . . . your Shakespeare, Byron, and Shelley . . . you were shameless . . . *shameless!*
GARDNER *(Eyes closed)*:
"I will find out where she has gone,
And kiss her lips and take her hands . . ."
FANNY: And then there was your own poetry to do battle with; your sonnets and quatrains. When you got going with them, there was nothing left of me! You could have had your pick of any girl in Boston! Why you chose me, I'll never understand. I had no looks to speak of and nothing much in the brains department. . . . Well, what did you know about women and the world? . . . What did any of us know . . . ?

Silence.

FANNY: GOD, MAGS, HOW LONG ARE WE SUPPOSED TO SIT LIKE THIS? . . . IT'S AGONY!
MAGS *(Working away)*: You're doing fine . . . just fine . . .
FANNY *(Breaking her pose)*: It's so . . . boring!
MAGS: Come on, don't move. You can have a break soon.
FANNY: I had no idea it would be so boring!
GARDNER: Gee, I'm enjoying it.
FANNY: You would . . . !

A pause.

GARDNER *(Begins reciting more Yeats, almost singing it)*:
"He stood among a crowd at Drumahair;
His heart hung all upon a silken dress,
And he had known at last some tenderness,
Before earth made of him her sleepy care;
But when a man poured fish into a pile,
It seemed they raised their little silver heads . . ."

FANNY: Gar . . . PLEASE! *(She lurches out of her seat)* God, I can't take this anymore!

MAGS *(Keeps sketching Gardner)*: I know it's tedious at first, but it gets easier . . .

FANNY: It's like a Chinese water torture! *(Crosses to Mags and looks at Gardner posing)* Oh, darling, you look marvelous, absolutely marvelous! Why don't you just do Daddy!?

MAGS: Because you look marvelous too. I want to do you both!

FANNY: Please! . . . I have one foot in the grave and you know it! Also, we're way behind in our packing. There's still one room left which everyone seems to have forgotten about!

GARDNER: Which one is that?

FANNY: You know perfectly well which one it is!

GARDNER: I do . . . ?

FANNY: Yes, you do!

GARDNER: Well, it's news to me.

FANNY: I'll give you a hint. It's in . . . *that* direction. *(She points)*

GARDNER: The dining room?

FANNY: No.

GARDNER: The bedroom?

FANNY: No.

GARDNER: Mags' room?

FANNY: No.

GARDNER: The kitchen?

FANNY: *Gar?!*

GARDNER: The guest room?

FANNY: Your God-awful study!

GARDNER: Oh, shit!

FANNY: That's right, "Oh, shit!" It's books and papers up to the ceiling! If you ask me, we should just forget it's there and quietly tiptoe away . . .

GARDNER: My study . . . !

FANNY: Let the new owners dispose of everything . . .

GARDNER *(Gets out of his posing chair)*: Now, just one minute . . .

FANNY: You never look at half the stuff in there!

GARDNER: I don't want you touching those books! They're mine!

FANNY: Darling, we're moving to a cottage the size of a handkerchief! Where, pray tell, is there room for all your books?

GARDNER: I don't know. We'll just have to make room!

MAGS *(Sketching away)*: RATS!

FANNY: I don't know what we're doing fooling around with Mags like this when there's still so much to do . . .

GARDNER *(Sits back down, overwhelmed)*: My study . . . !

FANNY: You can stay with her if you'd like, but one of us has got to tackle those books! *(She exits to his study)*

GARDNER: I'm not up to this.

MAGS: Oh, good, you're staying!

GARDNER: There's a lifetime of work in there . . .

MAGS: Don't worry, I'll help. Mum and I will be able to pack everything up in no time.

GARDNER: God . . .

MAGS: It won't be so bad . . .

GARDNER: I'm just not up to it.

MAGS: We'll all pitch in . . .

Gardner sighs, speechless. A silence as Fanny comes staggering in with an armload of books, which she drops to the floor with a crash.

GARDNER: WHAT WAS THAT?!   MAGS: GOOD GRIEF!

FANNY *(Sheepish)*: Sorry, sorry . . . *(She exits for more)*

GARDNER: I don't know if I can take this . . .

MAGS: Moving is awful . . . I know . . .

GARDNER *(Settling back into his pose)*: Ever since Mum began tearing the house apart, I've been having these dreams. . . . I'm a child again back at 16 Louisberg Square . . . and this stream of moving men is carrying furniture into our house . . . van after van of tables and chairs, sofas and love seats, desks and bureaus . . . rugs, bathtubs, mirrors, chiming clocks, pianos, iceboxes, china cabinets . . . but what's amazing is that all of it is familiar . . .

Fanny comes in with another load, which she drops on the floor. She exits for more.

GARDNER: No matter how many items appear, I've seen every one of them before. Since my mother is standing in the midst of it directing traffic, I ask her where it's all coming from, but she doesn't hear me because of the racket . . . so finally I just scream out . . . "WHERE IS ALL THIS FURNITURE COMING FROM?" . . . Just as a moving man is carrying Toots into the room, she looks at me and says, "Why, from the land of Skye!" . . . The next thing I know, *people* are being carried in along with it . . .

Fanny enters with her next load; drops it and exits.

GARDNER: People I've never seen before are sitting around our dining-room table. A group of foreigners is going through my books, chattering in a language I've never heard before. A man is playing a Chopin polonaise on Aunt Alice's piano. Several children are taking baths in our tubs from Cotuit . . .

MAGS: It sounds marvelous.

GARDNER: Well, it isn't marvelous at all because all of these perfect strangers have taken over our things . . .

Fanny enters, hurls down another load and exits.

MAGS: How odd . . .

GARDNER: Well, it *is* odd, but then something even odder happens . . .

MAGS *(Sketching away)*: Tell me, tell me!

GARDNER: Well, our beds are carried in. They're all made up with sheets and everything, but instead of all these strange people in them, *we're* in them . . . !

MAGS: What's so odd about that?

GARDNER: Well, you and Mum are brought in, both sleeping like angels . . . Mum snoring away to beat the band . . .

MAGS: Yes . . .

Fanny enters with another load lets it fall.

GARDNER: But there's no one in mine. It's completely empty, never even been slept in! It's as if I were dead or had never even existed . . .

Fanny exits.

GARDNER: "HEY . . . WAIT UP!" I yell to the moving men . . . "THAT'S MY BED YOU'VE GOT THERE!" But they don't stop; they don't even acknowledge me. . . . "HEY, COME BACK HERE . . . I WANT TO GET INTO MY BED!" I cry again and I start running after them . . . down the hall, through the dining room, past the library. . . . Finally I catch up to them and hurl myself right into the center of the pillow. Just as I'm about to land, the bed suddenly vanishes and I go crashing down to the floor like some insect that's been hit by a fly swatter!

Fanny staggers in with her final load; she drops it with a crash and then collapses in her posing chair.

FANNY: THAT'S IT FOR ME! I'M DEAD!

Silence.

FANNY: Come on, Mags, how about you doing a little work around here.

MAGS: That's all I've been doing! This is the first free moment you've given me!

FANNY: You should see all the books in there . . . and papers! There are enough loose papers to sink a ship!

GARDNER: Why is it we're moving, again . . . ?

FANNY: Because life is getting too complicated here.

GARDNER *(Remembering)*: Oh, yes . . .

FANNY: And we can't afford it anymore.

GARDNER: That's right, that's right . . .

FANNY: We don't have the . . . *income* we used to!

GARDNER: Oh, yes . . . *income!*

FANNY *(Assuming her pose again)*: Of course, we have our savings and various trust funds, but I wouldn't dream of touching those!

GARDNER: No, no, you must never dip into capital!

FANNY: I told Daddy I'd be perfectly happy to buy a gun and put a bullet through our heads so we could avoid all this, but he wouldn't hear of it!

MAGS *(Sketching away)*: No, I shouldn't think so.

Pause.

FANNY: I've always admired people who kill themselves when they get to our stage of life. Well, no one can touch my Uncle Edmond in that department . . .

MAGS: I know, I know . . .

FANNY: The day before his seventieth birthday.he climbed to the top of the Old North Church and hurled himself face down into Salem Street! They had to scrape him up with a spatula! God, he was a remarkable man . . . state senator, president of Harvard . . .

GARDNER *(Rises and wanders over to his books)*: Well, I guess I'm going to have to do something about all of these . . .

FANNY: Come on, Mags, help Daddy! Why don't you start bringing in his papers . . .

Gardner sits on the floor; he picks up a book and soon is engrossed in it. Mags keeps sketching, oblivious. Silence.

FANNY *(To Mags)*: Darling? . . . HELLO? . . . God, you two are impossible! Just look at you . . . heads in the clouds! No one would ever know we've got to be out of here in two days. If it weren't for me, nothing would get done around here . . . *(She starts stacking Gardner's books into piles)* There! That's all the maroon ones!

GARDNER *(Looks up)*: What do you mean, *maroon* ones?!

FANNY: All your books that are maroon are in *this* pile . . . and your books that are green in *that* pile! . . . I'm trying to bring some order into your life for once. This will make unpacking so much easier.

GARDNER: But, my dear Fanny, it's not the color of a book that distinguishes it, but what's *inside* it!

FANNY: This will be a great help, you'll see. Now what about this awful striped thing? *(She picks up a slim, aged volume)* Can't it go . . . ?

GARDNER: No!

FANNY: But it's as queer as Dick's hatband! There are no others like it.

GARDNER: Open it and read. Go on . . . open it!

FANNY: We'll get nowhere at this rate.

GARDNER: I said . . . READ!

FANNY: Really, Gar, I—

GARDNER: Read the dedication!

FANNY *(Opens and reads)*: "To Gardner Church, you led the way. With gratitude and affection, Robert Frost." *(She closes it and hands it to him)*

GARDNER: It was published the same year as my *Salem Gardens*.

FANNY *(Picking up a very worn book)*: Well, what about this dreadful thing? It's filthy. *(She blows off a cloud of dust)*

GARDNER: Please . . . *please*?!

FANNY *(Looking through it)*: It's all in French.

GARDNER *(Snatching it away from her)*: André Malraux gave me that . . . !

FANNY: I'm just trying to help.

GARDNER: It's a first edition of Baudelaire's *Fleurs du mal*.

FANNY *(Giving it back)*: Well, pardon me for living!

GARDNER: Why do you have to drag everything in here in the first place . . . ?

FANNY: Because there's no room in your study. You ought to see the mess in there! . . . WAKE UP, MAGS, ARE YOU GOING TO PITCH IN OR NOT?!

GARDNER: I'm not up to this.

FANNY: Well, you'd better be unless you want to be left behind!

MAGS *(Stops her sketching)*: All right, all right . . . I just hope you'll give me some more time later this evening.

FANNY *(To Mags)*: Since you're young and in the best shape, why don't you bring in the books and I'll cope with the papers. *(She exits to the study)*

GARDNER: Now just a minute . . .

FANNY *(Offstage)*: WE NEED A STEAM SHOVEL FOR THIS!

MAGS: Okay, what do you want me to do?

GARDNER: Look, I don't want you messing around with my—

Fanny enters with an armful of papers, which she drops into an empty carton.

GARDNER: HEY, WHAT'S GOING ON HERE?!

FANNY: I'm packing up your papers. COME ON, MAGS, LET'S GET CRACKING! *(She exits for more papers)*

GARDNER *(Plucks several papers out of the carton)*: What is this . . . ?

MAGS *(Exits into his study)*: GOOD LORD, WHAT HAVE YOU DONE IN HERE?!

GARDNER *(Reading)*: This is my manuscript.

Fanny enters with another batch, which she tosses on top of the others.

GARDNER: What *are* you doing?!

FANNY: Packing, darling . . . PACKING! *(She exits for more)*

GARDNER: SEE HERE, YOU CAN'T MANHANDLE MY THINGS THIS WAY!

Mags enters, staggering under a load of books, which she sets down on the floor.

GARDNER: *I* PACK MY MANUSCRIPT! I KNOW WHERE EVERYTHING IS!

FANNY *(Offstage)*: IF IT WERE UP TO YOU, WE'D NEVER GET OUT OF HERE! WE'RE UNDER A TIME LIMIT, GARDNER. KITTY'S PICKING US UP IN TWO DAYS . . . TWO . . . DAYS! *(She enters with a larger batch of papers and heads for the carton)*

GARDNER *(Grabbing Fanny's wrist)*: NOW, HOLD IT! . . . JUST . . . HOLD IT RIGHT THERE!

FANNY: OOOOOWWWWWWWW!

GARDNER: *I* PACK MY THINGS!

FANNY: LET GO, YOU'RE HURTING ME!

GARDNER: THAT'S MY MANUSCRIPT! GIVE IT TO ME!

FANNY *(Lifting the papers high over her head)*: I'M IN CHARGE OF THIS MOVE, GARDNER! WE'VE GOT TO GET CRACKING!

GARDNER: I said . . . GIVE IT TO ME!

MAGS: Come on, Mum, let him have it.

Fanny and Gardner struggle.

GARDNER *(Finally wrenches the pages from Fanny)*: LET . . . ME . . . HAVE IT! . . . THAT'S MORE LIKE IT!

FANNY *(Soft and weepy)*: You see what he's like? . . . I try and help with his packing and what does he do . . . ?

GARDNER *(Rescues the rest of his papers from the carton)*: YOU DON'T JUST THROW EVERYTHING INTO A BOX LIKE A PILE OF GARBAGE! THIS IS A BOOK, FANNY. SOMETHING I'VE BEEN WORKING ON FOR TWO YEARS! *(Trying to assemble his papers, but only making things worse, dropping them all over the place)* You show a little respect for my things. . . . You don't just throw them around every which way. . . . It's tricky trying to make sense of poetry; it's much easier to write the stuff . . . that is, if you've still got it in you . . .

MAGS: Here, let me help . . . *(Taking some of the papers)*

GARDNER: Criticism is tough sledding. You can't just dash off a few images here, a few rhymes there . . .

MAGS: Do you have these pages numbered in any way?

FANNY *(Returning to her posing chair)*: HA!

GARDNER: This is just the introduction.

MAGS: I don't see any numbers on these.

GARDNER *(Exiting to his study)*: The important stuff is in my study . . .

FANNY *(To Mags)*: You don't know the half of it . . . *not the half* . . . !

GARDNER *(Offstage; thumping around)*: HAVE YOU SEEN THOSE YEATS POEMS I JUST HAD . . . ?

MAGS *(Reading over several pages)*: What is this? . . . It doesn't make sense. It's just fragments . . . pieces of poems.

FANNY: That's it, honey! That's his book. His great critical study! Now that he can't write his own poetry, he's trying to explain other people's. The only problem is, he can't get beyond typing them out. The poor lamb doesn't have the stamina to get beyond the opening stanzas, let alone trying to make sense of them.

GARDNER *(Thundering back with more papers, which keep falling)*: GOD-DAMMIT, FANNY, WHAT DID YOU DO IN THERE? I CAN'T FIND ANYTHING!

FANNY: I just took the papers that were on your desk.

GARDNER: Well, the entire beginning is gone. *(He exits)*

FANNY: I'M TRYING TO HELP YOU, DARLING!

GARDNER *(Returns with another armload)*: SEE THAT? . . . NO SIGN OF CHAPTER ONE OR TWO . . . *(He flings it all down to the floor)*

FANNY: Gardner . . . PLEASE?!

GARDNER *(Kicking through the mess)*: I TURN MY BACK FOR ONE

MINUTE AND WHAT HAPPENS? . . . MY ENTIRE STUDY
IS TORN APART! *(He exits)*
MAGS: Oh, Daddy . . . don't . . . please . . . Daddy . . . *please?!*
GARDNER *(Returns with a new batch of papers, which he tosses up into the
air)*: THROWN OUT! . . . THE BEST PART IS THROWN
OUT! . . . LOST . . . *(He starts to exit again)*
MAGS *(Reads one of the fragments to steady herself)*:
"I have known the inexorable sadness of pencils,
Neat in their boxes, dolor of pad and paper-weight,
All the misery of manila folders and mucilage . . ."
They're beautiful . . . just beautiful.
GARDNER *(Stops)*: Hey, what's that you've got there?
FANNY: It's your manuscript, darling. You see, it's right where you left
it.
GARDNER *(To Mags)*: Read that again.
MAGS:
"I have known the inexorable sadness of pencils,
Neat in their boxes, dolor of pad and paper-weight,
All the misery of manila folders and mucilage . . ."
GARDNER: Well, well, what do you know . . .
FANNY *(Hands him several random papers)*: You see . . . no one lost
anything. Everything's here, still intact.
GARDNER *(Reads)*:
"I knew a woman, lovely in her bones,
When small birds sighed, she would sigh back at them;
Ah, when she moved, she moved more ways than one:
The shapes a bright container can contain! . . ."
FANNY *(Hands him another)*: And . . .
GARDNER *(Reads)*: Ahh . . . Frost . . .
"Some say the world will end in fire,
Some say in ice.
From what I've tasted of desire
I hold with those who favor fire."
FANNY *(Under her breath to Mags)*: He can't give up the words. It's the
best he can do. *(Handing him another)* Here you go, here's more.
GARDNER:
"Farm boys wild to couple
With anything   with soft-wooded trees
With mounds of earth   mounds
Of pinestraw   will keep themselves off
Animals by legends of their own . . ."
MAGS *(Eyes shut)*: Oh, Daddy, I can't bear it . . . I . . .

FANNY: Of course no one will ever publish this.

GARDNER: Oh, here's a marvelous one. Listen to this!

"There came a Wind like a Bugle—
It quivered through the Grass
And a Green Chill upon the Heat
So ominous did pass
We barred the Windows and the Doors
As from an Emerald Ghost—
The Doom's electric Moccasin . . ."
SHIT, WHERE DID THE REST OF IT GO . . . ?

FANNY: Well, don't ask *me*.

GARDNER: It just stopped in mid-air!

FANNY: Then go look for the original.

GARDNER: Good idea, good idea! *(He exits to his study)*

FANNY *(To Mags)*: He's incontinent now, too. He wets his pants, in case you haven't noticed. *(She starts laughing)* You're not laughing. Don't you think it's funny? Daddy needs diapers. . . . I don't know about you, but I could use a drink! GAR . . . WILL YOU GET ME A SPLASH WHILE YOU'RE OUT THERE . . . ?

MAGS: STOP IT!

FANNY: It means we can't go out anymore. I mean, what would people say . . . ?

MAGS: Stop it. Just stop it.

FANNY: My poet laureate can't hold it in! *(She laughs harder)*

MAGS: That's enough . . . STOP IT . . . Mummy . . . I beg of you . . . *please stop it!*

Gardner enters with a book and indeed a large stain has blossomed on his trousers. He plucks it away from his leg.

GARDNER: Here we go . . . I found it . . .

FANNY *(Pointing at it)*: See that? See? . . . He just did it again! *(Goes off into a shower of laughter)*

MAGS *(Looks, turns away)*: SHUT . . . UP! . . . *(Building to a howl)* WILL YOU PLEASE JUST . . . SHUT . . . UP!

FANNY *(To Gardner)*: Hey, what about that drink?

GARDNER: Oh, yes . . . sorry, sorry . . . *(He heads towards the bar)*

FANNY: Never mind, I'll get it, I'll get it.

Fanny exits, convulsed. Silence.

GARDNER: Well, where were we?

MAGS *(Near tears)*: Your poem.

GARDNER: Oh, yes . . . the Dickinson. *(He shuts his eyes, reciting from memory, holding the book against his chest)*
"There came a Wind like a Bugle—
It quivered through the Grass
And a Green Chill upon the Heat
So ominous did pass
We barred the Windows and the Doors
As from an Emerald Ghost—"
(Opens the book and starts riffling through it) Let's see now, where's the rest? . . . *(He finally finds it)* Ahhh, here we go . . . !
FANNY *(Reenters, drink in hand)*: I'm back! *(Takes one look at Gardner and bursts out laughing again)*
MAGS: I don't believe you! How you can laugh at him?!

They all speak simultaneously as Mags gets angrier and angrier.

FANNY: I'm sorry, I wish I could stop, but there's really nothing else to do. Look at him . . . just . . . look at him . . . !
MAGS: It's so cruel. . . . You're so . . . incredibly cruel to him. . . . I mean, YOUR DISDAIN REALLY TAKES MY BREATH AWAY! YOU'RE IN A CLASS BY YOURSELF WHEN IT COMES TO HUMILIATION!
GARDNER *(Reading)*:
"The Doom's electric Moccasin
That very instant passed—
On a strange Mob of panting Trees
And Fences fled away
And Rivers where the Houses ran
Those looked that lived—that Day—
The Bell within the steeple wild
The flying tidings told—
How much can come
And much can go,
And yet abide the World!"
(He shuts the book with a bang, pauses and looks around the room, confused) Now, where was I . . . ?
FANNY: Safe and sound in the middle of the living room with Mags and me.
GARDNER: But I was looking for something, wasn't I . . . ?
FANNY: Your manuscript.
GARDNER: THAT'S RIGHT! MY MANUSCRIPT! My manuscript!
FANNY: And here it is all over the floor. See, you're standing on it.

GARDNER *(Picks up a few pages and looks at them)*: Why, so I am . . .

FANNY: Now all we have to do is get it up off the floor and packed neatly into these cartons!

GARDNER: Yes, yes, that's right. Into the cartons.

FANNY *(Kicks a carton over to him)*: Here, you use this one and I'll start over here . . . *(She starts dropping papers into a carton nearby)* BOMBS AWAY! . . . Hey . . . this is fun!

GARDNER *(Picks up his own pile, lifts it high over his head and flings it down into the carton)*: BOMBS AWAY. . . . This *is* fun!

FANNY: I told you! The whole thing is to figure out a system!

GARDNER: I don't know what I'd do without you, Fan. I thought I'd lost everything.

FANNY *(Makes dive-bomber noises and machine-gun explosions as she wheels more and more papers into the carton)*: TAKE THAT AND THAT AND THAT!

GARDNER *(Joins in the fun, outdoing her with dips, dives and blastings of his own)*: BLAM BLAM BLAM BLAM! . . . ZZZZZZZZ-RAAAAAA FOOM! . . . BLATTY-DE-BLATTY-DE-BLATTY-DE-KABOOOOOOOOOM! . . . WHAAAAAAA . . . DA-DAT-DAT-DAT-DAT-DAT . . . WHEEEEEEEE AAAAAAAAAAAAA . . . FOOOOOO . . .

They get louder and louder as papers fly every which way.

FANNY *(Mimes getting hit with a bomb)*: AEEEEEEIIIIIIIIIIIII! YOU GOT ME RIGHT IN THE GIZZARD! *(She collapses on the floor and starts going through death throes, having an absolute ball)*

GARDNER: TAKE THAT AND THAT AND THAT AND THAT . . . *(A series of explosions follow)*

MAGS *(Furious)*: This is how you help him? . . . THIS IS HOW YOU PACK HIS THINGS?

FANNY: I keep him company. I get involved . . . which is a hell of a lot more than you do!

MAGS *(Wild with rage)*: BUT YOU'RE MAKING A MOCKERY OF HIM. . . . YOU TREAT HIM LIKE A CHILD OR SOME DIMWITTED SERVING BOY. HE'S JUST AN AMUSEMENT TO YOU!

FANNY *(Fatigue has finally overtaken her. She's calm, almost serene)*: And to you who see him once a year, if that . . . what is he to *you*? . . . I mean, what do you give him from yourself that costs you something? . . . Hmmmmmmm? . . . *(Imitating Mags)* "Oh, hi Daddy, it's great to see you again. How have you been? . . . Gee, I love your hair. It's gotten so . . . *white!*" . . . What color do you expect it to get when he's this age? . . . I mean, if you care so much how he looks, why don't you come and see him once in a while? . . . But oh, no . . . you have your paintings to do and your shows to put on. You just come and see us when the whim strikes. *(Imitating Mags)* "Hey, you know what would be really great? . . . To do a portrait of you! I've always wanted to paint you, you're such great subjects!" . . . *Paint* us?! . . . What about opening your eyes and really *seeing* us? . . . Noticing what's going on around here for a change! It's all over for Daddy and me. This is it! "Finita la commedia!" . . . All I'm trying to do is exit with a little flourish; have some fun. . . . What's so terrible about that? . . . It can get pretty grim around here, in case you haven't noticed . . . Daddy, tap-tap-tapping out his nonsense all day; me traipsing around to the thrift shops trying to amuse myself. . . . He never keeps me company anymore; never takes me out anywhere. . . . I'd put a bullet through my head in a minute, but then who'd look after him? . . . What do you think we're moving to the cottage for? . . . So I can watch him like a hawk and make sure he doesn't get lost. Do you think that's anything to look forward to? . . . Being Daddy's nursemaid out in the middle of nowhere? I'd much rather stay here in Boston with the few friends I have left, but you can't always do what you want in this world! "L'homme propose, Dieu dispose!" . . . If you want to paint us so badly, you ought to paint us as we really are. There's your picture!

Fanny points to Gardner, who's quietly playing with a paper glide.

FANNY: Daddy spread out on the floor with all his toys and me hovering over him to make sure he doesn't hurt himself! *(She goes over to him)* YOO-HOO . . . GAR? . . . HELLO?
GARDNER *(Looks up at her)*: Oh, hi there, Fan. What's up?
FANNY: How's the packing coming . . . ?
GARDNER: Packing . . . ?
FANNY: Yes, you were packing your manuscript, remember? *(She lifts up a page and lets it fall into a carton)*
GARDNER: Oh, yes . . .
FANNY: Here's your picture, Mags. Face over this way . . . turn your easel over here . . . *(She lets a few more papers fall)* Up, up . . . and away . . .

Blackout.

Scene 2

The last day. All the books and boxes are gone. The room is completely empty except for Mags's backdrop. Late afternoon light dapples the walls; it changes from pale peach to deeper violet. The finished portrait sits on the easel, covered with a cloth. Mags is taking down the backdrop.

FANNY *(Offstage; to Gardner)*: DON'T FORGET TOOTS!

GARDNER *(Offstage; from another part of the house)*: WHAT'S THAT?

FANNY *(Offstage)*: I SAID: DON'T FORGET TOOTS! HIS CAGE IS SITTING IN THE MIDDLE OF YOUR STUDY!

Silence.

FANNY *(Offstage)*: HELLO? . . . ARE YOU THERE?   GARDNER *(Offstage)*: I'LL BE RIGHT WITH YOU; I'M JUST GETTING TOOTS!

GARDNER *(Offstage)*: WHAT'S THAT? I CAN'T HEAR YOU?

FANNY *(Offstage)*: I'M GOING THROUGH THE ROOMS ONE MORE TIME TO MAKE SURE WE DIDN'T FORGET ANYTHING. . . . KITTY'S PICKING US UP IN FIFTEEN MINUTES, SO PLEASE BE READY. . . . SHE'S DROPPING MAGS OFF AT THE STATION AND THEN IT'S OUT TO ROUTE 3 AND THE CAPE HIGHWAY . . .

GARDNER *(Enters, carrying Toots in his cage)*: Well, this is it. The big moment has finally come, eh what, Toots? *(He see Mags)* Oh, hi there, Mags, I didn't see you . . .

MAGS: Oh, hi, Daddy, I'm just taking this down . . . *(She does and walks over to Toots)* Oh, Toots, I'll miss you. *(She makes little chattering noises into his cage)*

GARDNER: Come on, recite a little Gray's *Elegy* for Mags before we go.

MAGS: Yes, Mum said he was really good at it now.

GARDNER: Well, the whole thing is to keep at it every day. *(Slowly to Toots)*
"The curfew tolls the knell of parting day,
The lowing herd wind slowly o'er the lea . . ."
Come on, show Mags your stuff! *(Slower)*
"The curfew tolls the knell of parting day,
The lowing herd wind slowly o'er the lea . . ."

Silence; Gardner makes little chattering sounds.

GARDNER: Come on, Toots, old boy . . .

MAGS: How does it go?

GARDNER *(To Mags)*:
"The curfew tolls the knell of parting day,
The lowing herd wind slowly o'er the lea . . ."
MAGS *(Slowly to Toots)*:
The curfew tolls for you and me,
As quietly the herd winds down . . .
GARDNER: No, no, it's "The curfew tolls the knell of parting *day* . . ."!
MAGS *(Repeating after him)*: "The curfew tolls the knell of parting
day . . ."
GARDNER: "The lowing herd wind slowly o'er the lea . . ."
MAGS *(With a deep breath)*:
The curfew tolls at parting day,
The herd low slowly down the lea . . . no, *knell!*
They come winding down the *knell!*
GARDNER: Listen, Mags . . . *listen!*

A pause.

TOOTS *(Loud and clear with Gardner's inflection)*:
"The curfew tolls the knell of parting day,
The lowing herd wind slowly o'er the lea,
The ploughman homeward plods his weary way,
And leaves the world to darkness and to me."
MAGS: HE SAID IT. . . . HE SAID IT! . . . AND IN YOUR VOICE!
. . . OH, DADDY, THAT'S AMAZING!
GARDNER: Well, Toots is very smart, which is more than I can say for a
lot of people I know . . .
MAGS *(To Toots)*: Polly want a cracker? Polly want a cracker?
GARDNER: You can teach a parakeet to say anything; all you need is
patience . . .
MAGS: But *poetry* . . . that's so hard . . .

*Fanny enters carrying a suitcase and Gardner's typewriter in its case.
She's dressed in her traveling suit, wearing a hat to match.*

FANNY: WELL, THERE YOU ARE! I THOUGHT YOU'D DIED!
MAGS *(To Fanny)*: HE SAID IT! I FINALLY HEARD TOOTS RE-
CITE GRAY'S *ELEGY.* *(She makes silly clucking sounds into the
cage)*
FANNY: Isn't it uncanny how much he sounds like Daddy? Sometimes
when I'm alone here with him, I've actually thought he *was* Daddy
and started talking to him. Oh, yes, Toots and I have had quite a
few meaty conversations together!

Fanny wolf-whistles into the cage; then draws back. Gardner covers the cage with a traveling cloth. Silence.

FANNY *(Looking around the room)*: God, the place looks so bare.

MAGS: I still can't believe it . . . Cotuit, year round. I wonder if there'll be any phosphorus when you get there?

FANNY: What on earth are you talking about? *(She carries the discarded backdrop out into the hall)*

MAGS: Remember that summer when the ocean was full of phosphorus?

GARDNER *(Taking Toots out into the hall)*: Oh, yes . . .

MAGS: It was a great mystery where it came from or why it settled in Cotuit. But one evening when Daddy and I were taking a swim, suddenly it was there!

GARDNER *(Returns)*: I remember.

MAGS: I don't know where Mum was . . .

FANNY *(Reentering)*: Probably doing the dishes!

MAGS *(To Gardner)*: As you dove into the water, this shower of silvery green sparks erupted all around you. It was incredible! I thought you were turning into a saint or something; but then you told me to jump in too and the same thing happened to me . . .

GARDNER: Oh, yes, I remember that . . . the water smelled all queer.

MAGS: What *is* phosphorus, anyway?

GARDNER: Chemicals, chemicals . . .

FANNY: No, it isn't. Phosphorus is a green liquid inside insects. Fireflies have it. When you see sparks in the water it means insects are swimming around . . .

GARDNER: Where on earth did you get that idea . . . ?

FANNY: If you're bitten by one of them, it's fatal!

MAGS: And the next morning it was still there . . .

GARDNER: It was the damndest stuff to get off! We'd have to stay in the shower a good ten minutes. It comes from chemical waste, you see . . .

MAGS: Our bodies looked like mercury as we swam around . . .

GARDNER: It stained all the towels a strange yellow green.

MAGS: I was in heaven, and so were you for that matter. You'd finished your day's poetry and would turn somersaults like some happy dolphin . . .

FANNY: Damned dishes . . . why didn't I see any of this?!

MAGS: I remember one night in particular. . . . We sensed the phosphorus was about to desert us; blow off to another town. We were chasing each other under water. At one point I lost you, the brilliance was so intense . . . but finally your foot appeared . . .

then your leg. I grabbed it! . . . I remember wishing the moment would hold forever; that we could just be fixed there, laughing and iridescent. . . . Then I began to get panicky because I knew it would pass; it was passing already. You were slipping from my grasp. The summer was almost over. I'd be going back to art school; you'd be going back to Boston. . . . Even as I was reaching for you, you were gone. We'd never be like that again.

Silence. Fanny spies Mags's portrait covered on the easel.

FANNY: What's that over there? Don't tell me we forgot something!

MAGS: It's your portrait. I finished it.

FANNY: You finished it? How on earth did you manage that?

MAGS: I stayed up all night.

FANNY: You did? . . . *I* didn't hear you, did you hear her, Gar . . . ?

GARDNER: Not a peep, not a peep!

MAGS: Well, I wanted to get it done before you left. You know, see what you thought. It's not bad, considering . . . I mean, I did it almost completely from memory. The light was terrible and I was trying to be quiet so I wouldn't wake you. It was hardly an ideal situation. . . . I mean, you weren't the most cooperative models . . . *(She suddenly panics and snatches the painting off the easel. She hugs it to her chest and starts dancing around the room with it)* Oh, God, you're going to hate it! You're going to hate it! How did I ever get into this? . . . Listen, you don't really want to see it . . . it's nothing . . . just a few dabs here and there. . . . It was awfully late when I finished it. The light was really impossible and my eyes were hurting like crazy. . . . Look, why don't we just go out to the sidewalk and wait for Kitty so she doesn't have to honk—

GARDNER *(Snatches the painting out from under her grasp)*: WOULD YOU JUST SHUT UP A MINUTE AND LET US SEE IT?

MAGS *(Laughing and crying)*: But it's nothing, Daddy . . . *really!* . . . I've done better with my eyes closed! It was so late I could hardly see anything and then I spilled a whole bottle of thinner into my palette . . .

GARDNER *(Sets the portrait down on the easel and stands back to look at it)*: THERE!

MAGS *(Dancing around them in a panic)*: Listen, it's just a quick sketch. . . . It's still wet. . . . I didn't have enough time. . . . It takes at least forty hours to do a decent portrait . . .

Suddenly it's very quiet as Fanny and Gardner stand back to look at the painting. More and more beside herself, Mags keeps leaping around the room wrapping her arms around herself, making little whimpering sounds.

MAGS: Please don't . . . no . . . don't . . . oh, please! . . . Come on, don't look. . . . Oh, God, don't . . . please . . .

An eternity passes as Fanny and Gardner gaze at their portrait.

GARDNER: Well . . .
FANNY: Well . . .

More silence.

FANNY: I think it's perfectly dreadful!　　GARDNER: Awfully clever, awfully clever!

FANNY: What on earth did you do to my face . . . ?
GARDNER: I particularly like Mum!
FANNY: Since when do I have purple skin?!
MAGS: I told you it was nothing, just a silly—
GARDNER: She looks like a million dollars!
FANNY: AND WILL YOU LOOK AT MY HAIR . . . IT'S BRIGHT ORANGE!
GARDNER *(Views the painting from another angle)*: It's really very good!
FANNY *(Pointing)*: That doesn't look anything like me!
GARDNER: First-rate!
FANNY: Since when do I have purple skin and bright orange hair?!
MAGS *(Trying to snatch the painting off the easel)*: Listen, you don't have to worry about my feelings . . . really . . . I—
GARDNER *(Blocking her way)*: NOT SO FAST . . .
FANNY: And look at how I'm sitting! I've never sat like that in my life!
GARDNER *(Moving closer to the painting)*: Yes, yes, it's awfully clever . . .
FANNY: I HAVE NO FEET!
GARDNER: The whole thing is quite remarkable!
FANNY: And what happened to my legs, pray tell? . . . They just vanish below the knees! . . . At least my dress is presentable. I've always loved that dress.
GARDNER: It sparkles somehow . . .
FANNY *(To Gardner)*: Don't you think it's becoming?
GARDNER: Yes, very becoming, awfully becoming . . .
FANNY *(Examining it at closer range)*: Yes, she got the dress very well, how it shows off what's left of my figure. . . . My smile is nice too.
GARDNER: Good and wide . . .
FANNY: I love how the corners of my mouth turn up . . .
GARDNER: It's very clever . . .

FANNY: They're almost quivering . . .

GARDNER: Good lighting effects!

FANNY: Actually, I look quite . . . *young*, don't you think?

GARDNER *(To Mags)*: You're awfully good with those highlights.

FANNY *(Looking at it from different angles)*: And *you* look darling . . . !

GARDNER: Well, I don't know about that . . .

FANNY: No, you look absolutely darling. Good enough to eat!

MAGS *(In a whisper)*: They like it. . . . They like it!

A silence as Fanny and Gardner keep gazing at their portrait.

FANNY: You know what it is? The wispy brush strokes make us look like a couple in a French Impressionist painting.

GARDNER: Yes, I see what you mean . . .

FANNY: A Manet or Renoir . . .

GARDNER: It's very evocative.

FANNY: There's something about the light . . .

They back up to survey the picture from a distance.

FANNY: You know those Renoir café scenes . . . ?

GARDNER: She doesn't lay on the paint with a trowel; it's just touches here and there . . .

MAGS: They *like* it . . . !

FANNY: You know the one with the couple dancing? . . . Not that we're dancing. There's just something similar in the mood . . . a kind of gaiety, almost. . . . The man has his back to you and he's swinging the woman around. . . . OH, GAR, YOU'VE SEEN IT A MILLION TIMES! IT'S HANGING IN THE MUSEUM OF FINE ARTS! . . . They're dancing like this . . .

Fanny goes up to Gardner and puts an arm on his shoulders.

MAGS: They like it. . . . They like it!

FANNY: She's got on this wonderful flowered dress with ruffles at the neck and he's holding her like this. . . . That's right . . . and she's got the most rhapsodic expression on her face . . .

Getting into the spirit of it, Gardner takes Fanny in his arms and slowly begins to dance around the room.

GARDNER: Oh, yes . . . I know the one you mean. . . . They're in a sort of haze . . . and isn't there a little band playing off to one side . . . ?

FANNY: Yes, that's it!

Kitty's horn honks outside. Mags is the only one who hears it.

MAGS: There's Kitty! *(She's torn and keeps looking towards the door, but finally gives in to their stolen moment)*

FANNY: And there's a man in a dark suit playing the violin and someone's conducting, I think. . . . And aren't Japanese lanterns strung up . . . ?

Fanny and Gardner pick up speed, dipping and whirling around the room. Strains of a faraway Chopin waltz are heard.

GARDNER: Oh, yes! There are all these little lights twinkling in the trees . . .

FANNY: And doesn't the woman have a hat on? . . . A big red hat . . . ?

GARDNER: . . . and lights all over the dancers, too. Everything shimmers with this marvelous glow. Yes, yes . . . I can see it perfectly! The whole thing is absolutely extraordinary!

The lights become dreamy and dappled as Fanny and Gardner dance around the room. Mags watches them, moved to tears as slowly the curtain falls.

COASTAL
DISTURBANCES

ABOUT THE PLAY

Coastal Disturbances premiered at New York's Second Stage in 1986, under the direction of Carole Rothman. The Second Stage production reopened at Circle in the Square in 1987. The play was nominated for a Tony award.

Characters

LEO HART, the lifeguard, twenty-eight.
HOLLY DANCER, a photographer from New York, twenty-four.
FAITH BIGELOW, five months pregnant, thirty-five.
MIRANDA BIGELOW, her adopted daughter, seven.
ARIEL TOOK, Faith's guest, thirty-six.
WINSTON TOOK, her son, eight.
DR. HAMILTON ADAMS, an eminent eye surgeon, now retired, seventy-two.
M.J. ADAMS, his wife, an amateur painter, sixty-eight.
ANDRE SOR, owner of the Andre Sor Gallery, European born, forty-nine.

Time

The last two weeks of August.

ACT ONE
Scene 1: Tuesday morning, around ten.
Scene 2: Friday, noon.
Scene 3: Monday afternoon, around one.
Scene 4: Wednesday, two in the afternoon.
Scene 5: Friday, end of the day.

ACT TWO

Place

A private beach on Massachusetts' North Shore.

ACT ONE

Scene 1

A stretch of private beach on the North Shore of Massachusetts somewhere between Marblehead and Gloucester. There's sky, sand and ocean for as far as the eye can see. It's around ten on a hazy Tuesday morning, two weeks into August. A large wooden lifeguard's chair looms in the foreground. Wearing his customary orange trunks, Leo is holding onto one of the side frets doing leg-stretching exercises. As he completes his morning workout, Holly Dancer drifts onto the beach. Dressed in a tee shirt and gauze skirt, she gazes out over the horizon and eats a Milky Way. Leo immediately notices her and picks up speed on his exercises, interrupting her revery. Waves break in the distance.

LEO: Well . . . hi there.

HOLLY *(Laughing)*: Oh, I did-n't . . .

Pause.

LEO: What a day, what a day!

HOLLY: . . . I'm sorry . . .

Pause.

HOLLY: . . . notice you.

A silence as they stare at each other.

LEO: Skip a day of warmups and the old muscles just cramp right up on you . . .

HOLLY *(Eyes averted)*: I was trying to see if I could . . .

LEO: GLLLLITTTTCH! Forget it!

HOLLY: . . . make out the coast of Europe. You know . . .

Pause.

LEO: I'm sorry.

HOLLY: Nothing, nothing.

Pause.

LEO: No, no, go on . . .

HOLLY: I was just saying . . .

Pause.

LEO: Please?

HOLLY *(Laughing)*: Forget it, it's . . .

Pause.

HOLLY: You know, how if you look hard enough sometimes you can make out the coast of Europe on the other side . . . ?

LEO: Europe?!

HOLLY: Well, not cars or people or national flags or anything . . . *(Laughing)* Skip it, skip it . . .

LEO: No, no, I know exactly what you mean. A couple of days ago I could have sworn I saw an Egyptian pyramid in the distance . . .

HOLLY *(Trying to glide past him)*: Well, I think I'll head on down to the—

LEO *(Blocking her way)*: Hey, just a minute . . .

HOLLY: Oh, my pass, my pass! *(She starts fishing in her bag)* Hang on, I've got it right here. I'm staying with my aunt. Mabel Darling. You know, the tall lady with the floppy hat . . . DAMMIT, SHE HANDED IT TO ME RIGHT BEFORE I . . . . Mabel Darling . . . she comes down with a bucket to bring home water from the ocean . . . *(Plowing through her bag)* COME ON, COME ON, WHERE ARE YOU . . . ?! She likes to splash it on her legs while she sits in her garden. . . . GODDAMMIT, I JUST HAD IT!

LEO: Hey, take it easy, I'm not here to check people's passes.

HOLLY: I know the rules. This is a private beach . . . SHIT! *(She pulls out another Milky Way)* Care for a candy bar?

LEO: No, no thanks.

HOLLY: You sure? *(She offers it to him while still plowing through her bag)*

LEO: Look, I told you, you don't have to show me your pass.

HOLLY *(Waving the candy bar in front of him)*: They're very good. I just had one.

LEO: Okay, okay, what the hell . . . *(He unpeels it and takes a gooey bite)* Mmmmmmm!

HOLLY: What did I tell you . . . ? *(Suddenly freezes)* Hey, wait a minute. Since when has there been a lifeguard down here? This beach doesn't have a lifeguard.

LEO *(Enjoying his Milky Way)*: Jeez, this really *is* good!

HOLLY: Excuse me, but since when has there been a—

LEO: All it takes is one drowning.

HOLLY: There was a drowning?

LEO: All I know is, six weeks ago somebody tells me . . .

HOLLY: *Here*?!

LEO: . . . this group of families near Beverly Farms needs a lifeguard until Labor Day.

HOLLY: I don't believe it!

LEO: I figured, what the hell, the fishing business has been real slow.

HOLLY: I've been coming here since I was a child.

LEO: It would be nice to take it easy at the beach for a while.

HOLLY: My grandmother had this huge place . . .

LEO: I used to be a lifeguard in the summers. Well, I used to be a lot of things—a car mechanic, a double-A ball player, a contractor . . .

HOLLY: You're sure it was here? . . . At our little—

LEO: Yeah, some kid.

HOLLY: Oh no.

LEO: It really shook everyone up.

HOLLY: My aunt never told me. I guess she didn't—

LEO: He was real young, only—

HOLLY *(Hands over her ears)*: Don't!

A silence.

LEO: Yeah, it's weird. Even though everyone knows I'm here now, not many people show up. It's like they think it's catching or something.

A silence. Faith Bigelow, five months pregnant, and Ariel Took suddenly appear, their two children, Winston and Miranda, running ahead of them. Ariel's carrying a mountain of stuff including several beach chairs and a battered umbrella. Faith has a neatly folded quilt over her arm and carries a wicker picnic basket. Winston makes a beeline for Leo's chair.

WINSTON: HEY LEO, WHAT'S HAPPENING? . . . SEE ANY GOOD STUFF OUT THERE? . . . SEA MONSTERS . . . SHIPWRECKS . . . ?

ARIEL: WINSTON, get down! You know the rules!

WINSTON *(Scrambling up the ladder)*: HERE I COME, READY OR NOT!

MIRANDA *(Fuming, at the foot of the chair)*: No fair, no fair!

LEO: Morning, ladies.

Winston has found Leo's whistle and begins blasting on it.

ARIEL: WINSTON . . . STOP IT!

LEO: Okay buddy, cool it with the whistle.

Winston stops for the moment.

FAITH: Holly Dancer, is that you?

HOLLY: Oh my God, Faith! Look at you. *(She pats Faith's stomach)*

FAITH *(Laughing)*: I know, I know, isn't it wild?

HOLLY *(Embracing her)*: Oh Faith, congratulations!

FAITH: Finally, after all these years . . . do you believe it?

MIRANDA *(To Faith)*: How come he always gets to go up—

WINSTON *(Pretending he's Leo)*: All right everybody, clear the beach, clear the beach. *(He resumes blasting on the whistle)*

ARIEL *(Hands over her ears)*: WINNNNNNNNNSTON!

HOLLY: I'm so happy for you!

FAITH: How long are you down for?

HOLLY: Only two weeks.

FAITH: How's Mabel? I never see her anymore.

LEO *(To Winston)*: I SAID: KNOCK IT OFF!

ARIEL: WINSTON, I ASKED YOU TO GET DOWN!

WINSTON *(Imitating Leo)*: We've got some choppy-looking water out there, we don't want anyone getting hurt!

MIRANDA *(To Winston)*: BITCH!

FAITH *(To Holly)*: She isn't ill, is she?

HOLLY: No, no, she just doesn't come here much anymore, she doesn't really like the beach.

LEO *(To Winston)*: HEY CHARLIE, WHAT ABOUT GETTING DOWN SO I CAN GO TO WORK?

HOLLY: Hi Miranda, you've gotten so *big*!

WINSTON *(Still as Leo)*: Well ladies, make yourselves comfortable before the tide comes in.

ARIEL: YOU HEARD HIM, WINSTON . . . MOVE!

Winston doesn't.

FAITH *(To Ariel)*: You've met Holly Dancer, haven't you? Mabel Darling's niece . . . ?

MIRANDA *(To Leo)*: Couldn't I go up? Just once? I've never . . .

ARIEL *(Shaking hands with Holly)*: Oh yes, how do you do?

FAITH *(To Holly)*: You remember Ariel, she was my roommate at Wellesley. She's renting the Salisbury Place this summer.

HOLLY: Great! It's a pleasure to finally—

WINSTON *(Scanning the horizon dramatically)*: OH NO! *TIDAL WAVE! MAN THE LIFEBOATS!*

ARIEL *(To Holly)*: Excuse me a sec . . . WINSTON, IF YOU'RE NOT DOWN HERE BY THE COUNT OF THREE, I'M COMING UP AFTER YOU! *(To Holly)* I'm sorry . . .

FAITH *(To Ariel)*: Holly practically grew up on this beach. Her grandmother had a place down here. She's been coming every summer since—

ARIEL *(To Winston)*: ONE . . .

MIRANDA: I HATE YOU WINSTON, I *REALLY* HATE YOU!

ARIEL *(To Holly)*: How long are you here for?

LEO: WINSTON, DID YOU HEAR YOUR MOTHER?

HOLLY: Just two weeks.

ARIEL *(Not hearing)*: I'm sorry?

HOLLY: I said, only—

MIRANDA *(To Winston)*: BITCH! BITCH! BITCH!

FAITH: Look, if you're going to call him names, at least use the right gender. It's not "bitch," but "bastard"!

HOLLY:—two—

MIRANDA: BASTARD!

ARIEL *(To Winston)*: TWO . . .

FAITH *(To Holly)*: And how's wicked New York City! *(To Ariel)* She grew up in New York City, can you believe it? I mean, imagine *living* in New—

LEO *(To Holly)*: So, you're from New York, are you?

HOLLY: Sorry . . . ?

FAITH *(To Ariel)*: Her father's head of a big publishing company. I'm sure you've heard of it . . .

ARIEL: THREE! ALL RIGHT WINSTON, I'M COMING UP AFTER YOU!

Ariel doesn't move. A silence.

ARIEL *(To Holly)*: I'm sorry, he's just got a lot of energy . . .

LEO *(Bounding up the steps)*: OKAY BUSTER, SAY YOUR PRAYERS!

WINSTON *(Stops his blasting and begins laughing with apprehension)*: HELP . . . HELP . . . HELP!

ARIEL *(To Holly)*: You know boys. . . . So, how long are you down for?

HOLLY: Not that long. Only two—

LEO *(Slings Winston over his shoulder and starts climbing down the ladder)*: NO SUDDEN MOVES NOW, CHARLIE!

WINSTON *(Laughing wildly)*: HELP . . . HELP . . . HELP!

FAITH *(To Holly)*: We'll have to catch up later.

WINSTON: PUT ME DOWN! PUT ME DOWN!

LEO *(Sets Winston next to Ariel)*: Here you go, he's all yours!

MIRANDA *(To Winston)*: Bastard!

WINSTON: Bitch!

ARIEL *(Shaking Winston by the arm, out of control)*: NEXT TIME YOU DO AS I SAY WHEN I SAY IT. DO YOU HEAR ME?

WINSTON: Ow, ow, ow.

ARIEL: *I asked you a question!*

WINSTON: Okay, okay, I'll be good.

Silence.

FAITH: Well, what do you say we head for our spot? Come on, Miranda, get your stuff. *(To Holly)* Please give Mabel my love.

Faith and Miranda start down the beach.

HOLLY: I will.

MIRANDA *(Quietly to Faith)*: Why do you always have to invite them? They ruin everything.

ARIEL *(To Winston)*: NO SWIMMING FOR YOU TODAY!

FAITH: Honey, you know what I told you.

MIRANDA: But still . . .

FAITH: No "but stills." I'm doing it for Ariel. She's had a rough time.

ARIEL *(Over her shoulder to Holly)*: Nice meeting you.

HOLLY: Same here.

ARIEL *(To Winston)*: You're not setting foot in that water, do you hear me?

Ariel and Winston trudge off to their spot. Silence.

LEO *(To Holly)*: Well, it looks as if it's going to be another beautiful day.

HOLLY: God, I love this beach.

LEO: The fog's burned off.

HOLLY: It never changes.

LEO: I wasn't sure whether. . . . So, how long are you down for!

A silence.

HOLLY *(Lost)*: I'm sorry.

LEO: I was just wondering how long you're planning to—

HOLLY: Oh, Holly! Holly Dancer!

LEO *(Laughing)*: No, no, I asked.

HOLLY: I'm visiting my aunt, Mabel Darling. The tall lady that comes down to—

LEO: You know, you have amazing eyes.

A silence.

HOLLY *(Moving away from him)*: Well, I guess I'll be heading on down to the—

LEO *(Grabbing her arm)*: Wait!

Holly gasps and draws back, wide-eyed.

LEO *(Quickly dropping her arm)*: I'm sorry.

She stares at him.

LEO: I was just wondering how long you were . . . . Hey, hey, it's no big deal.

Holly looks more and more upset.

LEO *(Moving closer to her)*: What's wrong? . . . Is something the matter?

Blackout.

Scene 2

Friday, around noon. It's a gorgeous sunny day. Leo's up in his chair working on his tan, arms and legs outstretched, glistening with baby oil. Faith and Ariel are also out with their children. Faith is sunning herself; Ariel is crocheting something wildly colored and beautiful. Winston and Miranda are making sandcastles. Winston's is a huge formless mess. Miranda has a turreted plastic mold, so she turns out perfect tower after perfect tower. Also on the beach is M.J. Adams, who's created an entire home away from home complete with quilted flooring, oversize umbrella, roomy but creaky reclining chairs, food, cold drinks, extra blankets. She sketches on a water-color pad, wearing a wide-brimmed hat to keep the sun out. For the moment all one can hear is the rapid scratching of her pencil.

M.J. ADAMS *(After a furious assault, to herself)*: Rats! Why won't anything hold still? *(She erases vigorously and starts up again)*

Dr. Hamilton Adams, her husband, soundlessly approaches from the shoreline. He's wearing a beat-up Brooks Brothers short-sleeved shirt over ancient trunks. He's in very good shape. He dumps a stream of shells onto the quilt.

HAMILTON: Treasures from the deep . . .

Hamilton sinks down into his chair with a deep sigh. Silence as M.J. keeps sketching.

M.J.: How was the water? It looks cold.
HAMILTON: Sixty-five.

M.J. shudders. Hamilton is hiding something behind his back.

HAMILTON: I've got something for you.
M.J. *(Attacks her sketch with the eraser again)*: GODDAMMIT, WHY DOES EVERYTHING HAVE TO KEEP MOVING?
HAMILTON: Because we're outdoors.

M.J. *(Yelling at the vista)*: COME ON. . . . HOLD STILL, FOR CHRISTSAKES! *(She attacks her sketch again, growling)*

HAMILTON *(Thrusts two closed fists in front of her)*: Which hand?

M.J.: You and your shells!

HAMILTON: It's not a shell.

M.J.: Sponge, then. . . . Honestly, Hammy, a man of your age still picking up shells and things on the beach . . .

HAMILTON: It's *not* a sponge.

M.J.: Starfish then . . . sand dollar, whatever!

HAMILTON *(Opening his hand)*: Look!

M.J.: Really, darling, a person would think you'd have better things to do with your time.

HAMILTON *(Hands the object to her)*: Gently, gently . . .

M.J.: What is it?

HAMILTON: Well, look at it!

M.J.: But I'm doing something else now.

HAMILTON: Come on, just a tiny . . .

M.J. *(Looks at it, sighing)*: Plus ça change, plus c'est la même chose.

HAMILTON: Well, what do you think?

M.J.: Darling, I can't tell what this is.

HAMILTON: Use your imagination.

M.J.: It looks like waterlogged packing material.

HAMILTON: It's a piece of brain coral.

M.J. *(Quickly hands it back)*: Uuugh!

HAMILTON: Isn't it beautiful?

M.J.: Hammy, it's perfectly obscene and you know it!

HAMILTON: Its natural habitat is along the Gulf Coast . . . *(M.J. shudders again)* It's amazing it washed this far north.

M.J. *(Looking out over the ocean)*: Damned wind keeps shifting!

FAITH *(Rising)*: I don't know about you, but I could use a little exercise.

ARIEL *(Following her off the beach)*: Race you to Gloucester.

HAMILTON *(Glancing over M.J.'s shoulder)*: Oh, that's very nice, dear. Very nice.

M.J.: It's God-awful, and you know it!

HAMILTON: You've gotten the shoreline very well.

Holly steps onto the beach. She's wearing a battered cap, tee shirt and short shorts. She carries a large canvas bag. Eyeing Leo, she hangs back behind his chair so he won't see her.

M.J. *(Erasing again)*: Rats!

HAMILTON: You're a crackerjack at composition.

M.J. *(Recoils from him and rips the sketch out of the pad, scrunching it into a ball)*: HAMMY, I'VE ASKED YOU *NOT* TO WATCH ME AS I WORK! YOU KNOW HOW DISTRACTING IT IS!

HAMILTON *(Putting his hand on her arm)*: M.J. . . . M.J. . . .

M.J. *(Bolts out of her chair and heads for the shore)*: I'm taking a walk!

HAMILTON: I wish you wouldn't be so hard on yourself. You're really awfully good you know. M.J.? M.J. . . . ?

M.J. storms out of view. Hamilton watches her go and then settles into his chair, fondling his piece of brain coral. Holly steps forward a few steps and rips open a bag of M&M's. She pops them in her mouth while gazing out over the horizon.

LEO: Well, well, long time no see.

HOLLY: Oh, hi. *(Rattling her candy)* Care for some M&M's?

LEO: Where have you been?

HOLLY: What a day! Do you believe this air? *(She inhales deeply while downing more M&M's, then heads towards the water)* Well, see ya.

LEO *(Rising)*: Hey, wait a minute.

Holly slings down her canvas bag at the water's edge. She sits for a moment drinking everything in and finishing off her M&M's. She then rises, reaches into her bag and pulls out a folding tripod. She tries to set it up, but the legs keep jamming. She struggles with it, getting angrier and angrier.

HOLLY: DAMNED TRIPOD, WHAT'S WRONG WITH YOU! . . . OPEN! . . . COME ON . . . OPEN! . . . ARRGGGGH! *(Leo watches her with amusement)* WILL YOU OPEN FOR CHRIST-SAKES? *(She struggles further, then has a temper tantrum and starts kicking the tripod all over the sand)* SON OF A BITCH . . . OPEN! . . . WHAT'S WRONG WITH YOU? . . . GODDAMNED PIECE OF SHIT! *(She glares at it, then calmly walks over to Leo's chair)* Excuse me, I was wondering if you could help me with my . . . FRIGGING TRIPOD!

LEO: Easy, easy . . .

HOLLY: The lousy thing won't open.

LEO *(Bounding down his chair)*: So I noticed.

Leo and Holly head down the beach together.

HOLLY: I don't know what's wrong with me lately, I can't seem to do anything right!

LEO: So, you're a photographer?

HOLLY: I'm having a breakdown.

LEO: Now, now . . . (*He picks up the tripod and dusts it off*) Okay let's see what we have here.

HOLLY: A total, complete breakdown.

LEO: My brother Butchie used to have one of these. He was really good. Especially with candid shots.

HOLLY: I can't handle my equipment, I can't set up a decent shot . . .

LEO: There's this great one he did of a kid with a frog . . .

HOLLY: I can't even hold the camera steady.

LEO: I don't know how he got it, but the frog was sitting on the kid's head looking right into the camera.

HOLLY: It's very depressing.

LEO: The kid had this idiotic grin on his face. . . . It sounds stupid, but the frog had exactly the same expression. I'm telling you, that picture could have won a contest. (*He opens the tripod in one fluid move and hands it to Holly*) Here you go.

HOLLY (*Takes it absentmindedly*): Oh, thanks. (*She just stands there, staring at Leo's body*)

LEO: Well, you're all set.

A silence.

LEO: Aren't you going to use it?

HOLLY (*Startled*): What?

LEO: I said, aren't you going to . . . (*Gesturing towards the tripod*) You know . . .

HOLLY: Oh, oh, right. Thanks a lot.

Another silence.

LEO: Are you all right? (*Holly sighs deeply*) What's wrong?

HOLLY (*To herself*): I don't know, maybe it's time to move on.

LEO: I beg your pardon?

HOLLY: I can't keep doing nudes for the rest of my life.

LEO: You do, uh . . .

HOLLY: I mean, after a while there's only so much you can say about the . . .

LEO (*Inadvertently brushing close to her*): Nudes . . . ?!

HOLLY (*Jumping back as if singed*): . . . human body . . .

LEO: Whoops, sorry . . .

HOLLY: God, you're so . . .

LEO: Right, a body's just a body!

HOLLY: . . . *tan*!

LEO: I mean, what's the big deal . . . ?

HOLLY: I've never seen such a . . .

LEO: Everybody's got one! *(He laughs too heartily)*
HOLLY *(Weakly)*: . . . color . . . !

Silence.

LEO: And just who do you get to um . . . *pose?*
HOLLY: I just finished this series of myself. It was really . . .
LEO *(In a tiny voice)*: Yourself . . . ?
HOLLY *(In control again)*: Yeah, it's weird, but sooner or later anyone who's into nudes ends up doing themselves. It's just one of those progressions.
LEO: But how do you . . . I mean . . .
HOLLY: It's really not that different.
LEO: . . . set everything up?
HOLLY: You just feel a little stupid running around stark naked.
LEO: I mean, it must be tricky trying to pose and . . .
HOLLY: Well, you do a timed exposure of course.
LEO: Yeah, of course, I was just wondering how you . . .
HOLLY *(Dancing around him)*: You have to be fast on your feet, that's all. I mean, there are a lot of hilarious takes you wouldn't want anyone to see, believe me.
LEO: I believe you, I believe you!
HOLLY: But when it works, there's nothing like it. There's something about facing your own body that's . . . I don't know . . .
LEO *(More and more undone)*: Yeah, it must be . . .
HOLLY: It's exhilarating. *(Thrusting out her arms)* I mean, there you are just . . .
LEO *(Oogling her)*: I can imagine.
HOLLY *(Realizing what she's doing, quickly recovers)*: Well, another perfect day, do you believe it?

Holly laughs a bit too heartily. A silence.

LEO: Oh, your tripod. *(He offers it to her again)*
HOLLY: Oh, thanks. *(She takes it and starts setting up her camera)*
LEO *(Following her)*: Me, I can't stand having my picture taken. Ever since I was little, I've hated it. My baby pictures stop once I was old enough to crawl. I ducked out of view for all my homeroom pictures in grade school, and in high school, I left my yearbook page blank.
HOLLY: Yeah, I'm the same way really.
LEO: Now, a movie camera doesn't bother me. It's strange.
HOLLY *(Adjusting the tripod and looking through her viewfinder)*: I'm determined to photograph this beach!

LEO *(Blocking her view)*: Sorry, sorry. . . . Put me in front of a Super 8 and forget it! *(He does some spirited hijinks, almost knocking her tripod over)* Oh, sorry . . .

HOLLY: I don't know, I've been having a tough time lately. Well, when am I *not* having a tough time . . . ? With my work, I mean. I've been trying too hard. You know when everything comes out too perfect?

LEO *(Faking it)*: Oh yeah . . .

HOLLY: When result takes over intention? I'm hoping to regroup here. You know, relax a little. Take in more of the world—sandpipers, jellyfish, hermit crabs. Or at least take some pictures of other *people* for a change—widen my focus for God's sake . . . !

Winston and Miranda suddenly come running over to Leo and Holly.

WINSTON: Hey, whatcha doing?

LEO *(Trying to ward them off)*: Not too close now.

HOLLY: Setting up my camera.

MIRANDA: I've got a camera, a discomatic.

WINSTON *(Trying to crowd in)*: Can I look? Can I look?

HOLLY: Sure, just don't make any sudden moves.

WINSTON *(Peering through the viewfinder)*: HEY, NEATO, THERE'S A LITTLE BULLSEYE IN THE MIDDLE OF THE PICTURE.

MIRANDA: Let me see, let me see!

LEO: Easy, easy . . .

WINSTON *(Pushing her away)*: BACK OFF, MIRANDA, I GOT HERE FIRST!

LEO: Come on kids, watch it.

MIRANDA *(Starts posing like a model)*: Hey . . . do me!

WINSTON: Whoa, Mandy, way to go! *(Pretending he's a photographer)* Nice . . . nice. . . . Now give me a little profile . . . that's it . . . and let's see some leg . . . great!

Miranda's posing becomes more antic.

LEO *(Steadying the wobbling tripod)*: She said, no. sudden. moves!

WINSTON *(Runs to Holly and pulls on her arm)*: Hey, take our picture together!

MIRANDA *(Also pulling on her)*: Please? . . . Pretty please?

WINSTON: Just one?

LEO: Look kids, she didn't come here to—

The kids begin posing.

HOLLY *(Going to her camera)*: It's okay, this is the sort of thing I do to make a living.

WINSTON *(Upstaging Miranda)*: Hey everybody, look at me!

MIRANDA: WINSTON . . . STOP IT!

HOLLY *(Clicks away, entering the spirit)*: No, that's good, keep it up. The more spontaneous the better.

WINSTON: Lights . . . camera . . .   MIRANDA: OWWWW, you're ACTION!   hurting me!

LEO *(Moving closer to Holly)*: I have a boat, you know. If you ever want to photograph some beautiful scenery there are all kinds of places I could . . .

WINSTON *(To Miranda)*: He's got a boat. Uh-oh, you know what *that* means . . .

MIRANDA: Oh boy . . . ! *(Starts giggling)*

LEO: You know, I could take you around on my day off . . .

WINSTON: Kissy, kissy, kissy . . .

LEO: I worked for the coast guard a while back and could show you . . .

MIRANDA *(Sidling up to Leo, affecting a sexy voice)*: "Why, I'd just *love* to take a ride in your boat!"

Miranda and Winston mime smooching in front of Holly's camera.

WINSTON: Come to me baby . . .

MIRANDA: I've waited so long . . .

M.J. *(Returning from her walk)*: Good grief, what's going on here?

HOLLY *(Snapping away, laughing)*: We're just fooling around.

LEO: Come on kids, knock it off!

WINSTON *(Pulling Miranda to him with a romantic flourish)*: You're driving me crazy!

MIRANDA: Come on, Honey Lips . . . *do* it!

LEO *(Dying with embarrassment)*: I mean, no big deal. . . . We could head up towards Rockport. Have you ever been to Thatcher's Island or Paradise Cliffs?

Blackout.

Scene 3

Monday afternoon around one. It's nippy and overcast. It's Leo's day off. A sign hangs from his chair that reads LIFEGUARD OFF DUTY, SWIM AT YOUR OWN RISK. Faith and Ariel are the only ones visible on the beach. They sit high up on the sand wearing light jackets.

ARIEL: I love it when it's like this.

FAITH: Me too.

ARIEL: No one here but the true lunatics, the certifiables.

FAITH: Speak for yourself.

A silence.

ARIEL *(Glancing at Leo's chair)*: It's such a relief not having *him* around.

FAITH: What are you talking about?

ARIEL: He gives me the creeps.

FAITH: Gee, I think he's sexy.

ARIEL: He's so . . . I don't know . . .

FAITH: Provocative.

ARIEL: But in such a creepy way. He's always strutting around displaying himself.

FAITH: Ariel!

ARIEL: I think he stuffs himself.

FAITH *(Laughing)*: Ariel?!

ARIEL: Some guys do that.

FAITH: You *are* crazy!

ARIEL: Just take a good look at him sometime.

FAITH: He's a sweet guy. He's just rather well endowed in the uh . . . hoo-hah department. *(She starts laughing again)*

ARIEL: The "hoo-hah department" . . . ?!

FAITH: You know, the old ding-a-ling area . . . *(Laughing harder)* Oh God!

ARIEL: You see, you noticed too. I mean, what's a guy his age doing here? Lifeguards are usually high school kids or college students. It's creepy.

FAITH: We needed someone on short notice, and he was available.

ARIEL: It's still creepy.

FAITH: He lives somewhere in Essex. I heard he takes people out on whale watches.

ARIEL: I heard he was a professional sky diver.

FAITH: Right, right, I've heard that too! That he's broken all kinds of altitude records . . .

ARIEL: And he also races stock cars or something . . .

FAITH: I didn't know about that.

ARIEL: Oh yes, I think he won some important race in Europe a while back . . .

FAITH: Isn't his family in the shipbuilding business?

ARIEL: The Palme D'Or . . .

FAITH: That's a film award!

ARIEL: Whatever . . . ! He just gives me the willies the way he's always hanging around that friend of yours.

FAITH: You're just jealous.

ARIEL: Sure, sure.

FAITH: Come on, you've been separated from Fisher for almost four years now. You could use a little . . . male companionship.

ARIEL: Fisher gave me enough "male companionship" to last a lifetime, believe me!

Holly suddenly appears. She's wearing jeans and a gorgeous hand-knit sweater.

FAITH *(Jumping to her feet)*: HOLLY . . .

An embarrassed silence.

HOLLY: Oh hi, I was just . . .

FAITH: What brings *you* out this misty, moisty day?

ARIEL *(To Holly)*: I love that sweater!

HOLLY: Oh, thanks.

ARIEL *(Advancing towards Holly)*: What is it? . . . Mohair?

HOLLY: Gee, I don't . . .

FAITH *(Reaching towards Holly's earrings)*: Great earrings!

ARIEL *(Feeling the sweater)*: Yeah, that's what I thought.

FAITH *(To Ariel)*: Look at these . . .

ARIEL *(Touching the earrings, surprised)*: Ohhh, they're so light!

FAITH: You just can't get stuff like that around here.

HOLLY: Yeah, well . . .

A silence.

ARIEL *(Moving towards Leo's chair)*: KIDS, ARE YOU STILL UP THERE . . . ?!

A blanket covering the chair suddenly moves. Winston and Miranda erupt out from under it, giggling.

HOLLY *(Hand flying over her heart)*: Ohhhh! You frightened me!

FAITH: NO ROUGHHOUSING NOW! WE DON'T WANT ANY-ONE FALLING OFF THAT THING!

More giggling and horsing around. A pause.

HOLLY *(Starting to leave)*: Well, I think I'll head on down to the—

FAITH: No, no . . . join us.

ARIEL: Yes do.

HOLLY: I don't want to—

FAITH *(Pulling Holly over to them)*: Come on, I've barely seen you this summer.

HOLLY *(Sitting with them)*: Well, okay . . .

ARIEL *(To Holly)*: If you ever decide you don't want that sweater . . .

HOLLY: Yeah, isn't it beautiful? Someone gave it to me.

A silence.

HOLLY *(Leaning over and patting Faith's stomach)*: So, how are you feeling these days?

FAITH: Great! You know what I keep thinking about . . . ? How girl babies are born with all their eggs. It just blows me away—the image of a newborn being filled with these zillions of eggs . . .

ARIEL: And I thought *I* was the one just back from the funny farm . . .

FAITH: When we first got Miranda, I used to shake her like a cucuracha to see if I could hear them rolling around.

HOLLY *(Charmed)*: No . . . !

ARIEL *(Humoring Faith)*: All right . . .

FAITH: No, it's really astonishing. That a newborn girl has that child-bearing potential from the beginning. They're sort of like those nesting Russian wooden dolls. You open the first one and there's a smaller one inside . . . and inside that, an even smaller one, until finally there's only one left about the size of a thimble. "Well, this is it!" you say to yourself, idly pulling on the top to see if it will open and . . . BINGO! It's filled with all these little seeds with faces painted on them. When Miranda was tiny, I used to think of her as being one of those dolls . . . and *I* was one of her unborn seeds.

Holly laughs softly with delight.

ARIEL: Nothing wrong with her . . .

FAITH: No, this weird thing happens with your sense of continuity with girl babies. . . . You know, the Shakers had these cradles for the aged. I've seen them in museums. They're adult size for the very old. Now that I'm going to have my very own little girl, finally be part of that biological chain, I keep imagining us fifty years from now—I'll be this wrinkled crone lying in the cradle, and she'll be the mommy—rocking me back and forth and back and forth . . . and back and forth . . .

HOLLY *(Undone)*: Ooooohhhhh . . .

ARIEL: Okay . . .

FAITH: I'm sorry, I get carried away sometimes . . .

Holly tries to hide her tears.

ARIEL: We all have our moments.

FAITH: Miranda's almost more excited than I am.

The kids peek out from under the blanket and then dive back under again, laughing.

FAITH *(To Miranda)*: I SEE YOU! . . . She's amazing. She's never had any problems about being adopted.

The children begin roughhousing under the blanket again.

ARIEL: Come on kids, not too wild now!

FAITH: She knows how hard Charlie and I have been trying for this baby. She said the most moving thing when we told her I was finally pregnant. She said, "I feel as if all three of us made it."

HOLLY *(Enchanted)*: Ohhhh . . .

Ariel sighs, getting teary.

FAITH *(To Ariel)*: Yeah, it made Charlie cry.

ARIEL *(Hugging Faith, weepy)*: It makes me cry.

Holly looks longingly at them for a moment, then Miranda and Winston start acting up again.

FAITH *(Exasperated more than angry)*: EASY GUYS, YOU KNOW LEO DOESN'T LIKE YOU PLAYING UP THERE!	ARIEL *(World-weary)*: WINSTON . . . I ASKED YOU TO TAKE IT EASY!

The children quiet down.

HOLLY *(Rises, uneasy)*: Well, I'd better be—

FAITH: No, no . . . don't go.

Winston and Miranda erupt up from under the blanket again. Winston is now tickling her.

WINSTON: Tickle, tickle . . . tickle!

MIRANDA *(Laughing and trying to ward him off)*: Stop it Winston. . . . *Stop!*

FAITH *(More amused than angry)*: YOU TWO BE CAREFUL NOW, WE DON'T WANT ANY BROKEN BONES . . . ! *(To Holly)* Sorry . . .

HOLLY: It must be amazing watching them grow up.

MIRANDA *(Awash with laughter)*: HELLLLLLLLLLP!

FAITH: Come on kids . . . BEHAVE!

WINSTON *(Stops tickling)*: Okay. Hey, Mandy, let's play a game of War!

MIRANDA *(Ecstatic)*: ALL RIGHT . . . !

Miranda and Winston set up Leo's bench and begin playing cards.

FAITH *(To Holly)*: I'm sorry, you know kids . . .

HOLLY: No, no, I was just thinking how each child is really about eighty-five different people. I mean, the responsibility. . . ! How do you know what to do?

FAITH: You figure it out as you go along.

HOLLY: But what if you make a mistake?

FAITH: You try to be wiser the next time.

ARIEL: The whole thing is to hang in there.

FAITH: You said it!

Ariel growls with resolve. A silence.

HOLLY *(To Ariel)*: Are you planning to have more children?

ARIEL: I'm divorced at the moment.

HOLLY: Oh that's right. I'm sorry, I'm sorry.

ARIEL: Don't be. It's cause for jubilation. *(Pause)* No, my childbearing days are over.

FAITH: What are you talking about? You're nowhere near forty, even.

ARIEL: My equipment has dried up. I haven't had a period for almost two years. My shrink at "the farm" is convinced that's part of why I keep trying to off myself. You know, feelings of worthlessness and all that. Where other women's organs are chugging right along, mine are suddenly filled with dust. I'm like this walking sandbag.

FAITH: Come on!

ARIEL: Even if I were lucky enough to conceive, all I could squeeze out at this point would be a grasshopper or dragonfly.

FAITH: *Ariel?!*

ARIEL: I'm serious. I can see it now. After ten hours of hard labor, I'd push out this small gray . . . moth.

MIRANDA *(Comes down from the chair and cuddles up to Faith)*: Hi, Mommy.

FAITH *(Hugging her)*: Hello sweetheart, having fun?

MIRANDA: It's really great up there. You can see for miles.

Winston suddenly climbs up onto the railing that surrounds Leo's perch.

ARIEL (*Imitating the doctor who's trying to catch her flying baby*): "Well, congratulations, Mrs. Took . . . (*Missing*) Shit! Hold still, dammit! . . . It looks as if you've just given birth to a healthy ring-tailed . . . moth. GOTCHA!"
WINSTON (*Now standing tall on the railing, his arms out like a high-wire artist*): HEY, EVERYBODY, LOOK AT ME!
ARIEL (*Clutching onto Faith*): Oh my God . . . Winston . . . !
FAITH: Oh no . . . !
MIRANDA: WINSTON . . . WHAT ARE YOU DOING UP THERE?

Winston slowly raises his arms, poising himself for flight.

ARIEL: Honey, please . . .
FAITH: Winston . . .
HOLLY: I can't look!
ARIEL: Get. Down.
MIRANDA: You're going to kill yourself someday, you know that . . . ?
ARIEL: Winston . . . *please?!*

Everyone moves closer to the chair, spellbound with horror. Blackout.

Scene 4

Wednesday, two in the afternoon. Towering cloud formations dapple the beach with shadows. Leo's up in his chair wearing a light windbreaker. Ariel and Winston are having lunch and playing tic-tac-toe between bites. Hamilton is at the water's edge poking around for shells, and M.J.'s doing a series of five-minute watercolors which she's placed in a circle around her.

M.J. (*Turns from inspecting her paintings to trying to open an ancient thermos filled with iced tea*): HAMMY, WHAT DID YOU DO TO THIS THERMOS . . . ?! (*She struggles with the lid*) YOO-HOOOOO, HAMMY . . . ? Goddammit, I told him not to get sand in it! SWEETHEART, I NEED YOU! (*She resumes her struggle*)
LEO (*Clambering down his chair*): Here, let me help.
M.J. (*Trying with all her might to unscrew the lid; to Hamilton*): I CAN'T OPEN THE ICED TEA!
LEO: May I? (*He takes the thermos from M.J. and unscrews it in one deft move*) There we go. (*And hands it back to her*)
M.J. (*To Leo*): Thank you very much. (*To Hamilton*) IT'S ALL RIGHT . . . I GOT IT, I GOT IT! (*To Leo*) Poor thing's as deaf as a stone.

HAMILTON *(Walking towards M.J.)*: What's that? The thermos is stuck?

M.J.: NEVER MIND. I JUST SAID—

HAMILTON *(Reaching for it)*: Well, what seems to be the problem?

M.J.: Nothing, darling. Everything's fine. Just. Fine. You can go back to your shells.

HAMILTON: Hey, how about a little iced tea to wet your whistle . . . ? *(Pouring himself a cup)*

M.J. *(Sighing)*: No thanks, I changed my mind.

A silence.

LEO *(Gazing at M.J.'s watercolors)*: Hey, these are really good.

M.J.: Ugh, please.

LEO: No, they are! I mean it!

HAMILTON: Yes, she's awfully talented.

M.J.: I'm just a dabbler, just a dabbler.

LEO *(Reaching for one)*: May I . . . ?

HAMILTON: There's no talking to her about her work.

LEO: These are wonderful.

M.J.: Well, being married to a doctor all these years, I had to learn how to amuse myself.

HAMILTON: Now, now . . . *(To Leo)* Care for a spot of iced tea?

M.J.: He was never home.

LEO: No, no thanks.

HAMILTON: That's not true. Weekends I always—

M.J.: It certainly is true! You lived at that damned hospital. And when you weren't there . . . . Well, let's not get into that. . . . I don't recommend anyone marrying a surgeon, I don't care how winning their bedside manner is.

LEO: A surgeon . . . ?

M.J.: An eye surgeon, if you please. *(Leo shudders)* Oh yes, he was the best.

LEO: I believe you, I believe you.

M.J.: He had referrals from all over the world.

HAMILTON: M.J. . . .

M.J.: Everyone wanted him. Heads of state, popular entertainers, the ladies. Oh yes, especially the ladies!

A pause.

HAMILTON: Eye surgery is very routine business, she likes to embroider.

M.J.: Embroider, my foot! You should have seen him pop one of the Kennedy children's eyes back into its socket after it was knocked out during a touch football game with our kids. . . . He just marched right out onto the lawn, scooped it up in his hand and . . . *(Making a lurid sound)* screwed it back in.

HAMILTON *(Laughing)*: M.J., really!

M.J. *(Resumes painting)*: So, I cultivated my hobbies.

LEO: How many children do you have?

Pause.

M.J. AND HAMILTON *(Gleeful)*: Nine.

LEO: Jesus!

M.J.: Yes, even *our* families thought it was in poor taste.

LEO: Nine kids . . . !

M.J.: Well, I had help of course raising them.

LEO: But still . . .

HAMILTON: She's a remarkable woman.

LEO: I can see.

M.J.: Nannies and cooks.

HAMILTON: She kept us all going.

M.J.: I don't know what you're talking about. I wasn't a particularly good mother, and I had no patience with your hours. Just about the only thing I enjoyed was my pathetic little scribblings, and they *are* pathetic.

A silence.

M.J. *(Sunny again, to Leo)*: Well, I guess this is hardly the sort of job you envisioned when you took it: watching over a handful of old crocks all day.

LEO: Actually, I'm enjoying it.

HAMILTON: You see, M.J., you put much too dark a color on things.

M.J.: Don't you get bored? I should think you'd die of boredom.

LEO: I have my distractions.

M.J. *(Throwing Hamilton a pointed look)*: Yes, what would we do without our distractions . . . ? Hammy collects shells and sponges these days.

LEO: No kidding?

M.J.: Oh yes, Hammy's always been a great naturalist, had an eye for things of beauty . . . if you catch my drift . . .

An uncomfortable silence.

LEO: Well, I'd better be getting back to my—

M.J. *(Laughing)*: Don't get him started on the invertebrate shore life of North America, he'll talk your ear off.

Silence.

LEO: Well, I really ought to—

M.J.: Yes, please don't let us keep you.

HAMILTON: What a day! There won't be many more of these.

LEO *(Heading towards his chair)*: See ya.

M.J. *(Quite loud to Hamilton)*: What a nice young man.

HAMILTON: Well, I'm thinking of going in—

M.J.: How does he stand it? Chained up on that chair all day long—week in, week out. He can't swim he can't read—

HAMILTON: M.J., not so loud!

M.J.: Always the same vista, the same motley bathers, those dreadful children . . . !

HAMILTON: Well, the water's not going to come to me, that's for sure.

M.J.: The monotony must be crushing.

HAMILTON: You're here almost every day.

M.J.: Yes, but I don't have to be. It's my choice.

HAMILTON: Well, it's his choice too.

M.J.: But I have something to do.

HAMILTON: So does he, he's protecting us.

M.J.: But it must be so *boring*!

HAMILTON: In your eyes. Maybe this is just what he needs right now.

M.J. *(Sighs and pats Hamilton's knee)*: You're a good man, Hammy.

HAMILTON: Now, now, let's not get carried away.

M.J.: No, you really are. You're much more forgiving than I am.

Hamilton gazes out over the horizon. A silence. Back up in his chair, Leo can't seem to settle down. It's as if their talk about his boredom has suddenly made him aware of it. He sits, then rises, pacing like a caged animal. He suddenly picks up a copy of The Boston Globe *and starts flipping through it.*

LEO *(To Hamilton)*: Excuse me, I think I'll take you up on that iced tea, if you don't mind.

HAMILTON: Please, please. *(He pours some into the thermos top)* M.J. makes the best iced tea on the North Shore . . . she squeezes fresh orange juice into it. Makes all the difference, all the difference. *(He reaches the cup up to him)*

LEO: Thanks a lot, I really appreciate it.

Leo casually pours the iced tea into his newspaper, but it doesn't come out the other end.

HAMILTON *(In a whisper)*: Did you see that!
M.J.: I certainly did!

Winston now watches too as Leo opens the paper showing that the tea has vanished into thin air. He then casually pours it back into his cup, which he lifts towards the Adamses, and then drains.

M.J.: I'm amazed!
WINSTON *(Pulling Ariel out of her seat)*: Mom, come quick!
ARIEL *(Reluctantly following him)*: Winston, what are you . . . ?
HAMILTON *(Applauding)*: Why, Leo, I had no idea you could . . .
WINSTON *(To Leo)*: DO ANOTHER, DO ANOTHER!
ARIEL: What's going on here? . . . *(Laughing)* Winston?!
WINSTON *(Reaching for Ariel's hand)*: Just watch . . .
LEO: And now for the classic . . . Singapore Surprise! *(He makes fanfare noises)*

Holly suddenly materializes behind the chair. She's done something to her hair and is wearing a saucy little sundress, her camera slung over her shoulder. She drifts closer and closer.

LEO: Watch very closely. My hands will never leave my arms . . . *(He does a dazzling sleight-of-hand trick with an enormous surprise bouquet or flock of doves)*

WINSTON: FAR . . . OUT!   ARIEL *(Enchanted)*: Oh, Winston!

M.J. *(Applauding wildly)*: BRAVO, BRAVO!
HAMILTON *(Joining in)*: WELL DONE, WELL DONE!
WINSTON: MORE, MORE . . .
ARIEL: Now, honey . . . *(Eyeing Leo apologetically)*
M.J.: You could be on the stage.
LEO: Why, thank you.
M.J.: I had no idea you were so versatile.
HAMILTON: He's first rate, really first rate!
LEO *(To Holly)*: Oh hi . . . where have you been?
HOLLY: At my aunt's . . . *(To the Adamses, shyly)* Hi . . .
LEO: Boy, things must be pretty interesting over there. I mean, you spend a lot of time with her, don't you?
HOLLY: Yeah, I guess I do.
ARIEL *(Pulling Winston back to their spot)*: Come on honey, you still have half a tuna fish sandwich to finish.
WINSTON: Yukkk!
LEO *(To Holly)*: She must be a pretty interesting lady.

HOLLY: She is. She's wonderful! Whenever any of us are falling apart, we always come up and stay with her. She's just so . . . easy!

M.J., Hamilton, Ariel and Winston are riveted.

LEO: Falling apart . . . ?

Everyone quickly looks away. A silence.

HAMILTON *(Edgy)*: Well, I think I'm going to take a little stroll. *(To M.J.)* Care to join me?

M.J.: Not right now darling, you go ahead.

M.J. pulls out a copy of Quentin Bell's biography of Virginia Woolf and starts fitfully reading it. Hamilton exits.

HOLLY: Well not . . . *falling* . . . *apart* . . . ! I mean more . . . bottomed out. You know, everything just . . . . Whsst, forget it! *(She laughs)* Falling apart. *(Lowering her voice)* You know how sometimes you see people weeping uncontrollably in the street? *(She points to herself)* It's very scary.

All eyes are on Holly again.

LEO: You weep in the street?

Holly sighs deeply.

LEO *(Impressed)*: You're kidding?!

HOLLY: In the street, in the post office, at the drug store . . .

LEO: Jeez!

HOLLY: In the garage, the garden and tool shed . . .

LEO: The *tool shed* . . . ?!

HOLLY: I'm driving my poor aunt crazy.

LEO *(With a smile)*: So, *that's* what you do all day!

HOLLY: It's not funny.

LEO: I'm sorry, I'm sorry.

Holly sighs deeply again. A silence. Leo suddenly glowers at everyone staring at them. They all quickly look away.

LEO: Me, when I hit bottom, I go out in my boat.

HOLLY: Ohhhhh . . .

LEO *(Facing towards the ocean)*: It's no big deal, just a beat-up Rhodes 19. I've got an outboard on back, so I can take her through the inlets out to Crane's.

HOLLY: Oh, Crane's Beach is *the* most beautiful—

LEO: Well, you ought to see it when the sun's coming up. I get out about two miles, cut the motor and just drift with the sails down. Sometimes I come in real close to shore. You know how fine the sand is at Crane's. . . . Well, when that early morning sun catches it around 7:30, it's like mica city out there! You've never seen anything so beautiful. . . . I'm thinking about moving down to the Keys where you can be out on the water, year round . . . I'd like to get into the deep sea fishing business, maybe even have a spin-off with tourist cruises . . .

HOLLY: Gosh, that sounds—

LEO: Have you ever been to the Keys?

HOLLY: No, but I've got a cousin who has a place in Tampa.

Pause.

LEO: Oh, Tampa's . . . great.

HOLLY: I've never been there but . . .

A silence.

LEO: I just broke up with the girl I've been living with for three years.

HOLLY: Oh God, I'm sorry.

LEO: Yeah, it's been rough. I mean, we were going to get married and everything.

HOLLY: I'm really sorry.

LEO: She said it just wouldn't work out. Three fucking years and . . .

HOLLY: Oh God . . .

LEO: FOOM!

HOLLY: Maybe she'll change her mind.

LEO: Linda change her mind . . . ? No way!

HOLLY *(Touching his arm)*: I'm really sorry.

A silence.

LEO: Oh Christ, you're so beautiful, I can hardly stand on my feet.

Leo rises and stumbles towards Holly. All eyes are immediately on them again.

HOLLY *(Also rising, backing away, laughing)*: Hey, what are you . . . ?

LEO *(Lunging towards her)*: You just wipe me out.

HOLLY *(Raises her camera to ward him off)*: You're crazy!

LEO *(Starts chasing her)*: The things you say . . . your eyes and body . .

Holly starts snapping Leo's picture as he chases her around his chair and past the other bathers on the beach.

LEO: You've got the most beautiful eyes! They're transparent almost, like looking into cellophane. . . . And your skin . . . it *kills* me! I dream about it. Touching you. Your arms and face . . . sleeping with you . . . *(He practically falls into M.J.'s lap)* Sorry . . .

HOLLY: Long shot of the torso . . . medium shot of the chest. . . . Nice! . . . Tight in on the arms . . . . God, you've got great arms, you know that? I mean, they really are *something* . . .

Pause.

LEO: I shouldn't be saying all this, it's just you've been driving me crazy ever since you got here. . . . It's like I'm on fire all the time. It's even worse when I don't see you—if you knew how many times I've driven past your house at night trying to catch a glimpse of you. . . . Your back, your shoulders, anything . . .

HOLLY: Close in on the face. . . . Great! You've got a wonderful face, fabulous bones . . . okay. Hold still a sec and look at me. . . . That's it. . . . Just tilt your chin up a bit . . . PERFECT! . . . And again . . . NOW WE'RE COOKING . . . GREAT. . . . THAT'S IT . . . WHOA! . . . and again . . . GREAT!

Leo and Holly spin faster and faster around each other. Blackout.

Scene 5

Friday, the end of the day. Faith is flat out on her blanket trying to catch the last rays of the sun. Ariel's still working on her sweater. Both have fallen asleep. Miranda's sitting high up on the sand talking into a soda can telephone system she's rigged up with Winston, who's out of sight at the moment. Holly's squatting several feet away taking pictures of her. Leo rises in his chair, stretches and prepares to leave for the day.

MIRANDA *(Can to her ear)*: WHAT . . . ? I CAN'T HEAR YOU! WINSTON, YOU'LL HAVE TO . . . *(She starts shaking the can)* Wait a minute, the string's come undone. *(She fixes it and yells into the can)* HELLO, CAN YOU HEAR ME . . . ? HELLO? . . . HELLO, ANYONE THERE!

LEO *(Climbs down his chair, drifting near Holly)*: Well, see you all tomorrow. *(Holly's too engrossed to notice him)* Have a pleasant evening.

A silence. Leo moves a bit closer to Holly.

HOLLY *(Feeling Leo's presence, rises blushing)*: Oh, I didn't . . .

HOLLY: . . . hear you. I was just   LEO: I'm sorry, I didn't mean to
um . . . taking a few—   interrupt—

Winston suddenly storms between them holding his can.

WINSTON: JESUS MANDY, WHAT'S YOUR PROBLEM?!

MIRANDA *(Can to her ear)*: Hey, I can hear you, I can hear you. Say
something else.

LEO *(To Holly)*: Well, I guess I ought to be getting along . . .

WINSTON *(Grabbing Miranda's can)*: I TOLD YOU: DON'T HOLD
IT RIGHT UP TO YOUR MOUTH!

HOLLY *(Flustered)*: I was just taking some . . .

WINSTON *(To Miranda)*: You've got to keep it at least three inches away.
Like this.

HOLLY: . . . pictures.

MIRANDA: Well, sor-ee!

LEO *(To Holly)*: Okay. . . . See ya.

They exchange a long look as Winston shouts into Miranda's can.

WINSTON: TESTING. ONE, TWO, THREE, TESTING. GOOD
EVENING AMERICA, THIS IS WINSTON TOOK TELLING
YOU ALL TO GO STUFF IT! *(Shoves the can back in Miranda's
face)* See, it works fine. Now you try.

A silence.

LEO: Well, so long. *(He exits)*

MIRANDA: I don't want to play anymore.

WINSTON: But it works now.

MIRANDA: I said, I'm not playing.

WINSTON: Mandy . . . !

MIRANDA: No!

WINSTON: Come on, it'll be fun.

MIRANDA: I don't want to. Leave me alone. *(She rises and starts running
away from Winston)*

HOLLY: Miranda!

WINSTON *(Chasing her)*: Mandy . . . !

MIRANDA: I'm not playing!

WINSTON: You penis!

MIRANDA: Faggot! *(She suddenly steps on something and drops to the sand,
howling)* OW, OW, OW . . . I STEPPED ON SOMETHING!

HOLLY *(Running toward her)*: Oh Mandy . . . !

FAITH *(Waking with a start)*: What happened, what happened?

HOLLY: I'm coming, I'm coming.

ARIEL *(Sitting bolt upright)*: Who got hurt?

MIRANDA *(Starts to cry)*: I stepped on something, I stepped on something. Ow, ow, ow . . .

FAITH *(Rushing over to her)*: Oh honey . . .

WINSTON *(Trying to crowd in)*: Let me see, let me see!

ARIEL *(Trying to pull him away)*: Back off, Winston, you've already done enough.

WINSTON: What did I do? What did I do?

FAITH: Let Mommy look.

MIRANDA: Ow, ow, ow . . .

HOLLY: It looks like a piece of glass . . .

FAITH: Is the lifeguard still here?

HOLLY: Let me see if I can catch him. *(She runs off after Leo)*

FAITH: HURRY!

ARIEL: What happened?

FAITH *(On the verge of tears)*: She stepped on some broken glass.

MIRANDA: Ow, ow, it hurts, it hurts . . .

WINSTON *(Trying to sneak a look)*: Where is it? I don't see anything.

MIRANDA: Mommy, it hurts.

FAITH: Oh baby . . . HOW IN HELL DID BROKEN GLASS GET ON OUR BEACH?

MIRANDA: Do something.

ARIEL: You aren't safe anywhere these days.

FAITH *(Rocking Miranda)*: We're trying to get the lifeguard.

ARIEL: A friend of mine was at a neighbor's Fourth of July party in Ipswich and found a razor blade in their chili, I mean—

Leo and Holly come running back. Leo's dressed in civilian clothes for the first time—jeans and a tee shirt. He carries a serious-looking first-aid kit.

FAITH: Here they are!

HOLLY: I caught him just as he was about to leave.

MIRANDA *(Starts to howl)*: Ow, ow, it's going to hurt. It's going to hurt . . .

LEO *(Sinking down next to Miranda)*: Hey, hey, where's my brave girl?

HOLLY *(To Faith)*: How is she?

LEO *(To Miranda)*: Now tell me what happened.

MIRANDA: I was running away from Winston and —

WINSTON: Don't look at *me*; it wasn't *my* fault!

ARIEL: One of these days . . .

WINSTON: Well, it wasn't.

LEO *(To Miranda)*: Okay, you were running and . . .

MIRANDA *(Suddenly overcome)*: I STEPPED ON SOMETHING . . .

FAITH: It looks like a piece of glass.

WINSTON: Big deal, you can't even see it.

ARIEL *(Threatening)*: Winston . . . !

LEO: Okay, honey, just let me look, I'm not going to touch, I promise.

MIRANDA *(Backs away, terrified)*: No, no, no . . .

FAITH *(Trying to hold her still)*: Come on, he just wants to look.

MIRANDA: NO, NO, NO . . .

LEO *(Sneaking a glance)*: Oh, this is nothing.

FAITH: See, what did we tell you?

LEO: It's just a scratch.

WINSTON: Baby!

ARIEL: Can it, Winston. . . . Just . . . CAN IT!

A silence.

LEO *(Opening his first-aid kit)*: All I'm going to do is spray on a little medicine to take the sting away, okay? *(No response)* Okay? . . . See, here's the medicine. We just take the top off and . . .

Leo sprays the medicine into the air. Miranda starts to whimper.

WINSTON: What a baby!

ARIEL *(Grabs Winston and starts shaking him, furious)*: WINSTON, I'VE HAD IT UP TO HERE WITH YOU! THIS IS THE LAST TIME I'M BRINGING YOU DOWN HERE! WINSTON . . . DO YOU HEAR ME . . . ?!

LEO *(Trying to restrain Ariel)*: Hey, hey, take it easy . . .

ARIEL: GET. YOUR. HANDS. OFF. OF. ME!

Leo quickly releases Ariel.

ARIEL *(Whirling around to face Leo)*: JUST WHO DO YOU THINK YOU ARE . . . ?!

An awful silence.

ARIEL: Thank you. That's more like it.

Pause.

HOLLY *(Laughs nervously)*: Well . . .

LEO *(Circling the spray can around Miranda like a dive bomber)*: Nyyyyyyrrrrr . . . nyyyrrrrr. It's a bird, it's a plane . . . it's . . . MEDICINE MAN! *(Miranda starts to laugh)* Here he comes, faster than the speed of light with his trusty spray can. . . . Nyyyyyyrrrrrrr . . . nyyyyyyyrrrrrrrrr . . .

Ariel goes away from the group to sulk.

LEO *(Spraying Miranda's foot)*: Take that and that and that! DIE, YOU EVIL THING . . . ! Nyyyyyyr, dat, dat, dat, dat, DIE! Come on, help me. We need . . . MEDICINE GIRL for this . . . *(He hands Miranda the can)* QUICK, WE DON'T HAVE A MOMENT TO LOSE! ZAP THAT INFECTION BEFORE IT SPREADS!

Miranda starts spraying her foot.

FAITH: Yay, Medicine Girl!
HOLLY: It's Medicine Girl to the rescue!
LEO *(Grabbing Miranda's foot)*: Now let's move in for the kill before that evil infection has a chance to retaliate . . . *(Cackling in a sinister voice)* Think you can outsmart us . . . ? You toad, you varmint, you lowdown piece of crud! Well, Buster, you've got another think coming! *(He sneaks out a pair of tweezers and pulls the sliver out of Miranda's foot)* GOTCHA, RIGHT IN THE GIZ-ZARD!

A thin jet of blood spurts from the wound.

MIRANDA: Ow, ow . . . *Mommy!*
FAITH: Blood . . . !
HOLLY: I can't look!
WINSTON: GROSS!

Miranda whimpers softly.

FAITH *(Hugging Miranda)*: He got it out, he got it out, honey!
LEO *(Gently wiping off the blood and putting away the first-aid equipment)*: Let's get you cleaned up here and put this stuff away. You never know when you might need it again. You're some brave little girl, you know that?

Leo scoops Miranda up in his arms. She buries her head against his shoulder.

FAITH: Awwwwww . . .
HOLLY: Ohhhh, I can't breathe.

Pause.

FAITH *(To Leo)*: I don't know how to thank you.
LEO: Let me carry her out to your car for you.
FAITH: We would have been lost without you.
LEO: Come on, why do you think I'm here?

Leo starts walking off the beach carrying Miranda, then pauses for Faith, who's picking up their gear.

ARIEL: You go ahead, we'll get everything.
FAITH: Oh, thanks a lot.

Faith joins Leo and Miranda. Leo places his hand on the small of Faith's back and guides her off the beach as Holly watches, undone. A silence.

ARIEL: All right Winston, come on and help me pick up this stuff.
WINSTON *(Helping her)*: It wasn't my fault, honest.
ARIEL: Right, right . . .
WINSTON: But it wasn't.
ARIEL *(Getting weepy)*: I just don't know anymore.
WINSTON: Come on, Mom, lighten up.

Ariel struggles to control herself.

WINSTON: She's okay.

A silence. Winston keeps gathering up their things, then walks over to Ariel.

WINSTON: Hello?
ARIEL: You're right. She's okay. Faith's okay. You're okay . . . and even I'm okay. . . . More or less.
WINSTON: More.
ARIEL: Yeah?
WINSTON *(Putting an arm around her)*: Yeah, would I lie . . . ?
ARIEL *(With a sigh)*: Where would I be without you?
WINSTON *(Exasperated)*: Mom . . . !
ARIEL: Sorry, it was a stupid question. Well, you know me . . .

Pause.

ARIEL: . . . born with a silver foot   WINSTON: . . . born with a silver
in my mouth.   foot in your mouth.

Ariel and Winston exit. A silence. Holly sits alone on the beach, deeply affected by Leo's gallantry. He returns and walks over to her. A silence.

LEO: Well, that was quite a . . . *(He moves to sit next to Holly)* May I . . . ?
HOLLY: Sure.

They sit side by side. The sun begins to set, giving the sky a rosy glow.

LEO: Listen, about what happened the other day, I'm . . .
HOLLY: Hey, no problem.
LEO: . . . really sorry. I don't know what—
HOLLY: It's okay.

A silence.

LEO: I usually don't come on like that.
HOLLY: It's okay.
LEO: If you've been with somebody a long time, you forget how to . . . .
You know, three years is a—
HOLLY *(Putting her hand on his arm)*: You were really wonderful just
now.
LEO: Come on.
HOLLY: No, you were.

A silence.

HOLLY: The way you lifted her up in your arms . . .

Leo moves to kiss her.

HOLLY *(Edging away)*: Leo, no.
LEO *(Tries again)*: Holly . . .
HOLLY: I can't . . . *(She starts to cry)*
LEO *(Putting his arm around her)*: Holly . . .
HOLLY: Oh boy, here we go again . . .
LEO: What's wrong?
HOLLY: Once I get started I . . .
LEO: Hey, hey . . .
HOLLY: I'm sorry, I'm sorry, I didn't mean to. . . . Oh God! . . . See,
I'm just recovering from something myself. It's so . . . DUMB! I
mean, you lived with someone for three years. . . . Talk about
setting yourself up . . . ! He just owns the most important
photography gallery in the city, that's all. You know, power and
promises . . . beautiful women falling all over him . . . the whole
charismatic thing . . . sweeping into rooms and making everyone's
heart stop.
LEO: Ah, yes, there's nothing like the good old charismatic thing.
HOLLY: The sexy accent and swimming eyes . . . kissing you on either
cheek . . .

LEO: The good old charismatic-kissing-you-on-either-cheek thing.

HOLLY: Lowering his voice and swearing allegiance to only you.

LEO: The good old charismatic-kissing-you-on-either-cheek-swearing-allegiance-to-only-you thing.

HOLLY: Tying yourself in knots, trying to impress him all the time. I mean, who are we trying to kid . . . ? What if the man were a chef or a jockey instead . . . ? But of course he isn't. So round and round I go, trying not to be crazy, but then he walks into the room and . . . *(She starts weeping again)* I'm sorry, I'm sorry.

LEO: Yeah, well, what can you do . . . ? It's like with me and Linda. She keeps saying I'm too much for her, but instead of backing off, I just get crazier.

HOLLY: I know, I know.

LEO: It's a vicious circle.

HOLLY: Tell me about it.

LEO: You try and control yourself . . .

HOLLY: Forget it.

LEO: You try not to get upset.

HOLLY: Please!

LEO: You say, just wait till next time . . .

HOLLY: I know.

Leo sighs deeply. Holly sighs deeply. A silence.

HOLLY *(Stretching out on the sand)*: God, I love this beach.

LEO: Yeah . . .

HOLLY: It's so comforting to think it's always been here.

LEO: Mmmmm . . .

HOLLY: Before the Pilgrims . . . before Christopher Columbus . . . before the Indians even.

LEO: Yeah . . .

HOLLY: It's funny, you never picture Indians being at the beach, but they must have been. Can't you just see it . . . ? Teepee cabanas dotting the sand . . . braves surfboarding on totem poles . . . squaws sunning themselves on Navajo blankets . . .

Leo starts drizzling sand over her legs.

HOLLY: And before them, cavemen and saber-tooth tigers . . . three-toed horses tiptoeing across the sand like little pigs . . . *(She makes little rooting noises and laughs)* Ohh, that feels good. . . . You know what I read in a book . . . ? That the island of Atlantis was really inhabited by dolphins.

LEO: Come on . . .

HOLLY: No, it's true. They used to have legs and live on land.

LEO: Sure, sure.

HOLLY: I'm serious. If you dissect a dolphin, you'll find these residual flippers tucked up beneath its stomach. They used to be legs, but when Atlantis sank, the dolphins had to go with it and adapt.

LEO: And if a cat had a square ass, it would shit bricks.

HOLLY: I'm telling you, it's a fact! Dolphins used to walk around just like people. They wore pinstriped suits and carried briefcases!

LEO: Whatever you say . . .

HOLLY: Come on, everyone knows dolphins are more like us than any other species. So, the resemblance has slipped a little, they probably had colonies right here—on this very spot. I can feel it! . . . They were tremendously social, you know. They loved to party.

Leo begins burying her in earnest.

HOLLY: During the mating season, out came the dancing shoes and there'd be this . . . stampede down the Atlantic coast. The men, or *bulls,* I guess you'd call them, wearing seaweed tuxedos with mother-of-pearl studs, and the cows draping themselves with garlands of periwinkle and abalone. . . . Don't you love it how they always call male sea animals . . . *bulls*?! "Hey, I caught me a great *bull* walrus today!" . . . "Whoa, look at that *bull* manatee go!" . . . *(She starts laughing, breathless from the weight of the sand)* Oh God, I can just see it! . . . Wall-to-wall dolphins boogying from Miami clear up to Canada. . . . This pulsing silver tide for as far as the eye can see. . . . The surf creeping higher and higher, packing them in . . . lovesick couples sinking down to the ground . . . flippers arching, backs yielding, avalanches of seaweed and sand starting to roll. . . . Boy, do I feel weird . . . *(Laughing and giddy)* I'm so light-handed all of a sudden. I mean, *headed.* Lights in the head. Get it? *Headlights!* Boy, I really do feel strange . . .

Leo, finished with his handiwork, stands over her and sings a wavering note of triumph.

HOLLY *(Tries to rise)*: Hey, what's . . . ?

LEO *(Dancing around her)*: I've got you now.

HOLLY: I CAN'T MOVE!

LEO *(Circling her, rubbing his hands like a villain)*: You're mine, all mine!

HOLLY *(Struggling to get out)*: LEO, WHAT HAVE YOU DONE TO ME?

LEO *(Laughing tenderly)*: I wish you could see yourself.

HOLLY: It's not funny! Get me out of here!

LEO *(Starts to leave)*: Well, so long. Don't take any wooden nickels.

HOLLY: HEY, WHERE ARE YOU GOING? I'LL BE EATEN ALIVE BY SEA GULLS AND HORSESHOE CRABS!

Leo exits.

HOLLY *(Her voice getting weaker and weaker)*: HELP. . . . Help. . . . Hellllp . . . *(A silence; then in a sexy singsong)* LEO . . . ? Oh Leo . . . ?

LEO *(Popping back into view and settling beside her)*: You called?

HOLLY: You're a real son of a bitch, you know that?

LEO: Actually, I'm a very sweet guy.

HOLLY: Sure, sure.

LEO: No, that's my problem. I just come on a little strong. But underneath . . .

HOLLY: You're crazy, you know that?

LEO: I'm a nice guy.

A silence.

LEO: So, how're you doing?

HOLLY: I've got an itch on my nose.

LEO *(Scratches it)*: How's that?

HOLLY: Thank you.

LEO: Anytime, anytime.

HOLLY: Actually, you *are* a sweet guy, you just have a peculiar way of . . .

LEO: Holly, I'm falling in love with you. I don't know what to do.

Silence.

LEO: I don't know, I can't get my signals straight. I keep thinking you feel the same way. I have these dreams and you're always beckoning to me, opening your arms and smiling. I'm so confused all the time.

HOLLY: Leo, don't . . .

LEO: No, I've got to say it. Last night you began undressing me and whispering all these things . . .

HOLLY *(Losing more and more ground)*: Please . . .

LEO: Like all that shit just now about dolphins making it on the beach. I had the feeling something else was going on. You know what I mean . . . ? That you were telling me you wanted me—all that crap about arching backs and waving flippers. I mean, Jesus Christ . . .

HOLLY: Leo, no . . .

LEO: So, admit it.

HOLLY: Don't . . .

LEO: Just admit it, for Christsakes!

Holly sighs long and deeply.

LEO: Come on, what are you afraid of . . . ?

HOLLY: I'm just so . . .

LEO: I can't take this anymore. I mean, are you playing with me or what?

HOLLY: No, no, I'm . . .

LEO: So then I'm right.

HOLLY: Oh God . . .

LEO: You do . . . you know . . .

HOLLY *(In a whisper, shutting her eyes)*: Oh yes, yes. If you knew how much.

LEO *(Kneeling down next to her)*: Holly, Holly . . .

HOLLY: Leo!

Leo eases down over Holly, covering her face with kisses.

LEO: Oh baby!

Waves crash in the distance as the curtain quickly falls.

ACT TWO

Scene 1

Dawn, the next day. A foghorn moans in the distance. Holly sits on her blanket midst a tangle of castoff clothing from the night before. She's wearing Leo's lifeguard sweatshirt. He stands over her, back in his trunks. She's clinging to his leg.

HOLLY: Don't go . . . don't.

LEO: Come on, come with me.

HOLLY: But it's the middle of the night.

LEO: No it isn't, look at the sky.

HOLLY: It's the middle of the night and you want to go running.

LEO: This is the best time. Where's your spirit of adventure?

HOLLY: You're really nuts, you know that!

LEO *(Trying to pull her up)*: Come on, you'll love it.

HOLLY *(Resisting)*: Leo . . . !

LEO: You don't know what you're missing.

Leo kisses the top of Holly's head and jogs off down the shore. Holly gazes after him, then flops back onto the blanket. Faith steps onto the beach behind her and stops, losing herself in the view. Then recognizing Holly, Faith silently approaches her and touches her shoulder.

FAITH: *Holly,* what are you . . . ?

Holly sits up and screams, hand over her heart. Faith also screams.

FAITH: I'm sorry.

HOLLY: Oh God . . . !

FAITH: I didn't mean to sneak up on you.

HOLLY: *Faith* . . . !

FAITH: Are you all right?

HOLLY *(Laughing)*: I haven't had a scare like that for—

FAITH: I'm really sorry.

A silence.

FAITH: So, what are *you* doing down here . . . ?

HOLLY: Well, what brings *you* down here in the middle of the . . .

They both laugh.

FAITH: I couldn't sleep. I don't know, the foghorn gets me all keyed up.

HOLLY: Me too, me too.

FAITH: It's so plaintive. Like a lost child.

HOLLY: I know, I know.

FAITH: I just can't sleep when it's on, especially these days. I drive poor Charlie crazy, so rather than keep him up all night, I just—

HOLLY: How *is* Charlie? I haven't seen him in ages.

FAITH: He's fine.

HOLLY: Still a banker in Boston?

FAITH: Still a banker in Boston.

Silence.

HOLLY *(Starts moaning with the foghorn)*: Where is the foghorn, anyway?

FAITH: You know, I've never really known.

HOLLY: You think it's in Gloucester?

FAITH: I just don't—

HOLLY: It's probably somewhere off Little Misery. *(She glances down the shoreline and, seeing Leo in the distance, jumps)*

FAITH: Are you okay?

HOLLY: Fine, fine . . .

FAITH *(Noticing Holly's blanket)*: Hey, I'm not interrupting something, am I?

HOLLY *(Trying to hide Leo's clothes under the blanket)*: No, no, I was just . . . God, where does all this stuff come from? I don't believe all the shit I—

FAITH *(Flopping next to her on the blanket)*: What *is* it about the beach . . . ?

HOLLY: You'd think I was a bag lady or something . . . *(Suddenly noticing she's wearing Leo's sweatshirt, she whips it off and starts burying it in the sand)* I mean, this is ridiculous. All I want to do is take a few pictures of the sun coming up and . . .

FAITH: Did you ever notice how it's always women at the beach . . . ? Women sunbathing, women teaching the kids how to swim, women strolling along the shore . . . ? *Holly, what are you doing?*

HOLLY *(Frantically trying to make the sweatshirt disappear)*: Who me . . . ?

FAITH: Yes, you.

HOLLY: I'm not doing anything.

FAITH: You're trying to bury the lifeguard's sweatshirt.

HOLLY *(Laughing)*: I am?

FAITH *(Snatches the sweatshirt out of her hands and holds it up)*: Yes, you most certainly are.

HOLLY: Well, well, what do you know . . .

FAITH: Did you spend the night down here with him?

HOLLY (*Pulling out her camera*): See, the great thing about taking pictures at this time of day is—everything's *reversed*. The water's light and the sand and sky are dark, so your prints look like negatives.

FAITH: Holly . . . ?

HOLLY: I'm often tempted not to develop them but just mount them as they are . . .

FAITH: Yoo-hoo . . . ?

HOLLY: Boom! There's this classic beach scene with the sand and sky much lighter than the water . . . I mean, *darker*!

FAITH: Come on, I've seen how you've been eyeing each other.

HOLLY: Wait a minute, is that right . . . ?

FAITH: I don't believe it.

HOLLY: I'm all confused.

FAITH: You and the lifeguard . . .

HOLLY: That's the thing about the beach, it just—

Leo suddenly comes jogging into view, golden and windblown. He beckons to Holly.

LEO: Hey, Holl . . .

HOLLY (*Gasps and clutches onto Faith's arm*): Oh God . . . !

FAITH: He really *is* something!

LEO (*Running in place*): Come on, run with me. It's exhilarating.

FAITH: I'd better get out of here.

HOLLY (*Clutching onto her*): No, no, don't go.

FAITH (*Trying to pull away*): Holly . . . ?!

HOLLY (*Laughing like a schoolgirl*): Don't leave me.

FAITH (*Struggling to free herself, also starts laughing*): Ow . . . ! What are you . . . ?

LEO: Hey, Holl, come on . . .

FAITH: Go on, he's calling you.

HOLLY (*Holding on for dear life*): Oh God!

FAITH (*Laughing harder, tries to loosen Holly's grip*): Holly, what's wrong with you?

HOLLY: HELLLLP!

FAITH (*Laughing more and more, out of control*): Stop it!

HOLLY (*Clinging tighter*): He's just so . . . beautiful! Whenever he comes near me, I just . . . I don't know.

FAITH: Holly, stop it, I'm going to wet my pants!

HOLLY: Have you ever felt you were standing on the edge of a very high precipice?

They collapse onto the sand with laughter, Faith waving her arms helplessly.

LEO: Hey, you two, what's going on . . . ? *(He approaches them, holding out his hand to Holly)* Come on, run with me.

FAITH *(Trying to rise)*: Go on, go on . . . !

HOLLY *(Awash with laughter)*: Save me . . . save me!

FAITH *(To Leo)*: I don't believe this! Holly, get a grip on yourself!

Leo grabs Holly's hand and pulls her towards him in a swooning arc. Blackout.

Scene 2

Several hours later. The sun is up, but it's still early. Holly and Leo are the only ones on the beach. They sit side by side on his chair, wrapped in her blanket. They're laughing.

HOLLY: Stop, stop . . .

LEO: Wait, it gets better.

HOLLY: You're making the whole thing up.

LEO: Listen, when I want someone, I go after them . . . Juanita Wijojac—Christ, I haven't thought about her in years.

HOLLY: Leo . . . !

LEO: I was thirteen and she was eleven. Juanita Wijojac was the most exotic girl I'd ever seen. It wasn't just her beauty, which was phenomenal—her mother was Portuguese and her father was Hungarian or something, so she had all this hair—chalk white skin and clouds of black hair . . .

HOLLY: And she was a child prodigy . . . ?

LEO: Incredible.

HOLLY: She played the organ . . . ?

LEO: In-fucking-credible!

HOLLY: And she had an extra finger on each hand . . . ?

LEO: Several. That was her ace in the hole. I mean, when she got going on that thing, she sounded like a whole goddamned orchestra!

HOLLY: And just how *many* extra fingers did she . . . ?

LEO: It was hard to tell. They were so perfectly shaped, you couldn't . . . *(Holly groans)* No, no, you really didn't notice unless you started counting. *(Holly groans louder)* All the guys in school were in love with her. We used to fantasize: if she has extra fingers, what *else* does she have tucked out of view. . . ?

HOLLY: Leo, I don't believe one word of this! *(She takes a fresh Milky Way out of her bag and starts eating it)*

LEO: We couldn't figure out what she was doing in Essex. She must have been studying with some famous organist in the area. She didn't stay long. Only a year, but what a year. . . ! I used to climb the elm tree next to the First Congregational Church where she practiced in the evening and watch her. I lived in that fucking tree! On a clear night, there were as many as forty guys up there with binoculars. But no one was as loyal as me. . . . It's funny, I don't remember the music at all, and she was really good. I mean, when she cut loose with those preludes and fugues, she practically shook the stained glass right off the walls—those lambs and apostles jitterbugged like nothing you ever saw. . . . No, it was all her—the way she hunched over the keys, how her hair fell across her face, and of course all those flying fingers. Sometimes I counted as many as eight on a hand . . . *(Holly shudders)* Yeah, after a couple of hours up in that tree, the old imagination went nuts. I saw extra eyes, extra mouths. . . . Finally, I couldn't take it anymore, I had to do something. I'll never forget it. . . . One night I was up in my tree as usual, when all of a sudden I found myself marching right up into the organ loft and bam—there I was, face to face with her. She was so flushed and beautiful, I could hardly keep my balance. . . . I reached out to steady myself and set off this blizzard of sheet music. She lets out this piercing scream as if she's just met up with Jack the Ripper, I mean we are talking disaster city here . . . and then I notice some of her fingers kind of . . . disappearing down into her palm . . . *(Holly shudders)* and she's wriggling around on the bench as if she's trying to hide something.

HOLLY: Her extra leg, no doubt.

LEO: It was awful. I immediately regretted having come, but seeing her so flustered trying to reel everything in, just heightened my desire . . .

HOLLY: Leo, this is the most disgusting . . .

LEO: I threw myself at her feet.

HOLLY: Count 'em folks—one, two, three, four . . .

LEO: It's not funny. I didn't know what else to do. I began telling her that I loved her, that I'd always love her, that I wanted to marry her and be with her forever. But she didn't seem to understand, so I grabbed her.

HOLLY: Oh no.

LEO: I couldn't help it, she suddenly seemed so fragile. I wanted to protect her. By this time, she was screaming in every foreign language you've ever heard. The louder she screamed, the tighter I held on to her. It was a nightmare. Her heart suddenly started going crazy. It raced from her chest, to her side, down her legs, back up to her neck. I tried to steady it with my hands, but it was all over the place!

HOLLY: Leo!

LEO: Finally, some rector or deacon showed up and pulled us apart. It was shortly after that, that her family moved away. I thought I'd never recover. I mooned around for almost two years. I'll tell you one thing—she could have given one hell of a backrub.

HOLLY *(Kissing him)*: Oh, Leo.

LEO *(Pulling her close)*: Stay an extra week.

HOLLY: I can't!

LEO: Come on, run away with me. We'll take off in my boat . . .

HOLLY: But I have things to do.

LEO: Have you ever sailed up the coast of Maine? . . . It's unbelievable! The islands off Mount Desert . . .

HOLLY: I'm about to start a new project.

LEO: What, taking more nude pictures of yourself?

HOLLY *(Cuffing him)*: Leo!

LEO: It's a shame to waste it all on just a camera.

HOLLY: I don't happen to think working with a camera is a—

LEO: I'm sorry, I'm sorry, I didn't mean it that way. I was trying to say—

HOLLY: Yeah, I know what you were trying to say.

LEO: Come on, take off with me. We'll sail up Penobscot Bay like a couple of early French settlers—"Passez-moi zee caviar if you please . . . pourez-moi zee champagne . . ."

HOLLY: Some of us have work to do.

LEO: "Catch zee tiny, how you call them . . . ? *shreemp* in your hands!"

HOLLY: Important work!

LEO *(Grabbing her)*: "Fuck zee work, and sail with me back to zee beginning of time. I weel show you schools of singing whales and . . ."

HOLLY: All right, all right, I'll come!

LEO: You weel . . . ? I mean, you will?!

HOLLY: Don't ask me why. It's crazy . . . absolutely . . .

LEO *(Suddenly flings the blanket over their heads and lunges for her)*: SON OF A BITCH, YOU'LL COME WITH ME . . . YOU'LL REALLY DO IT . . . HOLY SHIT!

HOLLY: Leo, what are you . . . ? Oh my God, you can't take off your clothes up here. Leo . . . STOP IT . . . oh my God . . .

LEO: SHE SAID SHE'D COME . . . SHE'S GOING TO COME WITH ME . . . I DON'T BELIEVE IT. I JUST DON'T BELIEVE IT!

As Holly and Leo lurch around underneath the blanket laughing and trying to get comfortable, M.J. and Hamilton Adams suddenly appear. They creep towards the draped chair, mystified.

M.J. *(Gazing up at it)*: Morning. Is everything all right up there?

HAMILTON: Lovely day out, lovely day. Not a cloud in the sky.

HOLLY *(Peeking out from under the blanket)*: Oh my God, the Adams . . .

LEO *(Popping up from the blanket)*: Well, well, what do you know. . . ? It's the Adams! Morning Dr. Adams, Mrs. Adams . . . *(He quickly pulls himself together)*

HOLLY: I don't believe this. I just don't . . . *(She slowly starts to make her way down the ladder, still covered with the blanket)*

HAMILTON: Well, how's the water today? It looks a bit on the chilly side. . . . Well, that was some fog that rolled in last night . . .	M.J.: WHAT A BEAUTIFUL DAY! We almost didn't come because of all the fog this morning. You couldn't see your hand in front of your face.

Holly is still sneaking down the ladder.

M.J.: I told Hammy I thought we should skip it today. I can't stand the beach when it's damp and foggy. The color goes out of everything.

HOLLY *(Trying to pass by Hamilton)*: Excuse me . . . *(She gets into a dreadful hesitation dance trying to get past the Adamses)*

M.J.: And that wretched foghorn last night . . . ! I couldn't sleep a wink! *(To Holly)* Sorry . . .

Holly waddles down the beach and plops onto the sand like a deflated jellyfish.

M.J.: I hate the sound of the foghorn, it's so mournful. It makes me want to put a bullet through my head!

HAMILTON: Now, now . . .

M.J.: Well, it does. It's so damned New England! *(Pause; to Hamilton, referring to Holly)* Who was that?

HAMILTON: Yes, I was just about to ask the same thing.

LEO: Just one of the kids.

A pause.

M.J.: Ahhhh, smell that air!

HAMILTON: Nothing like it, nothing like it.

M.J.: Well, shall we dance?

HAMILTON: After you, Madame.

The Adamses head to their spot and start setting up their gear.

LEO *(Clambers down his chair)*: Here, let me give you a hand.

HAMILTON: That's not necessary.

M.J.: We can manage.

LEO *(Taking the umbrella from them)*: Please, it's the least I can do. *(He sets it up with a flick of the wrist)* There you go.

M.J.: Why, thank you very much.

LEO: My pleasure. *(He walks to the middle of the beach and flings his arms open)* What a day, what a day . . . !

Leo starts doing torso- and arm-stretching exercises. Andre Sor suddenly steps onto the beach behind him. He's dressed in a snazzy three-piece suit and knockout Italian shoes. He surveys the horizon, looking for someone. Leo finishes his exercises and casually walks over to Holly. He peels aside her blanket and offers her his hand. She takes it and he lifts her to her feet. They stand close together, laughing. The moment Holly's uncovered, Andre starts walking towards her. Unfazed by her involvement with Leo, Andre breaks in on them, taking her arm.

ANDRE: Holly . . .

HOLLY *(Astonished)*: ANDRE!

Andre kisses Holly on one cheek.

HOLLY: Andre?!

He kisses her on the other one.

HOLLY: What are you . . . ?

He clasps her in a bear hug.

HOLLY *(Starts laughing, exhilarated)*: I don't believe it.

ANDRE: I took the weekend off.

HOLLY: How did you ever . . . ?

ANDRE *(Covering her face with kisses)*: Holly, Holly . . .

HOLLY *(Laughing and crying)*: . . . *find* me . . . ?!

ANDRE: You must never leave me like that again.

HOLLY *(Returning his kisses)*: I've been so unhappy . . .

ANDRE: Mon ange . . .

HOLLY *(Suddenly aware of Leo, turns and faces him, stricken)*: Oh my God, Leo . . . I . . .

Leo drops his eyes and turns his back to her.

ANDRE *(Holds her tighter, whispering into her ear)*: Viens-toi petite. . . .
Tu me rends fou!

Blackout.

Scene 3

*Sunday, noon. It's murderously hot. The beach and ocean are bleached
white. The air doesn't move. Jellyfish bodies spangle the shore like mucous
frisbees. During the evening a beached and bloodied whale was washed
ashore. Its huge decomposing body dominates the waterfront. Faith,
Ariel, Miranda, Winston and Leo are all standing around it. Ariel
makes a shuddering sound.*

FAITH: I can't look.
WINSTON: Far out.
LEO *(Pulling Winston back)*: Come on, not too close.

Ariel shudders again.

MIRANDA *(Jumping away)*: It's moving, it's moving!
FAITH: Where did it come from?
ARIEL: Ohhh, the smell . . . !
LEO: It looks like a sperm whale.
MIRANDA: EEEEEEEWWW, EEEEEEEEEEWWWWWWWWWW!
ARIEL: You never think about the smell . . .
WINSTON *(Approaching the whale)*: HEY, LET'S TAKE SOME OF ITS
TEETH!
LEO *(Pulling Winston back)*: I said: not too close!
WINSTON: Eben Bliss has a whole bowl of barracuda teeth. They're so
neat . . .
LEO: I've called the coast guard. They'll be by sometime this afternoon
to drag it back out to sea.
FAITH: I've heard of whales getting lost and beaching themselves, I just
never thought it could happen here.
LEO: I'd say this one had a run-in with a few sharks first.
WINSTON *(Breaks away and starts scooping handfuls of gunk off the whale's
body)*: Hey, *blubber!* Blub, blub, blub . . .

Leo, Ariel and Miranda react simultaneously.

LEO *(Jumping on Winston)*: HEY, HEY, HEY . . .
ARIEL *(Dragging Winston back)*: DON'T TOUCH, YOU COULD
GET A DISEASE!

MIRANDA: EEEWWWWW . . . EEEWWWWW!

ARIEL: It's full of contagion. You could catch something really horrendous!

FAITH: Come on kids, leave it alone.

MIRANDA *(Starts dancing around the whale)*: The Black Plague or Leprosy. . . . EEEEEWWWWWW, WINSTON COULD GET LEPROSY!

WINSTON *(Joins in, acting out the diseases)*: Or Sleeping Sickness . . . or Malaria . . .

MIRANDA: The Bubonic Plague . . .

WINSTON: St. Vitas Dance . . .

MIRANDA: Whooping Cough . . . whoop, whoop, whoop . . .

WINSTON: Dropsy!

MIRANDA: Rabies . . . !

WINSTON: Oh, *Rabies*! Rabies is great!

Winston scoops sand onto his face so it looks like he's foaming at the mouth. Miranda follows suit. They become more and more animalistic as they drop down on all fours and race around the body, barking like dogs. Faith and Ariel laugh uneasily, which just eggs them on.

FAITH: Kids, come on . . .

ARIEL *(Laughing)*: It's not funny.

LEO: Knock it off!

Winston barks louder and louder and wags his behind. In a fit of inspiration, he lifts his leg and feigns peeing on the whale.

ARIEL: *(Trying to hide her mirth)*: Winston . . . !

FAITH: Kids . . . !

LEO: Come on guys, show a little respect for once.

Miranda barks louder and louder.

ARIEL: Winston, calm down!

FAITH: Miranda, what are you doing?

Winston races over to Leo and nuzzles against his leg, yelping and wagging his behind. Miranda follows.

LEO: I said: KNOCK IT OFF!

Winston and Miranda pay no attention and mime peeing on Leo's leg in a delirium of laughing and barking.

ARIEL *(Also laughing)*: HONEY . . . PLEASE?!

FAITH *(Trying to control herself)*: KIDS . . . CUT IT OUT . . . !

LEO *(Roughly pulling the kids to their feet and sitting them down in front of him)*: JESUS CHRIST, WHAT'S WRONG WITH YOU PEO-PLE . . . ?! SOME POOR ANIMAL GETS RIPPED APART BY SHARKS AND IT'S ALL JUST A BIG JOKE TO YOU . . . ! Did you ever stop to think how it might have *felt* . . . ?! To be swimming along minding your own business—what a day, what a day, oh baby, this is the life—and then BLAM . . . you're blindsided out of nowhere . . . *(Kneeling down next to them)* You think everything's just out there for your own private amusement. Well, you don't have a clue about real life. Not. One. Fucking. Clue!

Blackout.

Scene 4

Monday, Leo's day off, mid-afternoon. It's drizzling and overcast. The foghorn is on. Leo's sign, LIFEGUARD OFF DUTY, SWIM AT YOUR OWN RISK, bangs forlornly against his chair. The whale is gone. Approaching voices are heard.

HOLLY *(Strolling into view with Andre)*: Pierro came to the show with Dina?

ANDRE: They've been seeing each other for quite some time now.

HOLLY: I don't believe it!

ANDRE: She's been invited to show at the Modern, you know.

HOLLY: The *Modern* . . . ?!

ANDRE: Her new stuff is spectacular. I hope to lure her into my next group show. Blossom, Io and Zinkaloff have already committed.

HOLLY: I had no idea Dina was so . . . . And how were Haskell's reviews?

ANDRE: *Fabulous!*

Holly's barefoot, dressed in her gauzy skirt and sweater—all in white. Andre's wearing his Italian shoes and a chic raincoat. He carries an umbrella.

HOLLY: Well, here we are again . . . the little beach where I spent all my summers as a child. It doesn't have anywhere near the sweep of Crane's where I took you yesterday, but . . . . Are you okay?

ANDRE *(Fussing with one of his shoes)*: So much for these shoes.

HOLLY: Take them off, you'll be much more comfortable without them. *(Stooping down to untie them)* Here, let me . . .

ANDRE *(Pulling Holly back up)*: No, no I'm fine this way . . . please . . .

HOLLY: But you'll be so much more—

ANDRE *(Still fussing with the shoe)*: It's just a little sand . . .

HOLLY *(Bending down again)*: You're sure I can't . . .

ANDRE: I'm fine, I promise you. *(He glances up at Leo's chair)* Here, why don't we sit up here . . . ? *(He starts climbing up)*

HOLLY: NO!

ANDRE: Come on, I've never been up on one of these.

HOLLY: You can't!

ANDRE: What do you mean, I can't? The sign says—

HOLLY: You just *can't*, that's all!

ANDRE *(Climbing the rest of the way up)*: But no one's here.

HOLLY: Andre . . . NO!

ANDRE *(Sits down and opens the umbrella, which he holds directly over his head)*: Oh, this is marvelous . . . ! *(He looks out over the horizon)* I feel like a king!

A silence as Andre freezes into a Magritte-like image.

HOLLY *(Eyes filling with tears)*: Please?

ANDRE: Quick, come up and join me. You can see for miles!

HOLLY: Andre, you can't sit up there!

ANDRE *(Stands, pretending he's a lifeguard)*: What ho, do I hear cries for help?

HOLLY: Get. Down!

ANDRE: Is that a maiden in distress I see out there?

HOLLY: Andre, *please* . . . !

ANDRE: Never fear, I will battle the giant squid to its death!

HOLLY: You can't stay up there!

ANDRE *(Rising)*: All right, all right, if it means so much to you. . . . Just a moment while I close this umbrella. *(He starts making his way down the chair)*

HOLLY: Thank you.

A silence as he walks over to her.

ANDRE *(Kissing the top of her head)*: You're such a child sometimes. I never know what you're going to do next.

A pause.

HOLLY *(Intense)*: You know what I'm thinking of getting into when I get back . . . ? X-rays! The next step beyond nudes—actually piercing through the skin to a whole new landscape of dappled rib cages and iridescent tendons . . .

ANDRE *(Laughing)*: Holly, Holly . . .

HOLLY: No, I've got a friend that works in a lab. He says he can always use an assistant. I mean, can't you see it . . . ? Mounting a whole show of pancreases, gall bladders, large intestines . . . ?

ANDRE *(Affectionate)*: And she's off . . . !

HOLLY: I'd turn the gallery into a kind of spook house with dim fluorescent lighting—hook up tapes of muffled breathing and erratic heartbeats. It would be like entering this night-blooming garden of forbidden delights . . .

ANDRE *(Hugging her)*: What an imagination you have! No one sees the world like you. *(Pause)* It's so good to see you again. . . . You can't imagine what I've been through since you left. Lydia . . . the gallery . . . Haskell's installation . . .

HOLLY: Yes, mounting two thousand polaroids can't be easy.

ANDRE: Two thousand five hundred! And they had to be placed in order, just so. If so much as one print was out of sequence, he exploded and threatened to pull out. This went on every day, eight hours a day for almost a week. That's why I'm looking forward so much to doing your show . . .

HOLLY *(Walking away, stony)*: Sure, sure . . .

ANDRE: Holly, Holly, you know what my scheduling problems are like. . . . I have longstanding commitments. Stephan's new show, Lillewasser's retrospective . . . *(Silence)* Sweetheart, you know how much I love your work. You must be patient. I want to present you in the spring. Timing is so important. And you'll have more work by then. Who knows, maybe even some nudes on this beach that means so much to you. I just want what's best for you, *believe* me!

HOLLY *(Subdued)*: I know, I know.

ANDRE: Holly, Holly, the prospect of driving up here to see you was the only thing that kept me going this week. You can't imagine how ghastly it's been—as bewitching as Lydia may be on a movie screen, she's something else entirely with divorce lawyers.

HOLLY *(Moving away from him)*: Yeah, well . . .

ANDRE: She wants blood. They always want blood.

HOLLY: It must be awful.

ANDRE: There's more. I have to go to Europe again.

HOLLY: Andre, no!

ANDRE: You think I want to go?

HOLLY: NO!

ANDRE: You think I enjoy these separations?

HOLLY: For how long?

ANDRE: Three weeks, maybe more.

HOLLY: *NO . . . !*

ANDRE: There's some new work in Paris and Brussels I've got to see.

HOLLY *(Running away from him)*: No, no, no . . .

ANDRE *(Catching her and wrapping his arms around her)*: Cheri, tenez. . . . Let me try and explain . . .

HOLLY: No!

ANDRE: Please, it's important.

HOLLY *(Struggling)*: Let me go!

ANDRE: Sweetheart . . . !

HOLLY: Andre . . . !

ANDRE: Try to understand . . .

HOLLY *(Suddenly clinging to him)*: Oh Andre, I love you so!

ANDRE: Holly, Holly. . . . Listen to me . . . sweetheart . . . ! *(Holly sighs deeply)* Once upon a time there was a man who was a diamond cutter in Antwerp, but like so many Jews, he was forced to flee his homeland at the outbreak of the war. The Nazis confiscated his entire supply of uncut gems, so all he could bring with him was his talent. I'm talking about my father of course . . . *(Holly nods with recognition)* He settled his family in Brooklyn. Life was hard because the streets were filled with refugees just like him—merchants without their wares, artists without their materials. . . . In the beginning he made his living as a handyman, repairing leaky faucets, upholstering furniture, sharpening scissors. There was rarely enough to eat.

HOLLY: What did he look like? You've never really described him.

ANDRE: My father. . . ? He had beautiful hands, like a cellist. He was slim, medium height with a beard. He always wore a hat. People often said he resembled Sigmund Freud.

HOLLY: No!

ANDRE: Oh yes, he was quite imposing.

HOLLY: And your mother. . . ?

ANDRE: Was very fat.

HOLLY *(Laughing)*: Oh Andre . . .

ANDRE: But with a magnificent singing voice that could charm the birds right out of the sky.

HOLLY: You're so lucky, my mother can't even carry a tune.

ANDRE: Oh yes, she would have had a great career if only the timing had been different.

HOLLY: All my parents can do is play tennis. It's so boring. Every weekend they play mixed doubles with Jack and Gabby Wainwright. Jack was on the Davis Cup team back in—

ANDRE *(With gentle impatience)*: Holly . . .

HOLLY: I'm sorry, I'm sorry . . . I got carried away.

ANDRE *(Affectionately)*: Holly Dancer. . . !

HOLLY: Go on . . . please . . . *please!*

ANDRE: For all our poverty and deprivation, we had two sources of great joy. . . . First, was our Sunday outings to Brooklyn Heights when we'd walk out on the piers to gaze at the view of lower Manhattan. Every Sunday—spring, summer, winter, fall—my father would cry, "Forois zum wunderland!" Which in Yiddish meant, "Come to our enchantment!" . . . and we'd scramble onto the trolley car, my sisters almost trampling me under their shoes. . . . My father knew the skyline by heart. As we stood there; he'd begin his litany—"There, the Woolworth Building, to its left, the Bank of Manhattan, Farmer's Trust, the Cities Service Tower, the Municipal Building . . . !" . . . "Slow down, slow down!" my mother would cry. "They'll never learn anything if you go so fast!" . . . "And over there?" he'd point—"the one with the golden roof shaped like a pyramid?" . . . "THE COURTHOUSE, THE COURTHOUSE!" we'd all clamor, eager to be the first with the right answer . . .

HOLLY: I can just see you jumping up and down shouting louder than everyone else.

Thunder rumbles in the distance and it starts to rain.

ANDRE *(Taking Holly's hand and heading under Leo's chair)*: Come on, let's run under here, it's starting to pour . . . *(Holding her as he leans against one of the frets)* There, isn't this better . . . ? Now, our second joy, yes . . . ? As I said, my father was a diamond cutter. His gems were prized by the most beautiful women of Europe. He was a master. It was his *eye!* He could see the jewel where none existed. As a handyman in this country, he acquired boxes of castoff junk—clock springs, sewing-machine parts, glass doorknobs, old eyeglasses. After a day of haggling in the streets, he'd haul out his boxes of treasures and lose himself in the minutae of small gold springs and moving parts . . .

HOLLY: You have such a lovely voice.

ANDRE: Well, three or four times a year as we were finishing our meager Friday evening Shabbas dinner, he would suddenly announce, "I have something to show you, my children." You see, my father was also an amateur watchmaker. He built fantasy clocks that played tunes instead of telling time—mechanical toys that flew around the room—ticking bifocals . . .

HOLLY: I could listen to you forever.

ANDRE: As our circumstances worsened, his creations became even more fanciful. They reached their height the winter my sister Sophie almost died of pneumonia. Just as she was fluttering back into consciousness, my father whispered, "Ich hab epes eich zu veissen, mein kinder." . . . He reached under the bed and pulled out this crystal sphere about the size of a softball. Inside it was a miniature rendering of our cherished view—the Woolworth Building, the Bank of Manhattan, Farmer's Trust . . . *(Holly gasps)* But what was most astonishing of all was . . . he'd fashioned it as a clock with tiny numbers around the circumference. *(Rotating and miming the movement)* Every hour on the hour, something within the sphere moved. At eight o'clock, the Woolworth Building bent at the middle and doffed its roof. At nine o'clock, one of the little barges suddenly sent off a blast of steam. At ten o'clock, a flock of seagulls wheeled up over the courthouse. . . . As you can imagine, there was no sleeping that night. My father's fancy had not only animated our secret world, it also made it tangible—something we could hold in our hands. For Sophie, it was like being given back her life again. For me, it was a testament to the transforming eye of the artist. I don't have those gifts. *(Pause)* I can only admire. Innocence eludes me. But you—you and my father—you walk with the angels. Think of it—living a life promoting a talent you'll never have, a beauty you'll never be able to create.

HOLLY *(Starts to weep)*: Oh Andre . . .

ANDRE: Non non petite, ne pleur pas. I accepted it a long time ago.

HOLLY: Don't leave again!

ANDRE: You give me great joy.

HOLLY: I can't stand these separations anymore.

ANDRE: Just be patient with me.

HOLLY: Two weeks in Europe, three weeks in South America . . .

ANDRE: We've waited so long . . .

HOLLY: Meetings in Tokyo . . .

ANDRE: Sweetheart . . .

HOLLY: You're not listening to me.

ANDRE: You have such talent, such freshness and beauty . . .

HOLLY: I can't go on like this.

ANDRE: Your skin and eyes . . .

HOLLY: You make me so unhappy.

ANDRE *(Holding out his arms to her)*: Come to me.

HOLLY: I can't go on like this.

ANDRE: Mon coeur, mon ame . . .
HOLLY: I just . . . *can't!*

As they stand frozen in their misery, Leo suddenly appears, walking along the shoreline. He sees them and stops as if hit by lightning. Blackout.

Scene 5

Tuesday, late afternoon. Enormous clouds hang motionless in the sky. Faith and Ariel are shaking out their blankets preparing to leave. Faith's wearing the sweater Ariel's been working on all summer. Winston and Miranda are writing their names in the sand. Leo's up on his chair, staring into space.

FAITH: Okay, kids, time to leave.
ARIEL: Chop, chop, Winston, let's get moving.
MIRANDA: Oh, do we *have* to . . . ?
FAITH: Daddy's coming home early tonight.
MIRANDA: He is . . . ? Oh goody!
FAITH *(Suddenly embraces Ariel)*: I really love this sweater you made me.
ARIEL: Oh, I'm glad. I've been on a tear lately. You should see what I've been working on at home. It started out as a shawl, but is turning into this gigantic . . . now, don't laugh . . . *house!* It's the damndest thing, but that's what it looks like. Winston and I joke around that when we get back to town, we'll actually move into it.
FAITH: Ariel?!
ARIEL: He's been helping me from the start. We haven't had so much fun in years . . . ! The first floor is made out of ragg wool and hemp, the second, out of mohair and angora. . . . It's so soft and spongy we laugh that if he starts jumping on his bed, he'll fly right out through the roof!
FAITH *(Laughing, shaking her head)*: You two . . .

Pause.

ARIEL *(Casually)*: You really saved my life, you know. *(Pause)* Well, only a few more days and summer's over. Labor Day's almost here. School will be starting soon.
FAITH: Don't . . . !
ARIEL *(Patting Faith's stomach)*: Just think, next year at this time . . .
FAITH *(Laughing)*: Oh God . . .

ARIEL: Okay, Winston, let's pack it in.

WINSTON: Wait. . . . Just one more game of tic-tac-toe . . . ? *(He draws a grid on the sand)*

ARIEL *(Affectionately)*: You loon!

WINSTON: Please?

ARIEL: Okay, but it better be quick.

Winston places an X in the middle box. Ariel places an O in the upper left-hand corner. Winston places an X in the upper right-hand corner. Ariel places an O directly beneath her first one. Winston puts an X in the bottom left-hand corner, then draws a line through them.

WINSTON: I won, I won!

ARIEL: No fair, I'm hopeless at tic-tac-toe.

FAITH *(Starting to trudge off the beach with Miranda)*: Come on guys, it'll be dark soon.

WINSTON: I'm just smarter than you, that's all.

ARIEL: You are smarter than me, come to think of it. That's always been the trouble between us.

WINSTON: Come on, I'm not *that* smart . . . !

ARIEL: No, you are. You're very quick. You're going to be a great man someday.

WINSTON: Jeez, you really *have* flipped your lid!

ARIEL: No, I'm serious. You've got a lot of spirit. Spirit counts for everything in this world!

WINSTON *(Suddenly looks up at Ariel)*: Race you to the car . . .

ARIEL *(Not in the mood)*: Winston . . .

WINSTON: Come on, one last time . . . ?

A pause as Ariel stands looking at Winston. Without warning she sprints off ahead of him.

WINSTON *(Struggling to catch up)*: Hey, no fair . . . no fair. You got a head start . . . . Mom . . . !

And they're gone. A stillness descends. Leo stretches and looks at his watch. He starts getting ready to leave for the day. Holly suddenly comes teetering onto the sand in high sling-back sandals and a jumpsuit. She stands slightly behind Leo's chair gazing out over the ocean. She stumbles closer.

HOLLY: Hi . . . *(Pause)* I wanted to stop by and see you before I . . . . Boy, the place is really deserted. You know in the old days the beaches around here used to be jammed. . . I'm talking thousands . . . *millions* of people. . . . At the turn of the century they had these special trolleys from Boston. . . . Revere Beach . . . ? You wouldn't believe it! Miles of boardwalk . . . dance halls . . . amusement palaces . . . diving-horse acts . . . fireworks . . . ! *(She starts to lose her balance and grabs onto his chair)* WHOOPS!

LEO *(Pulling on his jeans)*: So, you're going back . . . ?

HOLLY: I'm not used to wearing heels on the beach.

LEO: When are you leaving?

HOLLY: You know, all this time and I never took a picture of your chair. Do you believe it? I mean, of all the things to . . . *(She falls again)* Oh God!

Leo starts scrambling down the ladder to help her, but suddenly slips on something and pitches into the sand.

LEO: SON OF A BITCH!

HOLLY *(Crawling over to him)*: Are you all right?

For a moment, both are on their hands and knees, desperately trying to stand up.

LEO: One of the kids left their fucking shovel on the steps! *(He brandishes it in one hand)*

HOLLY *(Trying not to laugh)*: I'm sorry.

LEO: STUPID IDIOTS!

HOLLY: How do you stand it?

LEO: I don't, but I've only got a couple of days to go, so what the hell.

HOLLY: Then what will you do?

LEO *(Turning the shovel in his hands)*: I don't know. . . . I'd really like to try and make it down to the Keys, but I've got to get my hands on some money first. I have a friend who wants me to manage a seafood chain in Rockport. The money's real good, but I hate working indoors. I don't know, maybe I'll see what's going on in the construction business. *(He absent-mindedly hands Holly the shovel)*

HOLLY: Yeah, I hear you can make a fortune in it—a thousand dollars a day or something . . . and you don't have to show up when the weather's bad . . . there are all kinds of kickbacks and overtime bonuses . . . I don't know what I'm talking about.

A silence.

LEO: How can you stand that guy?

HOLLY *(Handing the shovel back to him)*: Here, I don't want this.

LEO: He's such a phony. He'll fucking eat you alive . . . ! Look, I know it's none of my business, but you're throwing yourself away—and for what . . . ? Some mythical show he keeps promising you . . .

HOLLY: Listen, I didn't come here to be lectured about . . .

LEO: Okay, okay . . .

A silence.

LEO: He's just such an operator. I know the type. All talk. I bet he wears a diamond pinkie ring.

HOLLY *(Tries to set out again, wobbly)*: I assure you, he's never even *seen* a—

LEO: And sixty-dollar cologne with names like "Whip" or "Surrender" . . . *(Grabs Holly's hand and leads her to the ladder of his chair)* You know, you'd have a much easier time if you took those off.

HOLLY *(Sitting with a thud)*: Shit!

Leo squats beside Holly and starts undoing one of her sandals.

HOLLY: What are you doing?

LEO: Taking off your shoes. Come on, hold still.

HOLLY *(Moving her foot away)*: Who said anything about taking off my shoes!

LEO: You keep falling down.

HOLLY: It has nothing to do with my shoes.

LEO *(Trying to grab her foot)*: Will you hold still . . . ?

HOLLY: Look, Leo . . .

LEO *(Struggling with her)*: Come on . . .

HOLLY: I know it looks bad with Andre, it *is* bad with Andre. He makes me crazy, but I'm just so alive with him. I can't explain.

LEO: And with me, you're only happy, right . . . ? *(Pause)* You're a real asshole, you know that?

A silence.

HOLLY: I knew this was a mistake. I knew I shouldn't have . . . *(She tries to walk again, but promptly falls)* WHOOPS!

LEO: Look, if you took off those shoes . . .

HOLLY *(Scrambling to her feet)*: I TOLD YOU: IT HAS NOTHING TO DO WITH MY GODDAMNED SHOES! IT'S YOU . . . ! *(She pulls off the shoes, takes a few tentative steps and immediately falls)* See . . . ? It's you. . . . There's only one way to do this . . . *(She hands Leo her shoes)* Here . . . stand back . . . ! *(She drops to her hands and knees and starts crawling off the beach)*

LEO *(Approaching her)*: Holly, what the hell are you . . . ?
HOLLY: I said: STAND BACK!

Leo does. A silence.

HOLLY *(Inching forward again)*: This may not be the most dignified exit in the world, but at least I'm moving. . . . The trick is to stay away from you. It's like you're electrified or something. Every time you come near me I . . . *(She makes sizzling and crackling sounds)*
LEO *(Immediately touches her)*: Holly . . .
HOLLY *(Starts laughing)*: See . . . ? Oh boy, here we go . . . ! Listen, I had a wonderful time with you, really wonderful . . .
LEO: I don't believe this.
HOLLY *(Crawling faster and faster)*: I *knew* this would happen. I *knew* I shouldn't—
LEO *(Has also dropped to all fours, chasing her)*: Jesus, will you . . .
HOLLY: It wouldn't work and you know it!
LEO *(Trying to catch her)*: . . . slow down?
HOLLY: Come on, let me go. . . . I'd never get anything done with you around. You'd always be sneaking up on me with that look in your eye—pulling the camera out of my hands and grabbing me in the darkroom. I know you . . . ! You have no idea how ferocious I get when I can't do my work . . . I mean, I get nasty! I snap at the mailman, I push old ladies down in the supermarket, I'm a real . . .
LEO *(Tackles her)*: Gotcha!
HOLLY *(Goes sprawling)*: . . . monster! *(Struggling to free herself)* Leo, please . . . ! I'd drive you crazy . . . ! I'm a terrible housekeeper, I don't know how to cook, I forget the days of the week, I'm moody. . . . Oh, am I moody! When I get stuck on something, forget it! *(She starts to cry)* Leo, please . . . he's picking me up in just a few minutes . . .
LEO *(Pinning her)*: Don't go. Don't . . .

A silence.

HOLLY: I could never live in the Keys. It sounds so scary. Deep-sea fishing, people tearing around in motorboats. I mean, what would I do there?
LEO: Hey, hey slow down. Nobody said anything about—
HOLLY: Take those dopey pictures of tourists holding up ten-ton dead tunas they just caught . . . ?
LEO: I just want to see you again.
HOLLY: "Hey, you in the Hawaiian shirt, want to move that tuna a little to the left, it's blocking your wife!"

LEO: Come on, give me your address and phone number in the city.

HOLLY: "Great! Now smile! Not the fish . . . *you!*" Actually, I'd probably make a lot more money than I do now . . .

LEO *(Starts going through Holly's bag)*: You must have a pencil and piece of paper in here . . . *(Candy bars start spilling out)* What have you got in here? A goddamned candy store?!

HOLLY: Leo, what are you . . . ?

LEO *(Pulling out a pencil and piece of paper)*: Ah, here we go. . . . Can I use this?

HOLLY *(Snatching the piece of paper)*: What *is* that?

LEO: How should I know, it's your—

HOLLY: Wouldn't you know it—it's the invitation to Haskell's opening—lucky bum! *(She thrusts it at Leo in disgust)*

LEO: Okay, shoot!

HOLLY: Leo, I really don't think this is a very good—

LEO: Come on, cough it up.

HOLLY: I mean, it would be so strange to see you in the city.

LEO: Let's go.

HOLLY: All right, all right . . . *(Mumbling, inaudible)* 197 East 4th Street . . .

LEO: I beg your pardon?

HOLLY: I said: 197 East 4th Street. Oh God, I don't believe I—

LEO: And your number . . . ?

HOLLY *(Resumes crawling away from Leo, moving very fast)*: Look, I really think this is . . .

LEO *(Following on his hands and knees)*: Yes . . . ?

HOLLY *(Inaudible)*: 212–533–0749. . . . Holly, what *are* you doing . . . ?!

LEO *(Trying to keep up with her)*: 212 . . . what?

HOLLY *(Going faster and faster)*: 533–0749 . . . *(She starts laughing and talking to herself)* You've really flipped your—

Holly suddenly bumps smack into the Adamses, who soundlessly appear in her path carrying folding chairs, a small table, a mysterious white beach umbrella, a bolt of gauzy material and party stuff in their picnic basket. Holly screams at the impact.

M.J. *(Also screams, jumping back)*: Holly Dancer, is that you?!

HOLLY *(Still on all fours)*: Oh, hi Mrs. Adams, I was just . . .

LEO *(Writing it down)*: 197 East 4th Street . . .

HAMILTON *(To Holly)*: Well, well, don't you look attractive.

LEO: 212–533–0749.

M.J.: Did you lose something?

HOLLY *(Finally rises and dusts herself off)*: No, no, I was just trying to get off the beach. It can be pretty tricky sometimes. *(A pause, she looks at her watch)* Oh, no, I've got to go . . . ! *(She retrieves her purse)*

LEO *(Following her)*: Baby, don't.

HOLLY: Oh God . . . *(She faces Leo motionless)*

LEO: Don't . . .

HOLLY *(Starts to cry)*: I've got to, I've *got* to . . . ! Don't look so sad, I can't bear it . . . *(Weeping, she puts her arms around Leo)* Let me go. Please let me go . . .

Holly kisses Leo, then wrenches away and runs off. A silence.

LEO: YOUR SHOES . . . ! *(He follows Holly a few steps, holding them up)*

HAMILTON: I had no idea she was so attractive.

M.J. *(Leaning over)*: You dropped something, dear. What is this? *(She picks the toy shovel up)*

HAMILTON: There's always been a lot of looks in that family. Her mother was a beauty.

LEO *(Still holding her shoes)*: Holly . . .

M.J.: A toy shovel.

HAMILTON: Mabel's no slouch either.

M.J. *(Dropping the shovel into her bag)*: Well, this will come in handy in the garden. Waste not, want not.

A silence.

HAMILTON: Wake up, M.J., we've got a lot of work to do. *(To Leo)* Today's our anniversary.

M.J.: Don't ask us which one, we've lost count.

HAMILTON *(Starting to open the umbrella)*: Every year we come down here and have a little celebration, al fresco.

M.J.: Poor Hammy, it's really not worth the effort.

HAMILTON: Now, now, you say that every year, but once everything's all set up, you change your tune. *(He digs the umbrella deep into the sand)*

M.J.: But look at you, you're like Lawrence of Arabia!

HAMILTON: Nothing ventured, nothing gained.

M.J. *(To Leo)*: Do you believe it . . . ? The man's over seventy and he still carries on like a three-year-old!

HAMILTON: Quit your yipping, M.J., and help me with this stuff.

LEO *(Still holding Holly's shoes, suddenly races up his chair and leans out over the railing)*: HOLLY, HOLLY . . .

Hamilton and M.J. stop and look up at him.

M.J.: Poor thing. *(Looking away)* I can't look.

LEO *(Racing around the railing)*: HOLLY WAIT . . . ! COME BACK!

M.J. *(Unable to move)*: Oh Hammy . . . !

A silence.

HAMILTON *(Fussing with his gear)*: These young people are always losing things. They can't hold on to anything.

M.J.: Remember what I put you through the day before our wedding . . . ? Took off on a steamship for Portugal, I was so terrified.

HAMILTON: You were slippery all right.

M.J.: I almost made it too if it hadn't been for my wretched sister spilling the beans . . . I've never forgiven her for it!

HAMILTON *(Unfurling the bolt of material)*: Okay, M.J., now give me a hand with this. Come on and grab the other end . . .

M.J. *(She does)*: Right, right . . .

HAMILTON: Atta girl . . .

M.J.: Okay, I've got it . . .

HAMILTON *(Starting to unravel the bolt)*: Here we go . . .

M.J.: Careful now . . .

HAMILTON: I'll just look for the other end here . . .

M.J.: Take it nice and slow. Remember what happened the last time . . .

Poor Hamilton makes a worse and worse mess of it, getting all tangled up in the voluminous fabric.

HAMILTON: HEY THERE, LEO, WANT TO GIVE US A HAND WITH THIS . . . ? THE DAMNED STUFF'S GOT A MIND OF ITS OWN! *(He inadvertently pulls M.J. off balance with his flailings)*

M.J. *(Goes flying)*: LOOK OUT, LOOK OUT!

HAMILTON: For pity's sake, M.J., what *are* you doing . . . ?!

M.J.: What am *I* doing . . . ? *You're* the one that's yanking me all over kingdom come!

HAMILTON: Look, all you have to do is hang on to your end while I—

M.J.: That's easy for *you* to say . . .

HAMILTON: COME ON THERE LEO, LET'S GET CRACKING!

LEO: Yes . . . ?

HAMILTON: Could you give us a hand here? *(He pulls on his end again)*

M.J. *(Tottering)*: Hammy, *please!*

HAMILTON: GODDAMNED CHEESECLOTH!

M.J. *(To Leo, who's come down from his chair)*: We go through this every year . . . every year.

HAMILTON *(To M.J.)*: If you could just do what I asked you . . .

M.J.: Sweetheart, I'm trying!

LEO: Okay, let's see what the problem is. *(He takes the material from M.J.)* May I . . . ?

M.J. *(To Hamilton)*: Really darling, don't you think we're getting too old for this!

HAMILTON *(Putting his arm around her)*: Speak for yourself, Madame!

Leo starts hanging the gauze over the umbrella as the Adamses watch.

M.J.: Oh, Leo, what would we do without you?

HAMILTON: I hate to think.

LEO: Oh, you'd manage.

M.J. *(Gazing at the tent)*: It's amazing how well it's stood up after all these years.

HAMILTON: Remember the summer we lugged it down to Singing Beach?

M.J. *(Laughing)*: Oh God!

HAMILTON: The whole thing collapsed on us when the tide came in!

M.J. *(To Leo)*: You should have seen it! We looked like a couple of parachutists who'd just come in for a crash landing!

HAMILTON *(Admiring Leo's handiwork)*: Ahhhh, looking good, looking good.

M.J.: I always forget how handsome it is once it's up.

HAMILTON *(To M.J.)*: "In Xanadu, did Kubla Khan, a stately pleasure dome decree . . ."

M.J.: "Where Alph, the sacred river ran, through caverns measureless to man, down to a sunless sea."

LEO: There we go, that should do it.

M.J.: I don't know how to thank you.

HAMILTON *(Heading into the tent)*: Okay, M.J., I've got the table and chairs. Let's get this show on the road.

Hamilton starts setting the furniture up as M.J. gathers the food.

HAMILTON: And the lantern . . . don't forget the lantern!

M.J.: Right you are. Vouloir c'est pouvoir! *(She sets the lantern on the table and turns it on. To Leo)* Would you care to join us for a little drink . . . ?

HAMILTON: Yes, do!

LEO: Oh, no thanks, no thanks.

M.J. *(Leaving the tent and coming up to Leo)*: We'd love to have you, really!

LEO: That's very kind of you, but—

HAMILTON: Come on, there's plenty of champagne.

M.J.: Oh, *do* join us!

LEO: No, no, another time. Really . . .

HAMILTON: You're sure?

LEO: Yeah.

M.J.: Well, don't feel you have to stick around on our account.

HAMILTON: Yes, please don't let us interfere with your plans.

LEO: That's okay, I feel like sitting awhile. *(He heads back up to his perch)*

HAMILTON *(Holding the tent flap open)*: Come on, M.J., get a wiggle on . . .

M.J.: I'm coming, I'm coming . . .

HAMILTON: . . . the mosquitos are going to eat us alive!

M.J. *(Scurrying inside)*: Hold your horses, I've only got three hands.

HAMILTON: Atta girl.

M.J. *(Collapsing into her chair)*: Uuugh, honestly darling!

HAMILTON *(Sitting in his)*: There, this is more like it! *(Starts rummaging around for the champagne)* Okay. . . . Upward and onward . . .

M.J. *(Setting up the glasses)*: Upward and onward . . .

HAMILTON: What a night, what a night!

M.J.: Good old Hammy, the last of the romantics.

HAMILTON: Smell that air!

The little tent glows merrily against the darkening sky as M.J. and Hamilton set up their feast.

M.J.: How many years *has* it been . . . ?

The lights start to fade around them, leaving Leo in an afterglow. He gazes wistfully at their tent, suddenly rising. He pulls Holly's number out of his pocket and slowly recites it to himself, breaking into a radiant smile.

LEO: Oh yes!

The curtain slowly falls.

ABOUT THE AUTHOR

Born in New York City in 1937, Tina Howe graduated from Sarah Lawrence and then lived in Paris. She wrote her first play in college; the most notable of her many works prior to 1976 are *The Nest* and *Birth and After Birth*. Howe has received an Outer Critics Circle Award, a Rockefeller grant, an NEA fellowship, an Obie Award for Distinguished Playwriting, a Tony nomination and an honorary doctorate from Bowdoin College. Two of the high points of her life were introducing Ionesco at the 92nd Street Y and watching the cast of *Coastal Disturbances* play softball in the Broadway Show League.

PERMISSIONS

"Le Monocle de Mon Oncle" by Wallace Stevens, copyright © 1923, 1951 by Wallace Stevens. Reprinted from *The Complete Wallace Stevens* by permission of Alfred Knopf, Inc. "The Sheep Child" by James Dickey, copyright © 1966 by James Dickey. Reprinted from *Falling, May Day Sermon, and Other Poems* by permission of Wesleyan University Press. "Fire and Ice" by Robert Frost, copyright © 1923, 1969 by Holt, Rinehart and Winston and copyright © 1951 by Robert Frost. Reprinted from *The Poetry of Robert Frost* by permission of Henry Holt & Co. "Dolor" and "I Knew a Woman" by Theodore Roethke, "Dolor" copyright © 1943 by Modern Poetry Assoc., Inc.; "I Knew a Woman" copyright © 1954 by Theodore Roethke. Reprinted from *The Book of Collected Poems* by permission of Doubleday & Company, Inc. Poem "#1593" by Emily Dickinson, copyright © 1951, 1955, 1979, 1983 by the President and Fellows of Harvard College. Reprinted from *The Poems of Emily Dickinson,* Harvard University Press, by permission of the publisher and the Trustees of Amherst College. The author would like to thank Miss Anne Yeats for permission to reprint "The Song of Wandering Aengus" by W. B. Yeats.

ACKNOWLEDGMENTS

TCG gratefully acknowledges its individual contributors, as well as the following corporations, foundations, and government agencies for their generous support: Actors' Equity Foundation, Alcoa Foundation, ARCO Foundation, AT&T Foundation, Center for Arts Criticism, Citicorp/Citibank, Columbia Pictures Entertainment, Consolidated Edison Company of New York, Consulate General of Spain, Eleanor Naylor Dana Charitable Trust, Dayton Hudson Foundation, Exxon Corporation, Home Box Office, Japan-United States Friendship Commission, Jerome Foundation, Joe and Emily Lowe Foundation, Andrew W. Mellon Foundation, Mobil Foundation, National Broadcasting Company, National Endowment for the Arts, New York City Department of Cultural Affairs, New York Community Trust, New York Life Foundation, New York State Council on the Arts, New York Times Company Foundation, Pew Charitable Trusts, Philip Morris Companies, Rockefeller Foundation, Scherman Foundation, Shell Oil Company Foundation, Shubert Foundation, L.J. Skaggs and Mary C. Skaggs Foundation, Xerox Foundation.